# Creative and Mental Growth

FOURTH EDITION

# Creative and Mental Growth

FOURTH EDITION

Viktor Lowenfeld

W. Lambert Brittain

The Macmillan Company, New York
Collier-Macmillan Limited, London

Sixth Printing 1967

Library of Congress catalog card number: 64-12531

THE MACMILLAN COMPANY, NEW YORK
COLLIER-MACMILLAN CANADA, LTD., TORONTO, ONTARIO

Printed in the United States of America

# Preface

"IN THIS BOOK an attempt has been made to show how the child's general growth is tied up with his creative development. . . . Creative expression is as differentiated as are individuals. This is as clearly evident in the minds of artists as it is in the minds of educators and psychologists. However, the child's creative expression during specific stages in his mental and emotional growth can only be understood and appreciated if the general causal interdependence between creation and growth is understood."

This paragraph from the first edition of *Creative and Mental Growth* is as pertinent for this fourth edition as it was in 1947. The current edition is written in the hope that it may provide the basis for deeper understanding of the art expression of children. Such understanding is important not only for teachers or those who are planning to teach, but also for all those

v

who wish better to comprehend the influences underlying every creative act, whether the product is a painting, drawing, construction, or something nonartistic.

The fourth edition was already planned when Dr. Viktor Lowenfeld died in the May of 1960. His dynamic contribution to the field of art education cannot be measured in terms of his numerous articles, his research, or his many books, or even the exciting and stimulating lectures he delivered all over the country; rather it can be measured more readily in the people who have been more personally affected by close association with a spirit that continues to live in each of them. Many were inspired by his contagious enthusiasm. He overwhelmed his listeners, both as individuals and as large audiences, with an intensity that was awe-inspiring.

It is with a great deal of humility that I have undertaken to fulfill his hopes for the latest edition of this classic book. I wish to express my deepest appreciation to Mrs. Viktor Lowenfeld for her continued encouragement and understanding and to Dr. John Lowenfeld for his support. I also wish to acknowledge the kind assistance of the many colleagues and friends who have helped give direction to the new edition. I have appreciated the notes, tape recordings of recent lectures, and suggestions from those who were close to Dr. Lowenfeld in recent years which helped me to get a truer feeling for changes that he would have made.

I also wish gratefully to acknowledge the following for their help in securing the illustrations for this volume: Albright-Knox Art Gallery, Buffalo, New York, Gift of Seymour H. Knox, Plate 13; Bettmann Archive, Figures 101 and 103; John T. Biggers, artist, Figure 90; Barrett Gallagher, photographer, Figures 2, 6, 26, and 88; Jack Grant, photographer, Figures 15, 17, 57, 61, 71, 84, 85, 87, and 89; Jean Holland, Duke of York School, Plates 2 and 7; Lynn Haussler, photographer, Figures 21, 22, and 23; Indiana State College, Penn., Plate 3; Museum of Modern Art, Figures 104 and 105; Gordon Myer, Art Department, High School, Ithaca, N.Y., Figures 84, 85, 87, and 89; New York State College of Agriculture, Cornell University, Figures 55, 72, 96, and 97; New York State College of Home Economics, Cornell University, Figures 3, 27, 93, and 95; Photo Science Studios, Cornell University, Figures 9, 10, 11, 16, and 60; Kathryn Royer, instructor, Figure 94; Irene Russell, *Research Bulletin,* The Eastern Arts Assoc., Vol. 3, No. 1, 1952, Figure 5; Jean Warren, photographer, Figure 37.

The preface to the third edition closed with the hope, which I share for this revision, that it would be used "flexibly and with the thought that nothing can replace the intuitive quality of a good teacher who places sensitivity to problems above knowledge and aesthetic experience above rules and who is continuously conscious of the importance of the individual child."

W. Lambert Brittain

*Department of Child Development*
*and Family Relationships*
*Cornell University*

# Table of Contents

# 3

## The Meaning of Art in the Classroom

# 4

Beginnings of Self-expression: The Scribbling Stage,
Two to Four Years

# 5

First Representational Attempts: The Preschematic
Stage, Four to Seven Years

# 6

The Achievement of a Form Concept: The Schematic
Stage, Seven to Nine Years

# 7

## The Dawning Realism: The Gang Age, Nine to Eleven Years

# 8

## The Pseudo-Naturalistic Stage: The Stage of Reasoning, Eleven to Thirteen Years

# 9

# The Period of Decision: The Crisis of Adolescence Seen in Creative Activity

# 10

# Adolescent Art

# Color Plates

# Creative and Mental Growth

FOURTH EDITION

# 1

# The Meaning of Art
## for Education

ART has a potentially vital role in the education of our children. The process of drawing, painting, or constructing is a complex one in which the child brings together diverse elements of his environment to make a new meaningful whole. In the process of selecting, interpreting, and re-forming these elements, he has given us more than a picture or a sculpture, he has given us a part of himself: how he thinks, how he feels, and how he sees. For the child this is a dynamic and unifying activity.

Formal education takes on a tremendously important role when we realize that our children—from the age of five or six to sixteen, eighteen, or beyond—are forced by law and job requirements to spend ten, twelve, sixteen, or even twenty years behind school doors. That is a pretty stiff sentence just for being born a child. Yet the serving of this sentence is supposed to qualify a youngster to take his place as a contributing and well-adjusted member of society. From some points of view education has done its task; looking around us today, we can see great material gains. But serious questions can be raised about how much we have been able to educate beyond the making and consuming of objects. Have we in our educational system really put emphasis upon the human? Or have we been so blinded by the material awards that we have failed to recognize where the real values of a democracy lie, in its most precious good, the individual?

In our present educational system most emphasis has been put upon the learning of factual information. To a great extent the passing or failing of an examination or of a course, or the passing on to the next grade, or even the remaining in school depends upon the mastery or memorization of certain bits of information that are already known to the instructor. The function of the school system would then seem to be that of producing people who can file away bits of information, and then repeat these at a given signal. Once the student has achieved a certain competency at producing the proper bits of information at the correct time, he is considered right for graduating from school. What is most disturbing is that the skill in repeating bits of information may have very little relationship to the "contributing, well-adjusted member of society" we thought we were producing.

We do not want to give the impression that by merely developing a good creative art program in the public schools, mankind is saved; but the values that are meaningful in an art program are those which may be basic to the development of a new image, a new philosophy, even a totally new structure to our educational system. More and more people are recognizing that the ability to learn differs from age to age and from individual to individual, and that this ability to learn involves not only intellectual capacity, but also social, emotional, perceptual, physical, and psychological factors. Altogether learning is very complex. Therefore, there may be no single best teaching method. Our tendency to develop the capacity to regurgitate bits of information may be putting undue emphasis on but one factor in human development, that which is now measured by the intelligence tests. Intelligence as we now know it does not encompass the wide range of thinking abilities that are necessary to the survival of mankind. The ability to question, to seek answers, to find form and order, to rethink and restructure and find new relationships, are qualities that are generally not taught; and in fact these seem to be frowned upon in our present educational system.

Figure 1.

It may be that one of the basic abilities that should be taught in our public schools is the ability to discover, to search for answers, instead of passively waiting for answers and directions from the teacher. The experiences central to an art activity embody this very factor. This is true whether it is in putting together a construction called "Spring" from straws, colored paper, and bottle caps, or in painting a picture that necessitates the mixing of colors and the invention of new forms.

If we look at very young children, we often find a freedom to act without regard for the amount of knowledge mankind has amassed regarding this action. Children learn to walk without an intellectual understanding of the motor control involved. What a person knows, or does not know, may bear no relationship to creative action. One sometimes hears that there are definite steps to the creative process and that preparation is a first important step. However, it can be seen that children create with whatever knowledge they happen to have at the time. The very act of creating can provide new insights and new knowledge for further action. Probably the best preparation for creating is creating itself. Waiting until a good factual preparation can be obtained before taking action, or stopping children from creating until they know enough about the subject to act intelligently, may inhibit action rather than promote action. *The opportunity for the child to create constantly with his present knowledge is the best preparation for future creative action.*

One of the basic ingredients of a creative art experience is the relationship between the artist and his environment. That is, the painting, drawing, or constructing is a constant process of assimilating and projecting: taking in through the senses a vast amount of information, mixing it up with the psychological self, and putting into new form the elements that seem to suit the aesthetic needs of the artist at the time. Now, if we look at formal education, we realize that the basis for the development of learning rests within 26 letters and 10 numerals. These 36 abstract figures are manipulated and reshuffled from kindergarten through college. The development of mental growth then tends to be an abstract function as these figures take on different and more complicated meaning. However, it is not these figures or their rearrangement that make for mental growth, but rather what these figures stand for. Being able to assemble letters in proper sequence to spell *rabbit* does not constitute an understanding of a rabbit. To really know a rabbit a child must actually touch him, feel his fur, watch his nose twitch, feed him and learn his habits (see Figure 2). It is the interaction between the symbols, the self, and the environment

**Figure 2.** Interaction of the child with his environment—
in this case, a rabbit with his twitchy nose and soft fur
—provides material for abstract intellectual processes.

that provides the material for abstract intellectual processes. Therefore, mental growth depends upon the relationship between a child and his environment; such relationship is a basic ingredient of a creative art experience.

Man learns through his senses. The ability to see, feel, hear, smell, and taste provides the means by which an interaction between man and his environment takes place. The process of educating children can sometimes be confused with developing certain limited predetermined responses. The curriculum in public schools tends to be little concerned with the simple fact that man, and the child too, learns through these five senses. The development of perceptual sensitivity, then, should become a most important part of the educative process. But, except for the arts, the senses are apt to be ignored. *The greater the opportunity to develop an increased sensitivity and the greater the awareness of all the senses, the greater will be the opportunity for learning.*

We know too well that factual learning and retention, if it cannot be used by a free and flexible mind, will benefit neither the individual nor society. Education has often neglected these attributes of growth that are responsible for the development of the individual's sensibilities, for his spiritual life, as well as for his ability to live cooperatively in a society. The growing number of emotional and mental illnesses in this nation, the largest in any nation, as well as our inability to accept human beings first of all as human beings regardless of nationality, religion, race, creed, or color, is a frightening sign and vividly points out that education so far has failed in one of its most significant aims. While our high achievements in specialized fields, particularly in the sciences, have improved our material standards of living, they have diverted us from those values that are responsible for our emotional and spiritual needs. They have introduced a false set of values, which neglect the innermost needs of an individual. In a well-balanced educational system, in which the development of the total being is stressed, each individual's thinking, feeling, and perceiving must be equally developed in order that his potential creative abilities can unfold. Art education, introduced in the early years of childhood, may well mean the difference between a flexible creative human being and one who, in spite of all learning, will not be able to apply it, will lack inner resources, and will have difficulty in his relationship to the environment. Because perceiving, thinking, and feeling are equally stressed in any creative process, art may well provide the necessary balance for the child's intellect and his emotions.

## The Importance of Art for Creativity

Art has long been looked upon as the stronghold of creativity within the public schools. In recent years, however, the more academic courses have begun to develop an interest in fostering creative thinking. The importance of encouraging and developing creativity cannot be overemphasized. Without question, one of the prime objectives of any art program is the development of individuals who are creative thinkers.

Research into creativity extends back only a few years. There are still people who look upon drawing and painting as being somehow removed from reality, and children seem to them to be touched with some magical power. This feeling that creativity is somehow tied up with the gods may be one reason why mere humans have found difficulty in attempting to fathom the mystery around this important area of human development.

We do not have to ponder very long upon the condition of the world today to realize that children who are presently in elementary school will be called upon to revise, change, and remake our world into an entirely new pattern of existence. Problems in human relations, growing populations, international understandings, and the problems resulting from rapid technological change make it imperative that the development of creativity becomes one of the most important considerations of our educational system. *To teach toward creativity is to teach toward the future of society.*

No child should be thought of as "uncreative." In some cases the potential may be buried beneath the surface, and it is up to the teacher to help the child break through the restrictions of conformity and insecurity. On the other hand, there is no "creative" child. This would assume that the creative power is already unleashed to its fullest extent in some children and we therefore can do little to further its development. This whole question is somewhat analogous to developing healthy bodies. In any class we will find children who are undernourished or less healthy than normal. We would hope that proper medical care, diet, exercise, and a change of environment might stimulate healthy growth. But we continue the nourishment and exercise for further development of the healthy body. At any age, we find many levels of physical proficiency. There are also many levels of creative performance, from the mere drawing of a line following the directions of the teacher, to the complex integrated composition that is done spontaneously. *At all levels of creative performance children need to have the encouragement to progress beyond their present capacities and to come closer to a genuinely creative spirit.*

Some research has been done that can help us understand some of the factors involved in the creative process. Eight basic aspects of creativity have emerged from studies in the arts[1] and in the sciences.[2] An understanding of how these relate to the teaching process may clarify some of the important elements involved. It should be remembered that these are not isolated components but are areas to consider as relevant to the encouragement of creative thinking.

One factor that has been identified in the creative process is *sensitivity* —a sensitivity to problems, to attitudes and feelings of other people, and to the experiences of living. This is the ability to use eyes not only for seeing but for observing, ears not only for hearing but for listening, and hands not only for touching but for feeling. This is a high degree of awareness of a material, a situation, or anything unusual or promising. Certainly this is a central experience in working with art materials, where being sensitive to a line or form can be encouraged and developed at all levels. A kindergarten child can be very aware of the feel of a piece of fur, the fifth grader can develop sensitivity toward colors as they mix on his page, and the high school boy may find the polished grain of wood an exciting material.

Another factor that has been identified is *fluency*. This is the ability to produce a large number of ideas in a short period of time, to be able to think rapidly and freely. Fluency can be thought of as being both verbal and nonverbal, but certainly the creative person has the ability to come up with numerous solutions or ideas on a problem. This ability can be seen in the numerous scribbles of a preschooler or in the dozen suggestions a high school boy may have about designing a mosaic table top.

Another important area is *flexibility,* the ability to adjust quickly to new situations or to change rapidly in one's thinking. This is the very opposite of being rigid, or stuck in the rut. The paint may spill or the chisel may slip, but the creator must adapt and take continuous advantage of the unexpected and shift his ideas and responses. The accident should provide a challenge and a new direction for thinking. The process of painting itself requires a constantly changing viewpoint as the painting progresses. Using a box of scrap materials to make a picture of "Daddy" today, and using the same materials tomorrow to make a collage of "My Feelings Toward School," certainly develops flexible thinking.

Probably the best-known attribute of a creative person is *originality*. This is the ability to think of new or novel responses and is the opposite of the usual or accepted. Very little opportunity is given within our school system for developing this trait. Too often the "correct" answer is the one that is commonly agreed upon. However, in the field of art, originality is stressed; responding in usual or common ways is not necessarily the best answer. Art at all levels should stress the unique response of the individual child, and the copying of examples of work from the teacher, books, or from other children is usually avoided like the plague.

Another factor that has been identified in the creative process is the capacity to *redefine* or *reorganize*. To be able to rearrange ideas and shift the uses and functions of objects, or to see them in a new light, is apparently a quality that utilizes what is known, but for new or different purposes. This is certainly basic in an art experience. When we transform paper bags into puppets, we redefine the material in a new way and thus give it new meaning. Cutting up a piece of lumber and putting the pieces together for a wood project utilizes this ability to reorganize. Rearranging and changing elements on a wall for a mural, or on a canvas for a painting, is a constant process of reorganization. Experimentation with new materials brings new discoveries (see Figure 3).

Other factors in creativity have been identified as being a part of this important process. Although these have been identified by different names, these include the ability to *abstract*, the skill of analyzing the various parts of a problem or seeing specific relationships; the ability to *synthesize*, or the ability to combine several elements into a new form or whole; and the ability to *organize*, that is, the ability to put parts together in a meaningful way. It hardly needs to be pointed out that these are some of the basic qualities of any art experience. In an art class, motivating toward a greater awareness of details and toward a discovery of differences develops the capacity for analysis. As single brush strokes unite to form new shapes and solid areas, synthesis occurs; and each student, through his own aesthetic awareness, develops a meaningful artistic organization.

There is no implication that by merely adding together the factors

Figure 3. Experimentation with new materials brings new discoveries.

that have been considered important in studies of creativity, we can discover creative thinkers. Rather, we should look upon these as factors to consider in planning an art program.[3] Most of these abilities come under the heading of *divergent thinking*. This is the opposite of *convergent thinking*. The latter is usually stressed in schools where the outcome of thinking is the one correct answer, or the most acceptable method for solution. Both kinds of thinking should be developed, and certainly the creative arts become extremely important in our educational system if only because the arts stress divergent thinking, in which there are no right answers, and any number of possible solutions to problems or any number of outcomes in painting or drawing are correct.

Some questions that are factual and demand specific answers might be "What are the primary colors? What are the secondary colors? Give an example of a split-complementary color scheme." Open-ended questions that stimulate divergent thinking might be "Which colors make you feel sad? How would you feel if you were purple? Which color would you like to be?" The importance of teaching toward divergent thinking is stressed by Robert Burkhart: "The value of the divergent question is that it requires the student to look at a content area from a variety of viewpoints and to participate in an imaginative way in answering the question."[4]

Some of the research on creativity in art has pointed out that teaching toward "capacity for creative action" is complex and may depend upon personal meaningfulness, upon encouraging self-reflective thinking, upon encouraging self-evaluation, and upon developing greater student-teacher interaction.[5]

It might be well to mention here that the philosophy in art education is distinctly different from that of the so-called fine arts. Whereas the emphasis in art education is on the effect that the creative processes have on individuals, it is the aesthetic value of the end product that is of importance in the fine arts. However, we cannot separate an individual from what he paints. With the improved creativeness of the individual, his greater sensitivity toward experiences, and his increased ability to integrate them, the quality of his aesthetic product will also grow. Focusing attention upon the painting, drawing, or construction puts emphasis upon the end product only and limits growth to present understanding of the field of art, and in particular to the taste of the individual teacher. Focusing upon the child, however, makes the creative process extremely important, not only to the potential artist but to every child, regardless of how or in what profession this creativity will be utilized.

## Methods of Approach

It should be stressed that there is no single approach to freeing children or adults in their creative potentialities or to making them more sensitive toward themselves and their environment. However, it can be said that whatever a teacher does in stimulating creativeness greatly depends on three factors: (1) his own personality, of which his own creativeness, degree of sensitivity, and flexible relationships to environment are an important part, (2) his ability to put himself into the place of others, and (3) his understanding and knowledge of the needs of those whom he is teaching. It is quite impossible to say that any one approach—by whatever fine-sounding name it is called—is good for all. At one time it may be better to have the children divided in groups working on group projects, at another time working simultaneously with different materials in one classroom or working individually on the same motivation. This all depends on individual needs. Every sensitive teacher feels when his group is keyed up to one experience they have just gone through. At that time it would not only be quite out of place but superficial to divide the group into smaller groups and motivate them to work with different materials. Let it be clear that our task is to help individuals in their identification with their own selves and to stimulate creativeness with whatever methods are most effective. For the same reason it is quite ineffective, or even frustrating, to use group approaches if the individual either feels the group is interfering with his own individual mode of expression or if he cannot conceive of group work, if he is not ready for it. It must always be kept in mind that the child's needs change and that the teacher must adjust to these changing needs.

A question is sometimes raised as to whether children are not restricted in their creativeness when the teacher is using classroom motivations, that is, when the whole group is motivated by one experience. We have to differentiate clearly between subject matter and mode of expression. As long as the child has the freedom to use his *own* mode of expression, his creativeness remains free. In fact, it has been proven experimentally that a motivation is not always most effective when given individually.

Every teacher knows how easily a classroom motivation can become contagious, getting hold of all children, much as a football game with a large attendance. The best game with poor attendance may have little excitement. Indeed, it has been established that the same motivations may have different effects under different circumstances and treatment.[6] The teaching situation, as well as the need of the children, should always be the decisive factor in choosing the method of approach, for it is the effect of the creative process on the child and not the final product that is of decisive significance.

## The Important Principle of Extending the Frame of Reference

In order to understand the effect of the creative process on the child, and how the various components of growth are part and parcel of it, let us actually try to find out what goes on in a child's mind while he is busy creating a picture. It is needless to say that neither the quality nor the intensity of the creative process depends on the material used.

First of all, when he begins he must think of "something." Often this "something" seems to us insignificant. For the child, however, it always means a confrontation with his own self, with his own experience. Some children cannot think of "something" because they either lack sensitive relationships to meaningful experiences or their minds are blocked and go around in circles. If they lack sensitive experiences, they need to be motivated. If their minds are blocked and move around in stereotypes, *their frame of reference needs to be extended.*

The extension of the frame of reference constitutes one of the most important principles in art education, or indeed, in education in general. To extend the frame of reference, we always have to start on the level of the individual—to extend the child's thinking, feeling and perceiving on *his* level and at the stage of *his* development. If, for instance, Mary scribbles small in a corner of her paper, it would be useless to tell her to scribble larger, or to cover the whole paper. Such suggestions would not enhance in her the freedom necessary for larger motions, nor would they permit her to discover the meaningfulness of the paper at her disposal. For that, her frame of reference for motions needs to be enlarged; that is, the scribbling motion has to be extended to a more meaningful motion, the area on the paper to other more meaningful areas. In this case one could ask Mary, "Have you been in a skating rink?" "Suppose you have the whole space for yourself, would you only skate in the corner?" "Show me how you would skate." "Suppose the sheet of paper is your skating rink. Let's skate with our crayon on it." One motion has been referred to another more meaningful motion and has thus achieved greater significance. One area has been related to another area in relationship to an experience more meaningful to the child than scribbling has been. This extension of the frame of reference has sensitized the child to his own motions as well as to the meaningfulness of the drawing area. Obviously only meaningful experiences will be effective.

"My child only draws airplanes." "My child only draws guns." These are remarks we continually hear, both from parents and from teachers. "Don't draw these silly guns!" would obviously not contribute to the child's greater flexibility and understanding of his environment. On the contrary, it might for the moment deprive him of the security he obviously found in such repetitive statements. By repeating the same thing over and over, the child merely expresses his inability to adjust to new situations. For him his stereotyped repetition constitutes an escape, which he always uses whenever he cannot face a new situation. This is also true for children who go into a tantrum, another escape mechanism, which the child introduces whenever he is unable to adjust to a new situation. Mary may be peacefully playing with her doll when you suddenly interrupt her and tell her that her time is over and that she has to go to bed. Because Mary cannot adjust quickly to the new situation, she may escape into a tantrum. There is nothing easier than to condition her gradually to what will come and thus prevent such a quick and drastic adjustment. "Mary, will your doll soon go to sleep? You know that soon you will have to go to bed, too." This can be repeated, depending on the adjustability of the child, until the final step will no longer represent a decisive change. In art education such conditioning to a new situation often constitutes an important part of the motivation, especially for the extension of the child's frame of reference. If Johnny draws airplanes only, the important fact is to make the airplane *meaningful,* to make it alive, by extending the child's frame of reference. Again we have to start on the level of the child. If the child draws all airplanes alike, it will be a discovery for him to distinguish between big and small planes. "Where does your plane fly?" "Where does it land?" "Where do people get out?" To make the plane and its environment meaningful to the child, the teacher has to identify with the child's needs, in particular in his relations and feelings for airplanes. In this way

**Figure 4.** The child draws from his knowledge, his observation, and his experience.

the teacher has extended the frame of reference from the child's stereotyped meaningless airplane symbol to an expression of meaningful variety of airplanes, from a meaningless background area to a meaningful space that has become part of the child's experience. It is needless to say that diverting the child from his problem by making him do different things in different materials will not help him. It has been proved that diversion may only add to his frustration. If he is limited to airplanes, their meaningfulness can be improved by an extension to another material, that is, from drawing to three-dimensional form. The new and fresh approach in new materials may often break down old established stereotypes.

Fortunately most of our children are free and not bound up with stereotypes. Johnny, for instance, *can* think of something, because he has experienced something. As he thinks of it, his thoughts concentrate on the experience to be painted. His thought process, the ability to think for himself and concentrate on something, becomes stimulated. This initial intellectual process is an important part in creative activities. It is self-evident that he will include only those things that he knows and that are important to him. Important to him, however, are only those things to which he has established some more or less sensitive relationship. Thus, his emotional relationship will be an important part in his creative process. Let us say that Johnny wants to draw how he plays with other children in the yard. For Johnny the apple tree in the yard may have big apples because he has been watching them grow. He includes the apples in his drawing because they are important to him. They are part of his knowledge, his observation, and his experience (see Figure 4). Bob uses the tree only for climbing; apples have no meaning and are therefore not included in his painting. Bob is interested in Mary's dress. He likes Mary. His painting indicates more details on Mary than elsewhere. He paints Mary much larger than anything else because she is important to him. His painting, like those of all children, is not an objective representation. On the contrary, it expresses his likes and dislikes, his emotional relationships to his own world and the world that surrounds him. It also expresses not only what he knows but also what he feels, sees, and touches, if he has become sensitively aware of these things.

In order to understand this fully, let us go back to our own experiences. We, too, can only recall things to the extent to which either our knowledge or our individual emotional relationships permit us. Let us think, for instance, of a traffic light. We all know that it consists of three different colored lights. Our knowledge has registered that. We will, however, not be so sure of the location of the colors if we have not become sensitized to them. Is the green light on top, or the red? Only the degree of intensity with which we have observed the location will be responsible for our recalling it. Once we have become sensitized toward this particular location by conscious observation, that is, by seeing in detail, we shall incorporate this newly gained relationship into our permanent understanding. More sensitive relationships can, however, be fostered by experience we have with things. For instance, if we were color-blind, we would have to depend on the location of the lights and would very soon have to become aware of the red light on the top. If we had to install the lights, we would by necessity have become aware of their location. But emotional experience with things will also intensify our relationships to environment. If we experience the vastness of the sea with an underlying feeling of loneliness, all by ourselves, it is not the same as if we were accompanied by the noise of countless people happily splashing in the oncoming waves. Needless to say, the more sensitive relationships we establish toward experiences in general, the richer is our life, for what is true about the traffic light is also true about flowers, trees, textures, colors, and all that surrounds us.

Johnny, therefore, has given us an intimate understanding, through his drawing, of the type of relationships he has established to the things he represented. Of course, as he grows, these relationships will change. He will know more about things, and his emotional interest will also shift. The greater the variety in his paintings, the more flexible he will be in his relationships and vice versa. *It must, however, be remembered that it is one of the most important tasks of the teacher to continually encourage and motivate sensitive, rich, and flexible relationships.*

As Johnny continues to draw his back-yard scene, he adds things according to the significance they have to him. Perhaps the swings on the apple tree come first to his mind. He loves to swing on them. But there is Bob. Johnny does not like Bob because he always teases Johnny. So, according to his likes and dislikes in color and placement, he gives expression to his dislike for Bob in his drawing. Johnny is weaker than Bob; he can never show his dislike directly, but in his drawing he can. He feels better afterward, just as we feel better after we have talked about a disagreeable thing with a good friend. It bothers us to keep things all to ourselves, to have them eat into us.

It is needless to say that everything Johnny does and to which he is exposed has some influence upon him. If in his creative work he continually attempts to relate all his experiences, such as thinking, feeling, perceiving (seeing, touching, and so on), to one another, it must also have a unifying effect on his personality.

As Johnny goes on to draw his back-yard picture, he includes Rowdy, his dog, and also Dad, who fixes the fence. Rowdy is digging a hole in the lawn. Johnny is quite aware that this may spoil the lawn and Dad does not like it. Dad fixes the fence; Johnny could not draw Dad without putting himself into Dad's place while fixing the fence. This makes him better understand Dad. He even thinks how Dad lifts the heavy hammer to drive the post into the ground. Dad must be strong. It is one of the important attributes of any creative process that we become more sensitive to things with which we are dealing. If Johnny thinks of his environment more sensitively, he has been taught to do one of the most important things that we need in the world today—*to become more sensitive to the needs of others*. This is one of the most vital prerequisites for a cooperative attitude. In putting himself into the place of Dad in his picture, Johnny has just experienced this vital need.

Johnny not only becomes more sensitive to the things he draws, he also develops a great sensitivity to the materials he uses. He learns by experience that the lines of a crayon are different if he puts different pressure on it, that he can use the broad side of the crayon—all this he learns by trial and error, and soon incorporates into his picture. To discover and explore *what different art materials can do,* to learn their behavior is one of the important trends the child develops through creative activities. Johnny even learns to predict their behavior: he knows exactly how much he can bend wood, what he can do with wire, what colors to mix in order to get the one he wants. He has become sensitive to the reactions of materials and he uses great skill in handling them. This development of skill that is a result of the urge for expression is also a vital part of the creative process.

When Johnny began to draw his back-yard picture, he had to decide where to put the tree, the swings, the fence, Mary, Dad, Rowdy, and Bob. Thus he had to organize all these things meaningfully. What he knew of the tree, the swing, Mary, the fence, Dad, and Bob had to be related to how he felt about these things, and this had to be related to the location of the things on the paper. He also gave some definite color and shape to the objects he drew. He had to invent and explore his forms in relationship to the material he used. Of course all this organization takes place in the child subconsciously. But it all belongs to Johnny's personality and is part and parcel of the creative process and the resulting aesthetic product, for aesthetic growth consists of the growth from a chaotic to a harmonious organization of expression in which feeling, perceiving, and thinking are completely integrated.

Virginia, for instance, cannot express herself as flexibly as Johnny. She is tense and has developed a certain emotional inflexibility. She cannot meet new situations, as Johnny can. Her mind does not adjust as easily to her environment, and therefore she has established a certain sameness of reactions. She always draws the same kinds of patterns. Her mind is fixed on one thing—and this she keeps repeating. This repetition gives her a certain security. She knows she can repeat it again and again. She also knows that she does not need to meet new situations when she draws. It is a false security into which she escapes whenever she cannot do justice to a situation.

Johnny, through his continued art motivation, could adjust flexibly to other situations he was facing. During the creative process he not only used his intellect in finding out about the tree, the swing, the fence, Rowdy, Dad, and the other things, but he gave expression to his emotional relationships to Mary, his dog, and even the tree, because he loved to climb it. He observed the apples, Mary's dress, and became more sensitive to his environment. He independently created his own forms and concepts. By putting himself in the place of others, he learned the needs of others; by using his art material sensitively, he actually learned to identify with its behavior—both are important parts of social growth. By organizing all his experiences into a creative product, he integrated all these experiences into a total inseparable whole, the aesthetic product. Johnny is different from Virginia and so is his creative expression.

For our children art should become their friend to whom they turn with their joys and sorrows, their fears and frustrations, whenever words become inadequate. Through such experiences a child's art expression becomes "an integral part of the whole stream of his living."[7]

NOTES

1. W. Lambert Brittain, "An Experiment Toward Measuring Creativity," *Research in Art Education,* Seventh Yearbook (Kutztown, Pa.: National Art Education Association, 1956), pp. 39–46.
2. J. P. Guilford *et al.,* "The Relations of Creative-Thinking Aptitudes to Non-Aptitude Personality Traits," *Reports from the Psychological Laboratory* (Los Angeles: University of Southern California, 1957).

3. Viktor Lowenfeld and Kenneth Beittel, "Interdisciplinary Criteria in the Arts and Sciences: A Progress Report," *Research in Art Education,* Ninth Yearbook (Kutztown, Pa.: National Art Education Association, 1959), pp. 35–44.

4. Robert C. Burkhart, *Spontaneous and Deliberate Ways of Learning* (Scranton, Pa.: International Textbook Co., 1962), p. 217.

5. Kenneth Beittel, "Construction and Reconstruction of Teaching Methods Through Experimental Research," *The Art Education Bulletin,* **XIX,** No. 4 (Apr. 1962), pp. 48–55.

6. L. F. McVitty, "An Experimental Study on Various Methods in Art Motivations at the Fifth Grade Level" (Unpublished doctoral dissertation, The Pennsylvania State University, 1954).

7. Manuel Barkan, *A Foundation for Art Education* (New York: Ronald Press Co., 1955).

# 2

# The Importance of
## Creative Activity
## in Elementary Education

IF children developed without any interference from the outside world, no special stimulation for their creative work would be necessary. Every child would use his deeply rooted creative impulse without inhibition, confident in his own kind of expression. We find this creative confidence clearly demonstrated by those people who live in the remote sections of our country and who have not been inhibited by the influences of advertisements, comic books, and "education." Among these folk are found the most beautiful, most natural, and clearest examples of children's art. What civilization has buried we must try to regain by recreating the natural base necessary for such free creation. Whenever we hear children say, "I can't draw that," we can be sure that some kind of interference has occurred in their lives. No Eskimo child would express such lack of confidence. These interferences might come from anywhere. To provide children with the kinds of stimulation necessary for their creative growth, it is important to examine some of the interferences that thwart such growth.

Art is not the same for the child as it is for the adult. Art for the child is merely a means of expression. Since the child's thinking is different from that of the adult, his expression must also be different. Out of this discrepancy between the adult's "taste" and the way in which a child expresses himself arise most of the difficulties and interferences in art teaching. We have heard educators, although intrigued by the beauty of children's drawings and paintings, asking for the "right" proportions and "good" color schemes. The child sees the world differently from the way he draws it. It is precisely from our analysis of this discrepancy between the representation and the thing represented that we gain insight into the child's real experience. Therefore it is easy to understand that *any* correction by the teacher that refers to objects and not to the child's experience interferes greatly with the child's own expression. This interference starts perhaps when children scribble and eager parents expect to see something that fits their own adult conception. How ridiculous to overpower these little children's souls!

The difference in the meaning of *imitation* has created misunderstandings. Psychologists as well as educators agree that imitation is an important factor in learning. One of the most important means of communication— language—is initially conceived by imitation. The importance of imitation as a means of learning, therefore, cannot be overlooked. Yet if we were to remain on the level of mere imitation, language would only become the repetition of words and man would go down to the level of a parrot, who repeats words without understanding their meaning or without any intent to express something. Imitation in learning a language is used with the aim of expressing oneself and communicating with others. Indeed, *imitation in any learning situation is only used as a means to an end* and never as an end in itself. In using imitative means, then, it is educationally important that teachers become aware of how imitation is used. As self-evident as this may appear, much confusion has been created by "methods" that promote "learning" in one direction but degrade the child to parrot-like imitation in another. The child can not be sliced into subject matter. What influences him in arithmetic may be seen in his art expression and vice versa. If the child becomes inhibited in one area, it may be felt in the other.

# The Effect of Stereotyped Workbooks and Coloring Books on Children

Certain workbooks commonly used in arithmetic and reading confront the child with the task of repeating the same concept again and again. "Add six birds to the three. How many do you have?" When a "number concept" is promoted by using stereotypes, the child may become inhibited creatively. One of the authors of such a workbook defended his method by saying, "I am only interested in promoting better arithmetic—I don't know anything about art." The obvious answer was that we are concerned with the child and not with art or arithmetic. The difference lies between a subject-matter-centered and a child-centered method of teaching.

Experimental research has given us ample evidence that imitative methods have a detrimental effect on the child's creativeness. As one of the many examples a commonly used arithmetic workbook has a child draw 76 repetitions of a stereotype of a rabbit, 88 of a bird, 62 of a kite, 80 of a balloon, 36 of a cat, and so forth. Such repetition of stereotypes foreign to the child's own concept regiments the child into one type of representation and deprives him of the expression of his own relationship to the representation. A study by Heilman shows clear evidence of the detrimental effects of the use of workbooks. His experiments in public schools indicated how very dependent some children can become upon workbooks, which can influence their natural form of expression: ". . . the statistical data reveal that the general growth pattern through creative work was seriously influenced by exposure to workbooks. . . ."[1] According to the experiments of Russell and Waugaman, 63 per cent of all children who had been exposed to coloring book birds lost their initially established sensitivity to birds and changed their concepts to resemble the stereotype (see Figure 5).[2] This is a devastating result of the influence of workbook methods. It is needless to say that such procedures are in complete disagreement with democratic methods of learning, for they completely neglect individual expression.

In order to understand the effect on children of coloring and workbooks that contain such repetitive stereotype forms, let us go through the process a child goes through while using them, and let us also find out the aftereffect this process may have on our children.

Let us assume that the first picture the child has to fill in is that of a dog. As soon as the child is confronted with the task of following a predetermined outline, we have prevented him from solving his own relationships creatively. His relationship to a dog may be one of love, friendship,

*a*

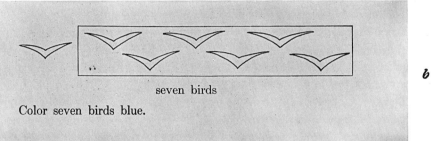

seven birds

Color seven birds blue.

*b*

*c*

**Figure 5.** Coloring books affect a child's creative expression. (Courtesy of Dr. Irene Russell, *Research Bulletin,* The Eastern Arts Association, Vol. 3, No. 1, 1952).
*a.* This bird shows one child's expression before he was exposed to coloring books.
*b.* Then the child had to color a workbook illustration.
*c.* After coloring the workbook birds, the child has lost his creative sensitivity and self-reliance.

dislike, or fear. There is no opportunity for him to express his relationship and thus relieve himself of tensions of joy, hatred, or fear. There is no place in coloring books to express anxieties. There is not even a place for the individual differences of Johnny and Mary. In filling the outline drawings, the children are regimented into the same type of activity, with no provision for their differences as individuals. Of course, some children, unaware of all these implications, and by nature somewhat lazy, enjoy coloring the dog; but as they color it with crayon, they realize that they could never draw a dog as well as the one they are coloring. They may even be very proud when they are through with their activity. After all, they have colored the dog. Next time, in school or elsewhere, when one of these children is asked to draw something, he remembers the dog in the coloring book. Realizing that he cannot compete, he says, quite logically, "I can't draw."

I have heard many teachers or parents say, "But my children love coloring books." This is quite true. However, children in general do not discriminate between things good for them and things detrimental. That they love things is not always an indication that those things are good for them. Many children prefer sweets to vegetables, and no doubt would always prefer them. But this does not mean that we should adjust their diets to sweets. Children once conditioned to overprotection love it too. In fact, they become so dependent upon it that they can no longer enjoy their freedom. There are cases where parents do everything for their children—children who simply stretch out their leg and their shoe is laced, then turn around and their hair is combed—almost automatically, as on the assembly line. These are the children who sit in the midst of their toys and don't know what to do with them, or go to camp and sit lonely in a corner while others enjoy their freedom and play.

A child conditioned to coloring books will have difficulties in enjoying the freedom of creating. The dependency that such methods create is devastating. It has been revealed by experimentation and research that more than half of all children exposed to coloring books lose their creativeness and their independence of expression and become rigid and dependent.

Although there is some question whether it is an important discipline, some teachers may still tell you that coloring books teach the child to stay within the lines. It has been shown by experiment that this is not true at all. More children color beyond the given boundaries of objects in coloring books than of objects they draw themselves. If Johnny draws *his* dog, he has much more incentive to remain within *his* boundaries than if he colors a dog in a coloring book to which he has no relationship.

Thus it has been proved beyond any doubt that such imitative procedures as found in coloring and workbooks make the child dependent in his thinking (they do not give him the freedom to create what he wants); they make the child inflexible, because he has to follow what he has been given; they do not provide emotional relief, because they give the child no opportunity to express his own experience; they do not even promote skills and discipline, because the child's urge for perfection grows out of his own desire for expression; and finally, they condition the child to adult concepts that he cannot produce alone and that therefore frustrate his own creative ambitions.

## Self-expression

The term *self-expression* has been misunderstood so often that it is necessary to clarify this term before using it. It would be wrong to think that self-expression means the expression of thoughts and ideas in general terms of content. This is the greatest mistake made in the use of this word. Thoughts and ideas can also be expressed imitatively. If one finds himself truly and originally occupied in any kind of medium, the outcome of this occupation and the mode of its expression are of decisive importance. What matters, then, is the mode of expression, not the content; not the what but the how. That is why scribbling, or in another field of expression, babbling, can be a means of self-expression as well as a potentially high form of creation. It can even happen that scribbling or babbling is a truer means of self-expression than a higher form of art if the work of art moves from the sincere mode of expression to a form based upon dependency on others, on imitation. In this connection it seems important to point out that the more primitive the stage of creative activity, the weaker the effect of such formal influences or interferences. The explanation of this fact seemingly lies in the nature of the more complex expression of art. Rarely can there be found a scribbling or babbling that is not a direct expression of a mental and emotional state. However, more complex forms of art expression can be influenced easily by stronger personalities. This influence often grows to such an extent that complex forms of art, even in spite of technical perfection, may lack completely the inner spirit or the mental and emotional state of the creator. They are, then, façades without substance, masks without life, condemned to die. However, this condemnation holds not only for the single art work, but also for the creator, who cannot live because he cannot breathe with strange lungs. In the same way that a babbling child is unable to pronounce words correctly, even if urged to do so, a scribbling child if forced to draw naturalistically can neither understand nor conceive what he is supposed to draw. Both would express themselves by strange means, which would not only inhibit them but block their further development. This applies to all stages and levels of creative activity. Education toward truth is one of the highest and deepest meanings of self-expression. This development toward freedom of expression, this great experience of individuals in finding themselves, rests upon the knowledge of what truth is in art education. This knowledge cannot be achieved without a thorough study of what we can expect in modes of expression in the different age groups and on the different mental levels.

## Self-adjustment

Any work that is forced upon a person creates tension and dissatisfaction. When the individual feels unable to perform a task, he becomes conscious of his own insufficiencies and develops lack of confidence, or even feelings of inferiority. This can happen if art education is applied improperly and if a child is urged to do something not appropriate to his development, or even if the child's work is criticized in a way that is not adjusted to the level of his ability to understand.

For instance, if a scribbling child, whose control of body movements is not developed to the extent that he can correlate them with his visual experiences, is forced to represent a definite object, he not only will be unable to perform a task that depends upon ability to achieve such correlation but he may also lose confidence in his own means of expression (scribbling). The child may even become aware that he does not represent anything real. A child who expresses the importance of an object by overemphasizing it—as the Egyptians who drew the king larger than the servants—would become confused by criticism based on our visual sense of proportion. The child not having another means to determine the importance of the object would first become aware of the "inadequacy" of his expression, would then lose confidence in his own experiences, and might finally start to measure proportions rigidly until blocked in his further development. Discouraged by such a stimulation, the child would then stop expressing himself altogether—"I can't draw."

However, if the child expresses himself adequately and freely by repeating his motions during scribbling with ever greater certainty, by expressing importance with his own adequate means, by feeling and expressing his own space experience (contradicting that of adults), he has great satisfaction in his achievement. And we all know how achievements create confidence. Since nearly every emotional or mental disturbance is connected with a lack of self-confidence, it is easily understood that the proper stimulation of the child's creative abilities will be a safeguard against such disturbances.

We have defined self-expression as the appropriate mode of expression according to the mental level of the child. Imitation, however, is expression according to adult, or at least foreign, levels. If the child expresses himself according to his own level, he becomes encouraged in his own independent thinking by expressing his own thoughts and ideas by *his own* means. The child who imitates becomes dependent in his thinking, since he relies for his thoughts and expressions upon others. The independent, thinking child will not only express whatever comes into his mind but will tackle any problem, emotional or mental, that he encounters in life. Thus his expression serves also as an emotional outlet.

Dependent thinking, however, restricts the child in his choice of subject matter as well as in his mode of expression. Since the imitative child cannot give expression to his own thoughts and emotions, his dependency leads directly to feelings of frustration. The child who uses creative activity as an emotional outlet will gain freedom and flexibility as a result of the release of unnecessary tensions. However, the child who feels frustrated develops inhibitions and, as a result, will feel restricted in his personality. The child who has developed freedom and flexibility in his expression will be able to face new situations without difficulties. Through his flexible approaches toward the expression of his own ideas he will not only face new situations properly but will adjust himself to them easily. The inhibited and restricted child, accustomed to imitating rather than expressing himself creatively, will prefer to go along set patterns in life. He will not be able to adjust to new situations quickly but rather will try to lean upon others as the easiest way out. Since it is generally accepted that progress, success, and happiness in life depend greatly upon the ability to adjust to new situations, the importance of art education for personality growth and development can easily be recognized.

The accompanying table summarizes the contrast between self-expression and imitation.

| Self-expression | Contrasted with | Imitation |
| --- | --- | --- |
| Expression according to child's own level. | | Expression according to strange level. |
| Independent thinking. | | Dependent thinking. |
| Emotional outlet. | | Frustration. |
| Freedom and flexibility. | | Inhibitions and restrictions. |
| Easy adjustment to new situations. | | Going along in set patterns. |
| Progress, success, purposefulness. | | Leaning toward others, dependency, stiffness. |

## The Significance of Self-identification Through Art

Today people have to a great extent lost their ability to identify with what they do and also with the needs of their neighbors. The reason for this increasing lack of ability for self-identification may be found in certain trends in industry and also in education. Mass production apparently does not stimulate individual self-identification, and mass education seemingly does not contribute toward it either. Yet it is an established fact that self-identification with the things we do is essential for any well-balanced individual, and self-identification with the needs of our neighbors is one of the most important assumptions for cooperation. To be able to identify with those we fear, those we do not understand, those who appear strange to us is a prime requisite for a peaceful society, which combines humans of different creeds, colors, and heritages.

In education the study of self-identification of the teacher with the needs of the child as well as that of the child with his own needs becomes a science—in our opinion, one of the most important sciences today. On its promotion the very future of our youth may depend, for nothing less is at stake than the ability of our youths to live cooperatively as well-balanced human beings in their society. Almost all fields in the social sciences can be understood better through self-identification than through a mere study of facts. Self-identification in teaching becomes the vehicle for any effective motivation, for without identifying with the needs of the growing child, we shall not be able to understand these needs.

No art expression is possible without self-identification with the experience expressed as well as with the medium by which it is expressed. This is one of the very intrinsic factors of creative expression. If we do not identify with these forces, art expression loses the very essence of its nature—its creativity.

The different trends in art education today depend entirely on the different emphases used by educators in identifying with the different forces determining creative processes. Some art educators identify predominantly with aesthetic criteria, art media and their application, the elements of design and their organization; others identify completely with the individual who produces. While the one group of educators concentrates on the organization of the creative product and its design values, the other identifies with the individual and his psychological needs only. In art education these trends must not be separated. They must be closely integrated, for it is the individual who uses his media and his form of expression according to his personal experiences. Since these experiences change with the growth of the individual, self-identification is a dynamic science. It embraces the understanding of *social, intellectual, emotional,* and *psychological* changes with the *creative needs* of the child.

### SELF-IDENTIFICATION IN TEACHING

To identify with the needs of the growing child is, then, imperative for any successful teaching. In art education it means that the teacher must know the child and his creative needs in order to understand him fully and also to motivate him effectively. This is not always easy. Two important attributes are essential for complying with this task.

**1. The teacher must be able to subordinate himself and his desires to the needs of the child.**

**2. The teacher must make himself acquainted with the physical and psychological needs of the child.**

For example, a teacher who sees a scribbling child must not only be able to identify with the needs of a child in this stage of development but he must also be able to identify with the *particular* needs of this *individual* child. Therefore, he must completely subordinate his adult needs or desires to those of the child. In order to be able to identify with the general needs of a scribbling child, he must make himself acquainted with the physiological as well as psychological characteristics of this developmental stage. Only then will he be able to identify with the particular needs of this individual child. Thus, it becomes essential that he study the needs of a scribbling child. If he discovers that the physical needs are of a purely kinesthetic origin, he will no longer motivate the child with visual imagery. He will then learn that an apple for this child is only something to eat, to smell, or to hold, and *not to draw*. The child in this stage of development has no desire to relate visual imagery to his drawing activity. He simply enjoys the motions on the paper. To go even further with the self-identification, the teacher should realize that the motions the child is making are for the child different in size from the way they appear to him. Sizes always are proportionate to our own self. He will then remember that a table or the square in his town that appeared large in size to him when he was a child now appears much smaller. Sometimes, then, a big motion on a big sheet of paper means almost the same as traveling or running on the paper to the child. The child's physical needs of *motor activity* therefore must be recognized in order to be properly motivated. It might even become significant to know that the child in the beginning stages of scribbling usually does not focus continuously on the motions he produces. To identify with this sensation, we would only have to scribble or draw with our eyes "blank"; that is, not focused at all, looking, as it were, into space. The teacher will then understand the *psychological* significance it has for the child when he discovers that there is a relationship between his motions and the lines on the paper. That the child *can* repeat this performance is of great significance to him, because it gives him self-assurance and self-confidence that he *can master* a situation.

Once the teacher has been able to identify with the general needs of a scribbling child, he will be able to discover the specific needs of a particular individual. He may find out that this child lacks freedom in his motions because he has been continually discouraged or has not been given an opportunity to experience his freedom in his motor activity. Another child may appear particularly timid, fearful to use his material. He might have been punished for breaking crayons or "spoiling" or "wasting" paper. There are many more such individual needs to be discussed in the chapter on scribbling, which can only be understood if the general physical and psychological characteristics typical of this stage of development are understood.

**Figure 6.**

Unless the teacher subordinates his own self to the desires of the child and knows the child's general as well as specific physical and psychological needs, no proper self-identification is possible. Without it, the teacher will never reach the child with his motivations (see Figure 6).

**SELF-IDENTIFICATION OF THE CHILD WITH HIS ART EXPERIENCE**

In spite of the teacher's fulfilling all the aforementioned prerequisites for an effective motivation, it may happen that the *child,* through improper influences, has difficulties in identifying with what *he* is doing. Usually such children laugh about their own products or are continually unsatisfied with them. For these children the final product apparently is of greater significance than the working process. The child has lost his connection with his *activity* and only is eager to "please" others or himself. False criticism or too great an emphasis on the final product may easily produce such an attitude. The child unable to identify with his own experience has lost confidence in his own creative activity. To try to boost the child's confidence in his *drawing activity* would only increase the child's frustration. "Yes, you can draw" or "See how beautifully you have done it" would only direct the child's attention to his own inefficiency. *The final product is only the result of the preceding experience.* If the child cannot identify with the experience, the final product will necessarily show it.

It is therefore imperative that every child be able to face his own experience. If he cannot identify with it, the motivation in his *experience* must be boosted and not the drawing activity! Not "You cannot draw picking flowers? Yes, you *can* draw it!" but "You do not *know* how to pick flowers? Show me how you would pick them." *The child must be able to identify with his own experience before he can be motivated to produce creatively,* as the urge for expression will only come through an intense experience.

Individual as well as classroom motivation must be presented in such a way that each child can identify with the given situation. Objective reports or illustrations are therefore unsuitable means for creating an inspiring atmosphere. The easier it is for the child to include himself in a given situation, the more readily will he identify with it.

Personality differences and different reactions toward experiences, then, count for the enormous variety in kind and intensity of self-identification. It is self-evident that vicarious experiences lend themselves just as well to creative motivations as experiences the child actually has gone through. For both types of experiences, however, it is important that as great a variety of sensations, perceptions, and other experiences are activated as is possible. It is apparent that the sensitive child will become sufficiently motivated through his own power of recalling sensations, but in most cases it is necessary to confront the child with as great a number of experiences as possible in order that he may discover his own way of self-identification. For example, "sitting in a swing" will immediately bring to consciousness, in the sensitive child, all kinesthetic feelings of swinging back and forth, even the tickling sensation in his stomach; he will feel the texture of the rope in his hands, and he will experience the corresponding up and down of his motions with that of the horizon. All that and more will immediately be available for self-identification in the wide-

**Figure 7.** "Mowing the Lawn," drawn by a six-year-old boy. The drawing shows a high degree of perceptual sensitivity.

awake child. In Figure 7 we see a pencil drawing by a six-year-old boy who has watched his father mow the lawn. Notice how very aware he is of the sound, of the grass ahead of the mower that still needs to be cut, and of the mechanical features of the mower. See too that the boy identifies so closely with his father that he puts his own sneakers on him, with the important laces he has just learned to tie.

However, a great number of children need to be faced with their experiences in order that they become strong enough for self-identification. This is still more true for experiences that are not directly drawn from the child's own life or are even vicarious. Since we do not know with which part or type of experience the individual child will identify, a great variety of sensations, perceptions, and imagery should be included in a good motivation. If a child lacks confidence in his art expression, the cause usually lies in too weak or too diffuse an experience. Such an experience is not detailed enough for self-identification; its vagueness does not allow the child to grasp it and project himself into it. Therefore, never be satisfied with such a general statement as "I can't draw it." It is imperative to find out which experience was too vague for self-identification. "What is it that you wanted to draw?" would be the proper investigation from the side of the teacher. If a child said, for example, "I want to draw skating," the teacher would know that most probably the child had difficulties in identifying with his experience. The proper stimulation then would be to draw from the child a detailed account of experiences in order that he identify with them. "You don't know how to skate?" "How is your body when skating?" "How are your legs—your arms?" "What do you wear?" "How does it feel?" are questions that motivate the child in his ability to identify with his experiences. It is this self-identification with experiences that is one of the most vital assumptions for producing creatively.[3]

## SELF-IDENTIFICATION WITH THE ART MEDIUM

Experimentation has been considered a most common principle in art education. "Give the child enough art material, and he will find his way of expression."

This attitude has done as much harm to the child as a meaningless restriction in the choice of art materials and procedures. Although it is commonly agreed that experimentation that may be harmful to physical growth is dangerous, we do not apply the same caution when we deal with the child's mental or emotional growth. For instance, we would never expose an infant to an unselected variety of foods in order to find out what is best for him. The child's ability to discriminate between "right" and "wrong," between materials that help him in his urge for expression and those that inhibit him is not developed, especially in early childhood. Yet psychologists agree that most of the influences affecting the child's mental or emotional growth occur during this decisive period. It is therefore important to investigate more closely the attributes art media must have to promote self-identification of the child with his experiences.

Before discussing these attributes, it seems imperative to clarify an existing confusion between what is commonly called *technique* and *procedure*.

## SELF-IDENTIFICATION WITH TECHNIQUE AND PROCEDURE

A technique is an individual's use of materials as a means of expression. Thus the same material may be used for different techniques, depending on the different ways it is used to express something. One child may use crayons only linearly; another may use the same material with the broad side. The one child may express himself by means of outlines; the other may require filled-in spaces to satisfy his needs. Thus a technique develops according to the individual's own needs. It is highly individual. *A technique, therefore, cannot be explained or taught.* Each child must develop his *own* technique. What can be explained is a procedure. A procedure consists of the different steps in the *general* principles in using a material. There are, for instance, general principles in making an etching. These principles refer to the preparation of the plate, the acid used for etching, the control of the process of etching, printing process, and so forth. These procedures can be explained to lead the student to a possible development of his individual technique. It is needless to say that a technique in etching cannot be developed unless the individual has an intimate understanding of the procedures and that a procedure such as etching would not only be too complex for children but would make them overconscious of the working process.

From what has been said it becomes apparent that any procedure or material used with children must fit their special need for expression, because only then will the child be able to identify with the medium he uses. A technique that does not help the child to express his particular desires is therefore not a good one. Since the child's desires for, and needs of, expression change with his development and growth, it becomes evident that he will identify with different art media during different developmental stages. Which are the attributes of an art medium that promotes self-identification? Three points seem to be the outstanding characteristics:

**1. The art medium must conform with the child's own desire for expression.**

**2. The art medium and art expression must become an inseparable whole.**

**3. No procedure or material should be replaceable by another one.**

Let us look, for example, at water color as the medium. The following seem to be outstanding attributes of this medium: water color is transparent when applied; it has a flowing, merging quality; since water colors merge easily, they can be mixed easily into the finest gradations; because of these mixing and merging attributes, water color changes easily in its characteristics; because of this changing condition, water color has a vibrating, atmospheric quality; because of this vibrating quality, it does not lend itself well to local color tones and surface appearance. The running and merging quality of the medium makes it unsuitable for purely linear expression; its transparency eliminates all types of working processes that call for work in layers, where one layer or brush stroke ought to cover the other. These are only a few attributes of the medium commonly called water color. In the light of these characteristics and the aforementioned three points necessary for the child's self-indentification with his art medium let us now look at the effect water color would have on a scribbling child, on an average child of eight years, on a child of twelve years, and finally, on a youth of sixteen years. A more detailed account of the relations between art media and expression will be given in each chapter on the different stages of creative development, but it seems important to show in one example the necessary care that must be taken in stimulating self-identification through art media.

**Figure 8.** To an involved child, scribbling is an important and meaningful activity.

Since the child's main urges during scribbling are to identify with motor activity, the material used should encourage free expression of kinesthetic sensations without any intruding technical difficulties. Although large crayons or thick tempera paint can be controlled (see Figure 8), water color, which has the tendency to run, would produce a blurred mass and render the child's motions as such indistinguishable. The child, unable to follow or gain control over his motions and unable to identify with them, would become discouraged and frustrated by such a technique. He needs an art medium especially suited to give easy expression to his urge for motor activity. If he scribbled with water color, the lines he produced with the wet brush would have to be interrupted frequently, as he would have to dip his brush into the water and paint. Such an interruption would, without any doubt, interfere with a search for motor control. As he continued to fill his paper with brush strokes, the brush lines would run into one another, merging into a blurred, indistinguishable mass of colors in which the kinesthetic sensation and the child's urge for controlling them would become entirely invisible. As the child could no longer see what he desired to do, he would become frustrated in his desire for self-identification and would stop scribbling altogether. Even at a later stage of his scribbling, when he has the urge to name his scribbles, when he has the desire to give his scribblings distinct meaning, water color would interfere with his experience. Motions that have different meanings can be separated much more easily in a linear technique than with blurring colors. Thus, it becomes clear that water color would greatly interfere with the needs of a scribbling child and is therefore an entirely unsuitable art material for this age level.

An eight-year-old child wants to express his experiences by means of drawings or paintings that resemble nature only as far as significant characteristics may appear in both the child's drawing and in nature. The child's relationship to his environment thus is signified by the child's search for his *own* concepts. Through repetition these concepts often become schema. Yet self-introduced repetition is of great importance to the child, as it is a reflection of his need for finding order within his environment. This structuring of his world is an important assumption for the development of abstract thinking. The stage in which the child repeats the same form concepts for trees or man has, therefore, a great psychological significance. If we did not give the child the proper motivation to identify with his individual concepts, we would not do justice to the child's creative needs during this stage of development.

Such form concepts of a tree or a man represent the child's knowledge of them and what is of emotional significance to him. Such form concepts consist of parts, all of which are meaningful to the child. These parts are not subject to any changes because of optical influences. A man or a tree will not change in sunshine or moonlight for a child of eight years. Illumination, light, or shadows do not influence the child's form concept. Therefore, any technical accident, such as unintentional shading or running of color, that destroys or changes his concept will interfere with his desire for expression. Unintentional changes are meaningless for the child of eight. They only destroy his concept, his relationship to his environment, his confidence, and his self-assurance that he *can* succeed in establishing definite relationships.

As has been said before, the transparency of water color serves best to paint atmosphere and not definite form concepts. Its running quality introduces many accidents that do not lend themselves to repetition. Such accidents could be of a happy nature if the child could make active use of them as visual stimuli. Since in his painting the child is more concerned with expressing his own ideas than with visual stimuli, such accidents would only frustrate him in his feelings of mastery. An accident cannot be repeated. At an age when the desire for repetition is most definite, the inability to repeat would only be disappointing. An unintentional change through the running of paint would render the child's established concept meaningless to him. What often seems of aesthetic quality to adults may seem spoiled to the child because he cannot identify with it. It appears that only an art material and a technique that allow the child to develop his individual concepts without unnecessary restrictions are suitable for this stage of development. The techniques used must permit him repetitions if he so desires. Since water color changes too easily in tone and hue and cannot be directed as easily as poster paint, for example, it impedes the development of free art expression in an average eight-year-old child.

A child of twelve years has discovered himself to be mentally and socially a part of the environment. He may still be a member of a gang. He loves to discover new things, to experiment, and to read fantastic stories. In art he will give expression to his new social and mental awareness. He will show his trend for search and experimentation. What formerly appeared an accident in painting will now be considered stimulating. The flowing, merging character of water color will be investigated. The child of twelve will soon find that he can get effects with water color that he cannot get with any other material. The child has become *visually* aware of his environment and will take great satisfaction in having found a medium by which he can give expression to this visual awareness. A dramatic sky will be made still more dramatic by letting the colors run as they want to. The dynamic quality of water color supports the twelve-year-old child perfectly in his search for new discoveries, for dramatic expression in nature, and above all, in his drive for visual stimuli. He may be surprised by what he can do through the many happy accidents that occur when the wet paint runs on the paper and merges in unexpected beauty. The visually aware child will benefit from such accidents.

A sixteen-year-old youth has become critically aware not only of his environment but also of the work he produces. He therefore has definite intentions, not only of what he wants to express but also of how his final product should look. He might want to paint his visual environment and thus take into consideration all the changing effects of shape and color in distance and atmosphere; or he might want to express his subjective emotional relation to experiences and thus use color and form as pure means of expression. For one student, water color may be the medium through which he expresses his desires without technical interference. Another student may not find in water color the strong opaque quality he needs for the interpretation of his subjective relationships. Water color may be an obstacle to his expression. Thus, when art expression reaches the realm of conscious art approaches, it becomes a specific art medium, suitable for a very definite type of self-identification. This shows very clearly that not all art students have to be able to use water color. Although it may be *the* medium for the one, it may be frustrating to the other, depending on the type of self-identification with art medium and experience.

Five points seem important in selecting art materials and developing techniques:

1. It is the job of the teacher to know and introduce the appropriate materials at a time when the child is most ready to use them in relation to his growth and free art expression.

2. Every material or technique must make its *own* contribution. If a task can be done more easily by a different technique with a better effect, the wrong technique has been applied.

3. The teacher should know that every child must develop his own

technique and that every "help" from the teacher in showing the child a "correct" technique will only restrict the child's individual approach.

4. An art material and its handling are only a means to an end. A technique should not be taught as such, separated from its meaning. Used at the right time, it should help the child in his desire for self-identification. Perfection grows with the urge for expression.

5. The simultaneous use of many different kinds of materials that fit the child's needs is of advantage because it exposes the child to the variety of procedures and makes him sensitive to various possibilities.

It is not the material approach which needs emphasis in a materialistic period such as ours, for the human spirit should transcend the material into creative expression.

### SELF-IDENTIFICATION AND APPRECIATION

Art on all levels is an expression of the human spirit. It expresses the relation of the artist to himself and to his environment. Since it expresses the experience of the creator with the thing and never the thing itself, it can only be understood and appreciated if we identify ourselves with the creator. This self-identification with the artist in understanding and appreciating his work will have to deal with three main factors, all closely interrelated:

1. The level of the appreciator.
2. The subject matter.
3. The means of expression.

1. *The Level of the Appreciator.* A creative product remains meaningless unless the individual can relate himself to it. As self-evident as this sounds, in most of the art appreciation practiced in our classrooms the level of understanding and emotional relationship of the appreciator are almost completely neglected. Art is handed over one-sidedly, and it is not infrequent that the teacher speaks of a work of art completely oblivious of the fact that his listeners have not the least understanding of the high-sounding adjectives he relates to it. We have witnessed classroom situations in which the teacher, so fully and sincerely involved in his *own* appreciation of the work, completely loses contact with his pupils by neglecting their level of understanding and comprehension. It has been demon-

strated that children react differently toward objects or pictures on different developmental levels.[4] Not taking into consideration the child's own needs by neglecting his responses would indeed be a frustrating experience. It is therefore important to base any aesthetic appreciation on the reaction of the pupil, and to expand his aesthetic level from there on. However, it must never be forgotten that the aim of art appreciation is not to "analyze" pictures or to "learn to understand" a work of art. It is much more important to make the individual sensitive to its values in order that he can relate to it meaningfully. "Relational statements are not on the plane of 'true' or 'false' intersubjectively. The same picture (or object) may inspire me and disgust you, but both our statements would have to be accepted as long as the relational 'to me' were understood to follow our judgments and as long as we both gave sincere reports. It is to be hoped that neither of us would end our appreciative experience there, but we would nonetheless begin there."[5] Simple questions, such as "How do you feel about this picture, or object?" "Of what does it remind you?" "Do you like it?" "Why?" "Why don't you like it?" may well be the starting point for an appreciation that leads to a greater sensitivity of perceptual, emotional, and intellectual relationships. This comprehension, however, is geared to the individual and *his* growing sensitivity to meaningful aesthetic discoveries and not to an evaluation of the aesthetic product.

2. *The Subject Matter.* The subject matter necessarily deals with contents. On all levels of art expression subject matter contents have always been of the greatest variety. They may have social significance, they may be of religious origin, they may be historic, scientific, entirely individualistic, or purely abstract in nature. In every instance it is imperative for the creation of a work of art that the artist identify with his subject matter. In order to relive or appreciate his intentions, we have to put ourselves into the situation of the creator. For example, we cannot identify with the intentions of a child who depicts his home environment without learning of his home atmosphere, that is, the subject matter he has chosen.

Although the choice of the subject matter has no influence on the intensity of self-identification, it is of prime significance for the creator. If the child chooses a subject in which he is not interested or to which he has little or no relationship, he will not be able to identify with it. The same holds true for the artist. Very often we hear that it does not matter what subject you choose for your creative production. "What is of final importance is the execution." To separate the content from its presentation would mean to deprive a body of its spirit. In a creative work subject matter and the way in which it is presented form an inseparable whole. In creative activity the urge for expression usually depends on the intensity of the experience. The more intensive the experience, the greater is the desire for expression. Since the child's spheres of interest change with his development and also with his environment, it is of prime importance that subject matter with which the child can easily identify be chosen. Conversely, the teacher will be able to see from the subject matter the child chooses just what the intellectual and emotional interests of the child are.

As has been said before, the subject matter may be concrete or abstract. Even in simple experiences like rowing a boat the child can identify purely with the motion he feels in the boat, the subjective kinesthetic sensation, or he may become visually bound up with the spectacle of the environment. The creative result may be an abstract expression of the kinesthetic feelings he had while rowing. He may completely identify the abstract motions he produces on the paper with his experience in the boat. However, he may also produce a pictorial representation of his relationship to the environment in which he was rowing. He may depict himself large or small depending on how significant he felt when he was rowing, or he may give us an account of his feeling for nature. In every instance we learn to understand and appreciate the child's relationship to his experience by identifying *ourselves* with his presentation.

What has been said for the appreciation of the child's creative work is basically true also for the appreciation of great works of art. In bringing them closer to the child, we have to know that we must first of all make it possible for the child to identify with the artist's relationship to his subject matter. It is therefore of little value for the appreciation of a work of art simply to determine the content of it. In so doing, we have separated the soul from its body. One cannot exist without the other. By trying to identify with the *intentions* of the artist, we shall come closer to the understanding and appreciation of his work. In this way we induce in the child the problems of the artist, and by so doing, we make him feel as did the creator.

3. *The Means of Expression.* Self-identification with the means of expression for the purpose of a better appreciation of creative works may appear to be difficult for one who is not producing creatively. It will immediately become easier if we try to assign "life" to the different means

of expression a creator has at his disposal. For example, if we think that a line is something living, it may move, it may live in friendship with another line, it may go visiting certain places, it may become excited, jump up and down, it may be quiet and calm, it may be aimlessly wandering about, or it may be "on business," going directly to a predestined place. It may even establish certain relationships with its environment, dominating it or being a part of it. The same and many more signs of such living quality can be seen in all other main elements of expression, as in color and space for example. This does not mean that we experience a particular color as happy, sad, or lonely in relationship to its environment; it means that we should identify with the color as something living in the same way as we would identify with our friends. To follow the fate of a tone or theme in music as it meets others, passes them, or unites with them to produce chords and harmonies is a wonderful way of learning to appreciate music in its own realm.

In the same way as we can identify with colors and tones, we can also identify with materials we are using. In fact every child does it, as when whittling a bow. First, he carefully tries to select the right branch—he predicts its behavior—he knows how much he can bend it. He would not do the same with wire. Wire behaves differently. He knows what to do with wood if wood wants to "feel beautiful," when it wants to show its grain at its best. How would wood "feel" when covered with paint? How insincere it would be for wood to look like marble!

To identify with art media becomes even more important for the older child, who is more consciously aware of the significance of the final product and the means with which he reaches it. Art materials and procedures will then always remain subordinated to expression. How materials behave under different circumstances and conditions will then become a fascinating part of art expression or art appreciation (see Figure 9). Instead of talking of skills or design characteristics, we would then be more justified in talking about the behavior of materials and elements of design under various conditions. This would immediately bring to light that lines, colors, spaces, or art materials have their own intrinsic characteristics and also their peculiar reactions just as if they were alive.

## SELF-IDENTIFICATION FOR SOCIAL ADJUSTMENT

It is well to remember that one of the major concerns of art education is its effect on both the individual and society in general. To live cooperatively as well-adjusted human beings in this society and to contribute

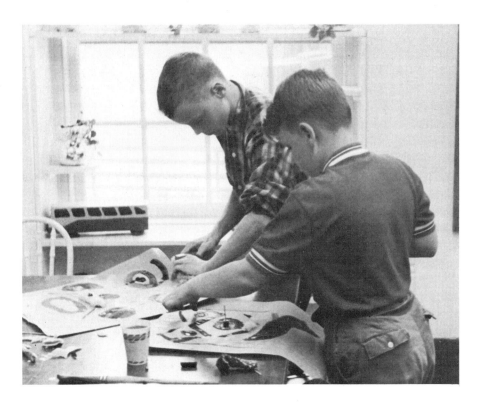

**Figure 9.** Through the creative use of materials, these boys are producing imaginative masks.

to it creatively have become most important objectives for education. It is impossible to live cooperatively and understand the needs of our neighbors without self-identification. As the child identifies himself with his own work, as he learns to appreciate and understand his environment by subordinating the self to it, he grows up in a spirit that necessarily will contribute to the understanding of the needs of his neighbors. As he creates in the spirit of incorporating the self into the problems of others, he learns to use his imagination in such a way that it will not be difficult for him to understand the needs of others as if they were his own. In identifying with art media, by experiencing them in their living quality, the child will gain appreciation and insight into the meaningfulness of art and culture. As the child develops creatively, the other subjects in his learning will necessarily gain in importance by this process. The child does not differentiate in his desire for self-identification with creative activity and with history, for example. History, too, will become alive for the child as he becomes a part of it. Most of all it is important for this world that educators realize that our ability to identify with our work and the needs of our neighbors may ultimately be responsible for our survival.

# The Meaning of Integration in Art Education

### THE INTEGRATED EXPERIENCE

In the process of total integration the single elements to be integrated unite to form a new entity. In art education integration takes place when the single components that lead to a creative experience become an inseparable whole, one in which no single experience remains an isolated factor. What are the single elements to be integrated in a creative experience? Four types of experiences seem to be outstanding:

1. **Emotional experiences.**
2. **Intellectual experiences.**
3. **Perceptual experiences.**
4. **Aesthetic experiences.**

None of them appears in pure form. It lies in the nature of a creative experience that they all unite to form an entity. This intrinsic value of any art experience seems to be of great educational significance, since it promotes the natural tendency of growth. The child neither grows in single subject matter areas nor does he grow in a separate way physically, emotionally, socially, or mentally. Yet in education simultaneity of growth has largely been neglected. Too early specialization, especially on the upper levels of education, has prevented the child's integrated growth and has made man one-track-minded. In some areas he has developed this specialization to such a degree that he has lost contact with the society that has to handle his "achievements." This is particularly true of the sciences; the inability to integrate them with our social growth has created the great discrepancy between social and scientific achievement from which our time so badly suffers. Integration in learning, therefore, becomes of major significance, since it may be responsible for leading our youth to a more unified and better adjusted life.

### THE INTEGRATION OF ART AND SOCIETY

If we want to understand a period and its characteristics, we should look at its cultural, social, and scientific achievements, and its art expression. If we want to understand a work of art fully, we should look at the time in which it was created, the circumstances that determined its style and art expression as well as the individual forces that led the artist to his form of expression. This interchange between social, political, and religious environment and art expression has always been of greatest significance for the understanding of a period. The total integration of all these aspects determines a culture.

If later generations were to look at our contemporary culture, they would get a most confused impression. Gothic cathedrals are built between skyscrapers, and most advanced fields in science are taught in buildings of architectural styles or pseudostyles long outmoded. In this way a discrepancy is created between contemporary teaching and the false façade of the environment. And the educators may not even be conscious of this discrepancy. We cannot expect confidence from our youth in one aspect of our advancing society if we show distrust in another. By so doing teachers deprive themselves of the proper functioning of a most effective educational means—environment. In a well-integrated culture such discrepancies do not exist.

It is clear that this is not a discussion of styles or even aesthetic attitudes, since both are only expressions of the time and its spirit. The influence that the environment has on growth is not a new discovery either of educators or of psychologists. An environment without relationship to the period in which it was created is like a building without a foundation, or like an individual who has lost connection with his own growth and now escapes into a world of meaningless stereotyped patterns. Only if we are unable to face a new situation do we try to find refuge in the repetition of conventional patterns. While teachers are generally aware of how education in pattern inhibits and restricts individuality—one of the most precious goods of a democratic society—they often fail to realize that a carrying over of styles meaningless to the spirit of the present day consists in nothing but an adherence to meaningless patterns.

This disunity between art and society, between education and environment, represents one of the factors from which our present time suffers. On the other side this disunity is clearly expressed by an art expression that because of its extreme individualistic character, almost loses its communicative meaning. Thus, two extreme antipodes can be found within one culture: the tendency toward a confirmation of traditional patterns and the extreme individualistic trend in contemporary art.

Home environment has always had the greatest influence on the growth and attitudes of youth. Here, too, later generations could find a most excellent expression of the lack of integration between contemporary life and culture. They would think that going from the dining room into the kitchen must have meant serious adjustments for the inhabitants. While the kitchen is the room into which the "modern age" has penetrated, the living room is usually filled with assembly line patterns of outdated pseudostyled furniture. Yet we are not at all aware of the adjustment that has had to take place in moving over the centuries from the functionally designed kitchen into the outdated living room. The lack of awareness, too, belongs to the serious educational deficiencies of our time, for we can only remedy mistakes if we see them. We fail to distinguish between conscious appreciation of former styles or even sentimental adherence to meaningful objects, and unaware acceptance of traditional patterns. These existing contradictions must seriously affect our emotional being.

It is obvious that no single individual can be made responsible for the lack of integration between our culture and scientific achievements, but these important characteristics of our time have to be understood especially by those who guide our youth. It is only when we see these discrepancies that we find the urge to change them.

In order to understand and appreciate the implications of these contrasting tendencies between art and society, let us compare some phases of the life of an educator of the present with one who lived in a previous culture. Whereas the Church was the main focal point of education during the Middle Ages, our schools have taken over this function today. During the medieval period the Church fostered the most contemporary architecture. The cloisters significantly influenced the building of their time. The children of this period learned in an environment as modern to them as any Frank Lloyd Wright or Saarinen architecture may be for our time. When the Cathedral of Florence was built, one of the most modern architects of that time was appointed, and Giotto began the famous campanile, which later was continued by Pisano. When, in 1462, Brunelleschi added the dome, the first of its kind, as an entirely different concept of style and building, he did something perhaps more revolutionary and modern than comparable architectural changes of our times, for there was no one who complained about the differences in styles even within the one building. At that time it was quite common in building to show several styles. St. Stephen's Cathedral in Vienna, which was started in Romanesque style, was continued in early and late Gothic, and finished in early Renaissance. While most of our public school buildings progressively move toward a new contemporary style, in most of the institutions of higher learning we do not dare to erect a contemporary building on a pseudostyled average college campus, because we are afraid to disturb a traditionally established pattern.

If the medieval educator wanted to leave his town, he could do so only by using horse-drawn coaches, the style of which was in complete agreement with the rest of his aesthetic environment. This uniformity of different areas of living determined the culture of the past. Today no one who has the choice of selecting an automobile would select an "outmoded" model. Obviously the latest streamlined model would be the first choice of the average American. Yet it is understood that no reference is made to the greater efficiency and power of later models, but to the aesthetic exterior, the upholstery, the styling of the dashboard, and so forth. Here we express a "taste" quite in contradiction to the one we expect in most of our homes. Are we then split personalities who accept different styles in different living areas—old-fashioned chairs at home, modern seating comfort in our cars, streamlined simplicity in the kitchen, and complex patterns of ornamentations in our bedrooms? Why is it that the utilitarian areas of living have accepted our modern style while our homes and social institutions still adhere to the past? Medieval man could pray in churches full of spiritual and religious power, built in the most contemporary styles. The best and most progressive architects were chosen to design them. If one period changed, the style changed with its spirit. Today we pray in churches that are, for the most part, poor imitations of times long past.

What is the reason for all these discrepancies in our modern social and cultural institutions? Apparently we have no confidence in these vital institutions, for if we felt the need to glorify them, the places that housed them would express this spirit. It seems that we have more confidence in our industrial power and institutions than in our religious forms, for we have quickly accepted the new styles for our factories. This, however, is significant in itself, as it reveals a most serious threat toward our ethics and civilization, especially as this is underlined by the fact that the home and family life of today have seemingly to find refuge in past periods. The apparent lack of confidence in our modern homes, too, constitutes a serious threat to our social forms of living. While the new look of our scientific buildings gives evidence of their living character, our educational buildings, especially those of higher learning, usually reflect the past, in an irresponsible adherence to an environment to which the youth of today has no relationship.

It is quite obvious that denying the present would only mean to deny the self, to play ostrich. The consequences of such self-denial, of such an adherence to the past, are too serious to be overlooked. It would not only widen the gap between our industrial and scientific achievements on the one hand and our social and religious institutions on the other but also seriously affect individual adjustments. All too rarely vital and sincere examples of contemporary church and school architecture give evidence of a real strength of spirit. Education must awaken before it is too late. If we cannot adjust our educational achievements to the environment in which they grew, our education will be doomed to die, and with it our social and religious institutions, while science and industry will triumphantly bury them.

## INTEGRATION AND LEARNING

From the foregoing the significance of integration for educational procedures can easily be seen, for without using integrative processes in educational procedures, we will never arrive at an integrated culture. Only when we begin with a well-integrated curriculum in early childhood will we be able to succeed.

*Integration means neither correlation with, nor interpretation of, other subject matters outside of art.* This represents the greatest misunderstanding of the meaning of integration. Teachers often think if history is illustrated, or interpreted in the art lesson, integration of the two subjects takes place. This is by no means true. In such a superficial situation neither is history explained nor does a creative experience become meaningful. In fact, both may have suffered. Yet integration might occur even in such a situation. Let us analyze the circumstances in which integration occurs and investigate the elements that promote or impede integration.

As has been said before, the single elements lose their identity in total integration. What are the single elements of a historic incident that becomes a creative experience? These elements may be of great variety and complexity; they consist of perceptual experiences such as visual, tactile, kinesthetic, smell, or taste sensations as well as aesthetic and other experiences. Let us for instance discuss the topic of the first settlers landing on our shores. An illustration of the incident in the literal meaning will neither integrate design elements (that is, how an experience is expressed in a definite medium) with the individual experience of landing at an unknown place, nor will it aid the integration of movement, like jumping from the boat, or the integration of the smell and coldness of the atmosphere with all the other experiences. All these experiences will either remain undeveloped, disregarded, or as separate parts in a purely literal interpretation of a subject matter. Both design and subject matter remain isolated. Design, the power to express an experience in a medium, has not become meaningful, nor has the subject matter succeeded in becoming a part of the individual's experience. Integration does not occur from the outside; integration is not "made" by "assembling" two subjects; *integration happens from within*. This shows clearly that integration can only take place by self-identification. The integrated art experiences will, therefore, be different with each individual, according to the type of self-identification with the settlers who landed on our shores. As a child expresses his fight with the waves as a kinesthetic motion, the design becomes the carrier of his experience—so much so, that one can no longer be separated from the other. As one child identifies with the fight with the waves when landing, another's experience may be focused around the sensation of stepping on land after endless sailing. The way all these experiences are expressed and organized in art media, however, is intensely personal. Such integration cannot take place when the teacher says, "Children, let's draw the landing of the first settlers." It can only take place if the child identifies with the experience. "How would *you* feel if *you* were in the group that landed; if *you* were the child of a settler, who would lower *you* from the big sailboat down into the rowboat, in a wet cold atmosphere of a dawning day?" "How would *you* feel being rocked in your boat up and down by the waves?" The wave may become the line, and the line, the wave; so intensely integrated that one can no longer be separated from the other. Such motivation of self-identification is necessary to create the urge for expression, which ultimately may result in an integrated art experience.

It has been demonstrated how integration occurs within the individual. Yet it has also been shown how such an integrative process may have its starting point in correlating different subjects. Research studies have shown that a close relationship exists between reading achievement and creative expression.[6] It has been demonstrated that the children who show good spatial coordination are better readers. In fact, one study indicates that the rating of reading readiness by the use of drawings is a better predictor of reading achievement than is the teacher.[7] Such studies should encourage teachers to become more aware of the meaningfulness of integrative experiences. This, of course, is not only true for reading; it can be done everywhere, providing better opportunity for integrative. experiences than can be done with separate, narrowly defined subjects. As long as learning is considered departmentalized, the child will develop inconsistently.

NOTES

1. Horace Heilman, "An Experimental Study of the Effect of Workbooks on the Creative Drawing of Second Grade Children" (Unpublished doctoral dissertation, The Pennsylvania State University, 1954).

2. Irene Russell and Blanche Waugaman, "A Study of the Effect of Workbook Copy Experiences on the Creative Concepts of Children," *Research Bulletin,* The Eastern Arts Association, **III,** No. 1 (1952).

3. L. F. McVitty, "An Experimental Study on Various Methods in Art Motivations at the Fifth Grade Level" (Unpublished doctoral dissertation, The Pennsylvania State University, 1954).

4. Jean Holland, "Childrens Responses to Objects in Daily Living, a Developmental Analysis" (Unpublished doctoral dissertation, The Pennsylvania State University, 1955).

5. Kenneth Beittel, "Appreciation and Creativity," *Research Bulletin,* The Eastern Arts Association, **V,** No. 1 (1954), p. 17.

6. Irene Russell, "A Study of Relationship Between Reading Achievement and Creative Expression," *Research Bulletin,* The Eastern Arts Association, **I,** No. 1 (1950).

7. Anna Grant Sibley, "Drawings of Kindergarten Children As a Measure of Reading Readiness" (Unpublished masters' thesis, Cornell University, 1957).

# 3

# The Meaning of Art
# in the Classroom

ART with all its variety and manifestations can become a fascinating and helpful study in any classroom. To delve into the various areas of development in art gives new meaning and understanding to child growth which is dynamic. A thorough knowledge of the meaning and significance of the creative process and the place of the product therefore becomes of great importance.

## The Importance of Creative Products

In studying the creative product of a child, we must first of all consider the purpose. Do we study it for our own purpose of gaining insight into the child's growth, his experiences, his emotions, his interest? Or do we want to evaluate the child's work for the purpose of showing him his strengths, his weaknesses, his creative abilities, his skillfulness or his lack of skill; in other words, to classify him?

One important factor should be kept in mind in discussing the meaning of creative products. Of prime significance is the influence of art education on child growth. It may happen that a most "primitive" (and from an adult viewpoint, ugly) work may be more significant to the child than a well-executed (to the adult's eye, pleasing) work. It may occur in many classrooms that a child "finds himself" in a painting, and an emotional block that inhibited him in his growth is removed. The child can identify with himself—maybe for the first time—in his creative work. Yet the work he produces may be aesthetically insignificant. It is obvious that such a change in his life is of far greater importance than any final product. To call the child's attention to the "poorness" of his product would only have a discouraging effect. It may even put the child back to his former status. It would also direct the child's attention to the final product and thus make him aware of "qualities," which are either meaningless or inconceivable to him. By encouraging the child in his work only because he has acquired greater skills in technical performances than others, we would signify that we are mainly interested in technical performances. We would thus neglect the most important meaning of art education in the elementary classroom—the promotion of the child's growth. On the other hand, if we recognize the significance to the child of his creative product, however "poor," we give the child confidence and encouragement and make him feel that he is on the right track. In this way he will gain the creative freedom that is necessary for his emotional growth and that encourages the type of independent thinking that is a part of his intellectual advancement. *Creative works must be understood on their individual merits.* This is highly significant and is true for all levels of teaching.

The understanding of children's creative works will not only differ from individual to individual but also from one stage of development to the other. An experience that may be significant but meaningless to a child of seven years may be meaningful to a child of twelve. It also becomes evident that a study of a child's creative works is made by the teacher to gain insight into the child's growth and not in order to confront him with his weaknesses or strengths. The first will help the teacher in understanding his pupils in their creative intentions and also in many phases of life outside art; the latter will only increase the child's difficulties in finding himself and gaining confidence in his creative expression. By discriminating "good" from "bad" without regard for the child's individual desires, we would only set rigid standards. These standards, well known to classroom teachers, encourage the child who lacks confidence in his own work to copy. Unable to compete, he will give up his work. The result of such practices is discouragement, lack of confidence, and inhibition of one group and a go-ahead signal to a selected few. This is in contradiction to any basic philosophy that intends to help the child in his creative and mental growth.

A study of the child's work is significant only if it helps the teacher to gain insight into the child's growth in order to effectively motivate the child in his creative needs.

### THE PSYCHOLOGICAL IMPORTANCE OF THE PRODUCT

One of the very first criteria in looking at a child's work of art should be whether the child identifies himself with what he does. Is there an *active desire* in the child to express himself, or does he just draw "something," or is he inhibited, saying, "I can't draw"? If an active desire for self-expression is present, it will not be difficult for the teacher to find the child's intentions. The easiest way of doing it is to ask the child, "Johnny, what are you doing? Tell me something about your painting." If Johnny is not verbally inclined, or does not want to talk, he should be encouraged to express himself verbally. This is a part of an integrated creative activity. "What does this mean in your drawing?" may start him off. Great care must be applied *not* to use suggestive questions: "Does this mean this or that?" is a question that will easily reveal to the child your lack of understanding. Let the child freely express and explain his work.

However, if the child just draws "something" and does not show any visible desire for active participation, it must first be determined whether there is no desire or whether an active desire for expression is "hidden." This, too, is not difficult to find out. It can best be seen in the type of discrepancy between his verbal expression and his projection. If he says, "There is just a tree and a house," and does not give another comment, even when encouraged, then in most of the cases he did not intend to draw anything specific but "something." However, if he tells of things not represented or visible, then we have to search for individual symbols, which may express what he said and often reveal even more. One child drew a man horizontally, and to his left drew two circles, one with some scribbles in it. Pointing at the circles, the child said, "The one is a glass of water and the other a plate with cookies I get to eat when I am hungry in bed." Immediately, this revealed the child's close identification with his drawing, which superficially looked meaningless, and also his perceptual experiences and his home atmosphere. It revealed that touching the upper circle of the glass was more important to the child than seeing it. It also revealed that the child apparently was often left alone, perhaps in darkness, and given a plate of cookies as a reward, which, together with the glass of water, was placed to his left on the night table. In the darkness the child apparently wanted to assure himself of their presence and repeatedly reached out to touch the objects. By touching them, he became more conscious of the top of the glass and the plate than of the "side view"; accordingly, he merely drew the two circles that he "felt" to the left of himself. Neither the bed nor the night table was included in the drawing.

Thus, the drawing revealed his complete experience, his relationship to his environment, his feeling in darkness, and his perceptual experience of a predominance of the sense of touch. It also revealed a home atmosphere, which, as it was found later, was a great disadvantage for the development of the child. Thus, apparently insignificant creative works that do not immediately show a close relationship between the child and his work are often very revealing. Before we consider that a child is detached from his work and just drawing "something" we must make sure of the child's intentions.

The child who just draws "something" has apparently no particular relationship to his experience. The establishment of a relationship therefore becomes of utmost importance. This is achieved differently for the various developmental stages, and specific methods of motivation appear in each of the chapters dealing with the stages of development.

To motivate children who at least draw "something," to establish a closer relationship between them and their work, will not be found as difficult as to encourage children who have *lost* connections with their expression altogether and simply react with the usual comment, "I can't draw." Some interference has occurred with their desire for self-identification as well as with their ability to project it. Many of these interferences occur in early childhood, when the initiative for self-expression is broken by showing the child how to do things. "What shall I do when my youngster of four years continually asks me to draw something for him? If I draw something for him he appears satisfied" is a common remark. Yet few parents realize that with such actions they may destroy the

**Figure 10.**

initiative of the child to express himself creatively. The reason for the
I-can't-draw child can also be found in the type of criticism based on
adult standards rather than on the child's own. At any rate if the teacher
wishes to evaluate creative work to aid a child in his growth, it will be

of great help to the teacher to find the cause of the child's inhibitions. For the establishment of self-identification of the child with his work it is necessary to give him confidence in his experience. Since the self is the center of the child's experiences, it is best to start with experiences that refer to the immediate self. In using the self and its relationship to environment, the teacher has also the best opportunity to control and boost the experience until the child has won confidence in his mode of expression. Even in stages beyond early childhood the motivation of experiences concerning the self is most effective in giving the individual enough confidence to project his experiences.

**THE MEANINGFULNESS OF CREATIVE PRODUCTS**

Another important criterion in the study of the child's creative work is its meaningfulness, or the *degree* to which the child identifies with his experience and its expression. Degrees of emotional intensity are always matters of subjective value judgments. The degree of intensity in a child's creative work can usually be found by comparing several examples. The sensitive teacher will have no difficulties in recognizing the creative works with which the child felt most intimately bound up. To watch the child during the working process is, however, the most exact measurement. The more children ask questions, the more they look around, the more they look at others' work, the less they are bound up with their own works. The child who is completely involved in his own work has no interest in asking questions, no time to look around; he has so much confidence in his experience that he does not need to look for inspiration from others' work (see Figure 10). He will work without interruption to a definite end.

Usually, technical performance goes hand in hand with the meaningfulness of the child's work. This should not surprise us, for it is the urge to express something meaningful that creates the desire for greater perfection. Technique grows out of the urge for expression. We know this very well also from other areas of activities. We have seen youngsters whittling bows and arrows, beginning in a very crude fashion but through an urge for greater perfection ending up with "professional" jobs. How can the meaningfulness be increased through motivation?

The meaningfulness of a motivation largely depends on two questions: (1) Is the motivation adequate to the *developmental stage?* (2) Is the motivation keyed to the *specific interest* of the child?

It is quite clear that a motivation that is not keyed to the child's level

does not become meaningful to him. For example, a scribbling child being
motivated by visual imagery would be unable to conceive of it, much as
an eight-year-old child could neither understand nor conceive of mechanical perspective. The only motivation meaningful to the child would be a
motivation adjusted to his stage of development. This, however, is not
enough for a meaningful motivation because it would also be useless or
even detrimental to his creative work if we were to divert a child from his
own interests. There are two types of interests that we always have to
keep in mind. The one depends on the general developmental stage, the
group interest; the other is determined by the single child, the individual
interest. For example, a child of six or seven years, according to his developmental stage, is necessarily self-centered. What is of immediate value
to *him* is significant. Everything is focused around the "I" and "my."
The meaningfulness of a motivation for a child of this stage of development will therefore depend on whether an experience is focused around
the "I" and "my." It may happen that a child has a new doll to play with.
Her individual interest and emotions are keyed to the doll. To divert her
from it by imposing something to which she has no relationship would
only be detrimental to her creative expression. This does not mean that a
child who is interested in her doll cannot be effectively motivated in other
spheres of her own interest. Such motivations, however, are only effective if the *whole* child is reached (see Figure 11).

## Art as a Means of Understanding Growth

Very often the mistake is made of evaluating the child's creative work
by only one component of growth, most often by external aesthetic criteria
—the way a creative product looks, its design quality, its colors and shapes
and their relationships. This is unjust not only to the creative product
but even more to the child, since growth cannot be measured by external
criteria of aesthetics only. Aesthetic growth, although very important,
constitutes only one fraction of the total growth of the child. However,
since art has traditionally been interpreted as relating mainly to aesthetics,
this concept is greatly responsible for the neglect of the other factors of
growth. In art education the final product is subordinated to the creative process. It is the effect of this process on the child which is significant
in his total growth.

It also needs to be pointed out that the different components of growth

**Figure 11.** The child with a new toy is eager to translate her feelings into creative expression.

are almost never equally distributed. A child may be very free emotionally, yet he may not be very original in his approaches, his thoughts and feelings, and therefore not be very creative. Another child may be very creative and inventive but may have little feeling for organization, for design. His aesthetic growth has not been adequately developed. Still another child may be highly endowed creatively and also aesthetically, yet his lack of motor control, shown in his lack of physical skills, may hold him back in his creative expression. There are highly intelligent children whose intellectual growth has far outranked the remaining qualities of growth. Such children may be hindered in using their intelligence creatively.

In order to understand and evaluate total growth better, an analysis of the significance of the different components of growth is given in the following paragraphs.

### EMOTIONAL GROWTH

The emotional release given by a creative work to its creator usually is in direct relation to the extent and to the intensity with which he identifies with his work. Neither the extent nor the intensity is easily measurable. Usually four steps of self-identification can be recognized:[1]

1. Stereotyped repetitions.
2. Pure objective reports or generalizations.
3. Occasional inclusion of the self or substitutes for it.
4. The inclusion of experiences of the self.

*Frequent stereotyped repetitions* are usually seen in the drawings of children who have adjustment difficulties. Every adjustment to a new situation implies flexibility, flexibility in thinking and also in imagination. In severe cases of emotional maladjustments the ability to adjust to new situations may be extremely low. There was a girl for whom the slightest change in her situation called for a serious adjustment. For example, when she was unexpectedly asked to get a glass of water, she withdrew into a cramped position, unable to respond to the request. For her, getting a glass of water meant changing her position, getting up, stretching, going, finding a direction, finding the sink, the faucet, turning on the water, and many more changes of her present situation. Unable to face these changes and to adjust to them, she withdrew into a stereotyped cramped position. In her drawings, too (see Figure 12), she felt most secure by repeating the same meaningless, stereotyped patterns of the same schema of a figure.[2] This, too, expressed an escape into a world in which she felt secure. Only when her drawing became meaningful to her did her inflexibility gradually disappear; only when she was able to adjust to a new situation did her drawing show more self-identification. Emotionally maladjusted children frequently escape into a pattern-like representation. Such stereotyped patterns are not adjusted to a particular experience of the child nor do they show a conscious desire for expression.

**Figure 12.** Meaningless repetition of a stereotype is symptomatic, here, of an evasion of reality.

The child simply repeats a schema in a rigid way because of his inability to adjust to a new situation. Such stereotyped, rigid repetitions thus express the lowest type of emotional release. Into this category of representation also belong all types of copy work. This, too, represents a stereotyped form of representation, a type of representation in which self-identification does not take place. Here, too, the child often is inhibited by adults, and unwilling or unable to express his own world of experiences, he escapes into a world of patterns. Copy work or tracing most often does not grow out of the child's inability to face new situations. Most often it is imposed and not a part of the child's behavior characteristics. Often, however, the continued use of copying methods deprives the child of his flexibility. The child accustomed to depending on given patterns no longer has the desire to adjust to new situations; he merely chooses the path of least resistance.

Yet if the child continues the use of given patterns, the end effect will be similar to the one of emotional maladjustment. Accustomed to dependency and rigidity in his creative work, the child's behavior reactions in general will reflect this tendency, because the child in his reactions does not distinguish between his different activities. They all reflect the total growth of the child. Thus, when copy work prevents the child from facing and expressing his own world of experiences, the child may ultimately lose confidence in his own work and resort to stereotyped repetitions as a visible escape mechanism.

It should, however, be kept in mind that there is a natural tendency for repetition in children's drawings during the schematic stage. Stereotyped repetitions, however, can easily be distinguished from the child's natural desire for repetition. Stereotyped repetitions do not show any deviations, whereas the repeated form concept during the schematic stage is used flexibly. From what has been said, it becomes evident that the degree of emotional release in creative activity depends largely on the creative freedom of the child: the more often stereotyped repetitions occur in the child's creative work, the greater is the inflexibility of the child.

Individual satisfaction that the child obtains from his work is not always indicative of its meaningfulness for the child's growth. A child who escapes into stereotyped patterns may gain much individual satisfaction from the drawing of meaningless repetitions. The very escape from facing a world of experiences is a form of individual satisfaction, no matter how detrimental it may be for the child's growth. As we know from experience, emotionally maladjusted children most often feel greatly disturbed when something interferes with their escape mechanisms. When left alone, one emotionally maladjusted girl found apparent individual satisfaction in countless repetition of stereotyped schema. Whenever she was diverted from them by being confronted with her own experiences, she became greatly disturbed. Yet ultimately this very disturbing factor brought her out of her own limitations and gradually adjusted her to life situations. Such cases are by no means rare. We find them daily in our schools—in children's and also in teachers' reactions. "But my children love to draw from coloring books" is a well-known remark. An escape into a pattern is a protection from exposure to the world of experiences. It is a false protection, the same overprotection that some parents impose upon their children. A continued overprotection conditions the child to it and deprives him not only of his freedom but also of his ability to adjust to new situations. An overprotected child sent to camp may sit in a corner and cry for his protection, unable to use and enjoy the freedom to which he is exposed. He apparently was individually satisfied in his overprotection, but such individual satisfaction is no indication of the value of such methods. A child who loves to trace or do copy work may gain individual satisfaction from such an occupation. However, such satisfaction is based upon a false feeling of security and the fear of being exposed to new experiences. Instead of being actively engaged in his own world of experiences, the child escapes into a passive state of mind, which is undesirable and unhealthy for life adjustment, citizenship, and a healthy personality.

If individual satisfaction does not go hand in hand with growth, it is of no value. If, however, individual satisfaction grows out of a feeling of achievement, if it is the result of one's ability to cope with a situation actively, it is a vital human experience that greatly contributes to the acquisition of self-confidence and happiness in life.

An emotionally dull or detached child will express his detached feelings by not including anything personal in his creative work. He will be satisfied by a mere objective report: "There is a tree, there is a house." Nothing is included that may indicate his relationship to these objects. There are no other intentions but to represent the objects. Such detached art expression can be seen in first stages of child art as well as in developed forms of art expression. In the beginning stages such detachments can easily be detected. Usually the child adheres to a mere schema: trees are all alike with little or no deviations; so are houses and other objects. Figures are usually not included at all; if so, they show neither action nor variety in characteristics. In more developed art expression the emotionally detached individual who objectively reports in his work without any participation on his part often covers this lack by skillful performances, or mannerisms.

An occasional inclusion of the self can be seen as soon as the child has achieved some emotional tie to his work and feels free enough to give it visible expression. By *inclusion of the self* we mean any form of inclusion, direct or indirect.

In a direct inclusion of the self the child actually participates in his drawings: he may appear directly in his creative work, or he may transfer his feelings to someone else. A child may indirectly include the self by characterization of objects: a house or tree that is meaningful to the child may have certain characteristics that other houses or trees do not have. A child who is emotionally free and uninhibited in creative expression feels secure and confident in attacking any problems that are derived from his experiences. He will closely identify with them and will with ease adjust to accidental situations that may arise from his work in dealing with different materials and media. Thus the emotionally stable individual is characterized by the great ease and flexibility with which he can identify with his own world of experiences.

### INTELLECTUAL GROWTH AS SEEN IN THE CHILD'S CREATIVE WORK

Intellectual growth is usually seen in the child's growing awareness of himself and his environment. In young children's drawings the details the child can think of are indicative of his intellectual alertness. The knowledge that is actively at the child's disposal when he draws may then indicate his intellectual level. This knowledge changes with the chronological age of the child. Yet even in children of the same age, a great variety of active knowledge can be seen. This difference usually indicates the difference in intellectual comprehension.[3] A child of five years who draws a man with only head and legs (Figure 13) is intellectually inferior to a child who also includes the body and features (Figure 14). A

**Figures 13 (left) and 14 (right).** There is a wide range of difference in active knowledge, as portrayed in these drawings of a man by five-year-old children.

careful account of the significance of details in normal development is given in each chapter of the different developmental stages in the latter part of this book. A drawing full of subject matter details comes from a child with high intellectual awareness. This may not necessarily be a "beautiful" drawing. The details may often be scarcely recognizable. The child's feeling for aesthetics or his ability for skillful execution may often lag behind his intellectual comprehension. As the child grows, details will have a different meaning to him. Details may then refer to a greater differentiation in color and a more detailed account of size and space relationship, or a recognition of social issues. Yet we must not make the mistake of thinking that lack of details of any sort in the creative expression of children *always* means low mentality. Very often emotional restrictions block the development of the child's intellectual abilities; or also, the child's "intellectualizing" of his experiences may restrict his emotional freedom. In both cases the child's creative expression may suffer. It is for this reason that we often hear of children who are "very good in drawing" and seemingly poor intellectually, and others who are apparently "poor in drawing" and intellectually superior. For the development of a healthy personality it is of utmost significance that a *proper balance be kept between emotional and intellectual growth.* If a child is found to be restricted in his creative expression and yet highly developed intellectually, he must be given more art motivation in order to achieve the mentioned balance. If a child is found to be rich in art expression but otherwise seemingly below his intellectual standard, he must be given help and confidence in his desire for intellectual achievements. Our present educational system suffers greatly from an overemphasis of intellectual growth. Learning, that is, the acquisition of knowledge, stands almost exclusively in the focus of education. It is just as important for the child to gain freedom in expression as it is for him to get more knowledge. In fact, knowledge will remain unused, frozen, unless the child develops the urge and the freedom to use it.

## PHYSICAL GROWTH IN CREATIVE ACTIVITY

Physical growth in the child's creative work is seen in his capacity for visual and motor coordination, in the way he guides the line, controls his body, and performs his skills.

In the beginning the mere coordination of body motion with the marks on the paper will be indicative of the child's physical growth from a state of passive enjoyment of uncontrolled motion to a level of coordinated body activity. In the later stages of development this coordination of body activities becomes more intricate. The sensitivity that is often necessary to make most minute changes needs the finest muscle coordination.

It is, however, not only this direct participation in body activities that indicates physical growth in creative activities; the conscious and unconscious projection of the body self into the creative work and the complete self-identification of the creator with his creation account for much of the body control growing out of this type of creative activity. It can easily be understood that a child who puts motion into an arm of a modeled figure feels this movement in his own body. Thus, the child with a high and sensitive consciousness of body experiences will not only show good coordination and control of lines and brush strokes in his work but will also project his ability for body control into his work. This conscious projection of body movements into creative art expression is accompanied by a kind of projection that apparently results from an unconscious presence of muscular tensions and general body feelings. Very often we can see that children with defects project these defects into their creative works. Some drawings by crippled children have clearly revealed the body defect by either an overemphasis or omission of the affected part. This projection, called *body imagery,* also shows the close relation between physical growth and creative activity.

### PERCEPTUAL GROWTH IN CREATIVE ACTIVITY

The cultivation and growth of our senses has been largely neglected in our educational system. Were it not for art education, the child would scarcely be reminded of the meaning and quality of his sense organs. Yet their proper use is of such vital importance, for the enjoyment of life and for vocational purposes, that we cannot afford such neglect.

In creative activity perceptual growth can be seen in the child's increasing awareness and use of kinesthetic experiences, from the simple uncontrolled body movements during scribbling to the most complex coordination of arm and linear movements in artistic production. It can be seen in the growing response to *visual* stimuli, from a mere conceptual response as seen in early child art to the most intricate analysis of visual observation as seen in impressionistic art in which form, color, and space are subordinated to the impression of the total picture. In this area of visual perception belongs the growing sensitivity toward color from the stage of mere enjoyment and recognition of color in early childhood to the ever changing relationships of colors in different light and atmosphere.

Even auditory experiences are often included in art expression (see Figure 7). This inclusion ranges from the mere awareness of sounds and their inclusion in children's drawings to sensitive reactions to musical experiences transferred into art expression.

Perceptual growth further reveals itself in the growing sensitivity to tactile and pressure sensations, from the mere kneading of clay and touching of textures to the most sensitive reaction in clay modeling and other forms of sculpturing and the enjoyment of the different qualities of surfaces and textures in interior decoration and other art forms. In addition to these factors of perceptual growth the extremely complex area of space perception must be added. To the child space means the immediate area around him, the area that has significance to him. As the child grows, the space around him grows, and the way in which he perceives it changes. Space can be perceived visually, by seeing objects at various distances, and also nonvisually, by actually moving in space. We then distinguish between visual orientation in space and kinesthetic orientation, which is used by people who have no sight, or do not use it. Both these orientations decisively affect art expression.

Children who make extensive use of perceptual experiences include in their creative expression kinesthetic sensations, tactile and visual experiences, and also a sensitive awareness of shapes, colors, and the environment that surrounds them. In contrast to them are children who are rarely affected by perceptual experiences. Their creative products show timidity in lines and brush strokes as an expression of lack of kinesthetic enjoyment; they show poor visual imagery, little or no ability to observe, and no inclusion of experiences relating to tactile or other sense experiences.[4]

## SOCIAL GROWTH IN CREATIVE ACTIVITY

One of the factors of foremost significance in human growth is the individual's growing ability to live cooperatively in his society. This ability cannot be developed unless the child learns to assume responsibility for the things he is doing. Unless the child identifies with his own experiences, this is not possible. Therefore, the first step in social growth is made by facing one's own experiences. There is scarcely a better means for taking this highly important step than creative activity. It lies in the very nature of a creative process that the individual identifies with it. In this way he not only discovers himself and *his* needs but also learns to identify with the needs of others. Though the child's immediate self and his home environment will be the starting point for creative experiences, he will soon discover that he is not alone and independent. The inclusion of others in his creative work, the close self-identification with the needs of others, will lead the child to the discovery of the group. He will find much satisfaction through group work, a very important part of creative activities. During the important period that we shall call the gang age, the child discovers his social independence with a group. The arts can greatly contribute, through cooperative work, in giving this newly discovered feeling a constructive meaning.[5] This feeling of social consciousness and responsibility is of great significance for the child's understanding of a larger world of which he will become a part.

In appreciating the arts of other cultures, the child will discover that "the arts are avenues by which the highest meaning of a whole society or culture can be felt, understood, and transmitted from one generation to the children and youth of the next."[6]

The creative works of children who are cooperative and conscious of their social responsibilities show a close feeling for self-identification with their own experiences and also with those of others. The products of children who are socially handicapped, or were suppressed in their desires for social participation, show their isolation by a lack of ability to correlate their experiences to those of others. Their works shows inconsistent, spatially uncorrelated items and the inability to identify themselves with others in subject matter as well as action.[7]

**AESTHETIC GROWTH**

Aesthetic growth is one of the inherent attributes of any form of creative activity. Herbert Read calls aesthetic education "the education of those senses upon which consciousness, and ultimately the intelligence and judgment of the human individual, are based. It is only in so far as these senses are brought into harmonious and habitual relationship with the external world that an integrated personality is built up. Without such integration we get not only the psychologically unbalanced types familiar to the psychiatrist, but what is even more disastrous from the point of view of the general good, those arbitrary systems of thought, dogmatic or rationalistic in origin, which seek in spite of the natural facts to impose a logical or intellectual pattern on the work of organic life. This adjustment of the senses to their objective environment is perhaps the most important function of aesthetic education."[8]

Aesthetic growth is thus essential for any well-organized thinking, feeling, and perceiving, and for expression of these in communicable form.

In fact, it is a part of any proper organization of whatever media we have at our disposal. Depending on the media, we then deal with the different art forms as expressions of this organization. The proper organization of words we call poetry; the harmonious organization of spaces we call architecture; of tones, music; of lines, shapes, and colors, painting; of body movements, dance. This organization does not start on any arbitrary line. It may start anywhere—in life, in play, in art. That is why our whole personality is affected by aesthetic principles. Wherever organization is lacking, the mind disintegrates. Aesthetics, therefore, not only affects the single individual but also our whole society. Aesthetic growth is organic with no set standards; it may differ from individual to individual and from culture to culture. It is this that distinguishes it from any arbitrarily set organization. Also in art, aesthetic criteria are based on the individual work. A creative work grows by its own aesthetic principles. If we attempt to regiment aesthetics, we arrive at dogmatic laws, which have their expression in totalitarian rules. This has important implications for aesthetic growth. It implies that all set rules, rigidly applied to any creative expression, are detrimental to aesthetic growth.

In the creative products of children aesthetic growth reveals itself by an increasing sensitivity to the total integration of all experiences concerning thinking, feeling, and perceiving. This total integration can be seen in the unity of a harmonious organization and expression of thoughts and feelings by means of spaces, lines, textures, and colors. Children who lack aesthetic growth show no feelings for organization either in their thoughts or feelings or in the expression of them.

From what has been said it can easily be understood that aesthetic education should be one of the main forces in a democratic society.

## CREATIVE GROWTH

One of the major distinctions between man and animal is that the man creates and the animal does not. Creative growth mainly consists of the power to use freely and independently and to apply the six aforementioned components of growth for an integrated effort. Creativity is an instinct all people possess, an instinct with which we were born. It is the instinct we primarily use to solve and express life's problems. The child would use it to express himself even if he were not taught to do so. Recent psychological studies reveal that creativity, the ability to explore and investigate, belongs to one of the basic drives, and is a drive without which man cannot exist.

Creative growth starts as soon as the child begins to document himself.

He may do it by inventing babbling noises, or he may do it by inventing his own forms, which he may call "man," "house," or "mountain." It is *his* form, *his* invention, and thus a creation. From this simple documentation of one's self to the most complex forms of creations there are many intermediary steps. It is with these steps that creative growth deals.

In child art creative growth manifests itself in the independent and original approach the child shows in his work. A child does not need to be skillful in order to be creative. Yet, for any form of creation, a certain degree of emotional freedom is necessary because there is no creativity without freedom and fearlessness in subject approach and in the use of various media. Experimental attitudes are evidences of creative-mindedness. Children who have been inhibited in their creativity by dogma, rules, or forces resort to copying or tracing methods. They quickly adapt styles of others as a sign of lost confidence in their own original power to create.

## The Importance of Materials and Skills

Even the most skillful child will become discouraged if he tries to express himself with wrong or inadequate means. The lower the developmental stage, the more the child needs guidance in the selection of the right material. A more experimental attitude in letting the child find his media is important on the upper levels, where the satisfaction from the final product becomes more significant. The way in which to guide the child in his desires for using a particular material for his expression may be approached from two points of view: (1) the *general* suitability of a material for the kind of expression appropriate to the developmental stage, and (2) the *specific* way that the individual uses a material.

The *specific* way in which the individual uses materials to express *his* experiences must be considered for each specific child. It is important for the teacher to know the *intentions* of the child before giving him any suggestions. If the intentions of the child are contrary to his use of the medium, it is obvious that the child needs guidance. If, for instance, a child who paints "A Fair" in monochrome colors is unhappy because he cannot get the noise expressed, a discussion of what is noise in color could follow. Or, if a child who wants to express racing and surrounds everything by a static outline complains about the lack of movement, he might be given the feeling that the outline might restrict movement just as a fenced-in space would restrict movement. Such individual guidance, however, must always be of a general character. It is up to the child to apply it specifically to *his* work.

In the evaluation of the adequacy of an art material both the *general* suitability for the stage of development as well as the *specific* way in which the individual uses a medium must be considered. *A material must be an integral part of the creative work.* This means that the use of a material or a procedure is never taught by itself, separated from the creative work. It is never merely a by-product. It must be a *part* of the creative work. Its perfection grows through the urge for expression. We all know of youngsters who can make innumerable slingshots and who will not stop until a perfect one has been accomplished. If this drive for perfection of a self-chosen object could be used also in the creative skills and techniques, we would accomplish the desired aim. A youngster does not learn how to whittle a stick without having a purpose in mind. But if he whittles a stick to make a slingshot, the use of the slingshot and the fun he will gain from it provide the drive for perfection. It is not grammar that we learn first. There would be no use for it, were it not for the sake of expression. Once the desire for expression is awakened, the urge for greater meaningfulness will develop the desire for grammar. To find out that a sentence might change its meaning through the use of a comma may be an exciting experience for a child in whom the urge for expression is awakened.

Learning an art procedure for the procedure's sake would be senseless and might even develop in the child an aversion toward it. The best food will not taste good if there is no appetite for it; it may even cause indigestion. The same is true of an imposed technique at all levels of art education. The drive for expression must precede the learning of artistic method. The more powerful the drive for expression, the greater is the urge for technical perfection. Especially on the upper levels this desire for greater technical perfection must be supported by the teacher. This support, however, must always be based on the individual desire of the student and determined by his work. There is no formula for drawing or modeling a figure; the study of it is intensely personal. There are scarcely two individuals who would look for exactly the same things. One might want to study shapes and forms, another the anatomical structure, a third the expression of it, a fourth might concentrate on movement, while a fifth might be interested in the figure as such only secondarily but would draw from it the inspiration for an abstract interpretation. The student has to be guided in the direction of *his* thinking. We find many students for whom "almost any definite formula for drawing a figure or fastening two pieces of material together is more pleasing than a spontaneous experiment,"[9] but this represents only an uncreative escape. This type of regimented learning is contrary to any democratic spirit and may lead ultimately to a regimented society. Where else should we learn creative approaches if not in art education? Yet skills and techniques are important, especially in the higher stages of development, where self-criticism and critical awareness lead the individual to a greater emphasis on the final product. Important as skills and techniques may be, however, they must always remain a *means to an end* and never become the end themselves. In a creative technique "the hand cannot be separated from the eye and brain. It includes skilled vision, skilled imagination, skilled planning, criticism, and concentration of energies. The fault of most academic training in art has been that it neglects most of the elements necessary for a full technique. It fails even to realize that there is such a thing as the technique of artistic perceiving and imagining. It leads students too directly and constantly to the final stages of execution and expression, with too little attention to the preliminary phases of creative thinking. . . . The mental and manual are intimately bound together. Perhaps this is the main distinction between the artist and the uncreative worker, however skilled the latter may be in a mechanical way. In the former, direction of the hands and outer medium is controlled by an inner, self-developed aim and vision, whereas the factory machine operator can at times almost let his hands work by themselves, without conscious control."[10]

Especially in our secondary schools, where compartmentalized teaching of subjects prevails to a great extent, we find the same tendency for specialization in art education. It must be possible for *all* children and youth to participate in art education. That is only possible if we recognize the creative potentialities in each individual.

## Grading the Child's Creative Product

Whenever the main attention is diverted from the child to the product he produces, injustice must result both to the child and to his work. A child who may have been inhibited and frustrated in his expression, and for the first time crudely reveals his experience, may produce a creative product that scarcely shows the importance of this action. For the child this may be the first tender beginning of a new life, a life in which he no longer has to escape into meaningless stereotypes, a life in which he can face his own self and freely express it. Yet the beginning is difficult. It may just consist of some slight deviation from his former mode of expression, scarcely recognizable to the naked eye. Yet for the child this first little step is decisive. We would not notice it in his final product unless we knew the child and his former mode of expression. By looking at the product only, we would not only do injustice to the child but also to the significance which the process of self-discovery has for him. By comparing his work with the work of others in the same grade, we would completely neglect the individual child.

Grading of creative products, however it is done, is harmful to the child because it turns his attention from the creative process to the final product. It may add another blow to an inhibited child who for the first time has found himself in his creative activity if his work does not compare with that of others. A poor grade, in addition to his inhibitions, indeed would not promote his freedom of expression.

Unfortunately, in most of our public schools grading is required. If rigid numerical grades can be avoided and replaced by descriptive grades, it will be of great advantage. In descriptive grades the child's problems can at least be revealed. If numerical grades are required, less harm may be done by grading the individual's progress rather than by establishing classroom standards. Such external standards only deal with the product and completely neglect the individual child and the effect the creative process had on him. By grading the child's progress, we at least deal with the child. By comparing the successive products, we can draw certain conclusions as to the child's efforts, the meaningfulness of his *experience,* the *organization* of it, and the *skill* with which he used his media. Even then we may punish him for his inhibitions if we do not take into account that we deal with human beings and not with products.

## Exhibits and Competitions

### NATURAL COMPETITION

In every healthy classroom situation the child feels a part of the classroom spirit. It is obvious, therefore, that he will have a natural desire to improve this spirit by his own contribution. This contribution starts as soon as the drive to express himself in one or another medium is awakened in the child. First, he competes with himself, finding out whether he can do better than he has done before. Growth ·is continuous competition with one's own standards and achievements. This is the most natural and healthy form of competition, especially at a time when the child does not approach his environment critically and with awareness. The family and the natural classroom situation confront the child with competitive experiences that often create difficult problems. The difficulties most often arise from the child's inability to conceive of achievements of others beyond his own level and to cope with them. If parents and teachers do not appreciate the child's own individual contributions on the child's own merits, complications such as jealousy or withdrawal from active participation may result. In creative expression not only the various stages of development differ but also individual modes of expression. Since the child's art activities merely are a means of expression, and his individual mode may differ greatly from that of his classmate, he often may be unable to conceive of and understand these differences.

The situation changes somewhat when the child grows older and the final product becomes more and more significant. For the younger child the natural competition in the home and in the classroom often confronts him with difficulties beyond his comprehension; for the older child natural competition is one of the best characteristics of a good and creative home or classroom atmosphere. In the upper grades of the elementary school and farther on, the stimulation children receive from each other's creative approaches is an invaluable contribution to creative teaching (see Figure 15). The child is simultaneously exposed to many different "styles" and modes of expression, which he now can evaluate in terms of his own experiences. Such natural competition that is not based on standards creates a most wholesome atmosphere.

## FORCED COMPETITION

By *forced competition* we mean the type of competition that does not grow from a natural situation but is introduced. Usually in forced competitions a certain standard must be met and prizes are given as stimulus and reward.

Since teachers often are confronted with this type of competition, an analysis of its educational meaning seems to be important. No doubt most of the competitions are sponsored with the best intentions—usually to give the child an additional stimulus to use the utmost of his abilities and to prepare him for life situations, according to the sponsors, for

**Figure 15.** The stimulation children receive from one another contributes to a creative atmosphere.

competition also plays an important part in life. Competitions further reward him for his efforts, apparently comparing favorably with life situations. Some even say that such preparation is essential, because life is not easy and is full of competition. They say that it would be artificial to protect the child from the struggle to which sooner or later he will be exposed. Finally, it is said that the child should see how his work compares with that of others.

Let us try to apply these arguments to the child's situation and the meaning of art education. Child art is highly differentiated. It is extremely individual. No two children express themselves entirely alike. One of the important aims of art education is to bring out the individual differences that make up the child's personality. Suppressing them would inhibit the child's personality. In order to have *all* children participate in expressing their individual differences creatively, art education emphasizes the freeing process of self-expression and not the final product. Any competition based on the final product is most harmful to the child since it confronts him directly with problems of evaluations of the final product which are inconceivable to him. A child who won a high award in one of the recent competitions could not recognize his own drawing. This is by no means rare. Children quickly change and therefore lose contact with their former mode of expression. Another child did not know at all *why* the first had won the prize; neither did the other children in the classroom. However, since the child had drawn his award-winning picture with the side of the crayon, *all* children in the classroom drew with the side of the crayon from then on. Thus competition not only directed the children's attention to the final product but stimulated them to imitate. John Michael, in a study of the effect of prizes, the effect of adult paintings, and the effect of other children's work, found that each of these influences decreased the aesthetic quality of students' work.[11]

A child does not understand why somebody else's drawing won a prize. For him there are no rights and wrongs in creative expression. If some standards are imposed upon him, they will only harm his personality, since they will suppress his individuality. Since the child does not use techniques consciously, an emphasis on the final product may make him conscious of techniques and take away his spontaneity. Very often the child expresses experiences in his creative products that are not visible even to experienced teachers, yet they may be highly significant to the child. In competitions the aesthetically beautiful and "original" drawings usually receive awards. Original, however, connotes standing out from others by means of external qualities. Those children who express themselves sincerely but neither originally nor aesthetically never have a chance to receive rewards in competitions. Yet they may be the children for whom creative activities are most important, for they need the freeing of their personalities most urgently. Competition does not provide such a release, since it is based on the final product whereas the child grows through the creative process.

The best preparation for the child's future life is to give him a fair chance for a healthy personality. No artifical stimulations—no matter how high the rewards are—can replace the sound *experience* necessary for any creative work.

For the upper levels, that is, when the child becomes more critically aware of himself and his environment, the meaning of competition may change somewhat. During puberty the child's attentions grow more toward the final product, so it can easily be understood that the result of the creative effort assumes greater significance. We must also contend with another factor, which completely counteracts this growing significance. With his increasing awareness during puberty, the youth becomes more conscious not only of the final product but also of his inability to achieve it adequately. We all know that this is the period when most of our youth lose confidence in their ability to draw or paint. Yet one of the main aims of art education on this level is to preserve creative freedom beyond childhood and make art an activity for *all*. Shall we then continue to *emphasize* the dividing line between those who are "gifted" and those who are shaken in their confidence to create? Do we need the added stimulus of rewards for the gifted, which harm the ones who have not found themselves creatively?

Competition may be a great incentive—and often also a discouragement—on the professional level. However, it seems a necessity that has not always brought out great genius, as the history of art will demonstrate. Nevertheless, exhibitions are one of the few means by which artists can reveal themselves to others. If we have especially gifted art students in secondary schools, why shouldn't they participate in competitive exhibits? Should we concentrate, however, on the few by neglecting the others? No jury can take into consideration the meaningfulness of a work to its creator. It is this meaningfulness that is most important to the development of a healthy personality, especially at a time when the individual's confidence is shaken.

There is another aspect of competitions that needs to be discussed— the time-consuming effort required to prepare for them and the pressure exerted to meet a deadline. Some schools seem constantly geared to work for competitions. The results are superficiality, stress on techniques, and overemphasis on the outcome. All this overpowers any serious attempt for self-identification of the youth with his own creative experiences. The natural competition that takes place in every good classroom atmosphere remains the most healthy type of competition.

## CLASSROOM AND SCHOOL EXHIBITS

In speaking of exhibits, we mean the showing of works with no competitive aims. Such exhibits may serve two purposes: (1) to reveal what has been done, and (2) to follow a certain educational purpose. Both objectives may be of great value.

Exhibits in classrooms are usually held for the children's sake. The child enjoys seeing a display of his own work more than the work of others. Which works should be displayed? Should we display them indiscriminately, or should a selection be made? From what has been said before it is quite obvious that no work should be displayed that does not express the child's own experiences. That is why all pattern or copy-work should be excluded. If we have to make any further selection, it should by no means be made from the viewpoint of adult taste. Often the most expressive drawings may not appear beautiful to the adult. *All* child art that expresses the child's own and sincere intentions should be displayed. Classroom exhibits should frequently be changed, for the child quickly loses the intimate relationship to his own work. It is senseless and may even be detrimental to display children's "developments" for them, because their feeling for past experiences most often is gone and old drawings have become meaningless. For the teacher and the parent such displays of developmental series may be highly educational. They give the teacher and the parent an excellent means of comparing different stages in the development of the children, to see the progress, or often to detect certain stereotyped repetitions or emotional blocks. Many important attributes that cannot be seen in the single work are revealed in the sequence of drawings.

An exhibit for an educational purpose needs careful labeling and the purpose should clearly be visible. Every exhibit is a visual organization of material. Not enough care can be given to its proper display. An exhibit in which too many things are shown is confusing. If the attention is supposed to be directed toward one piece, the piece should be clearly isolated. If a series of pieces belongs together, the sequence should be brought out through the display. The educational influence of a well-organized display is very great. The way the sign leading to the exhibit is lettered will affect the visitor's attitude toward the exhibit. A casual sign with poor lettering may immediately put him into a psychological state of nonattentiveness and casual reactions. A carefully labeled exhibit will create the feeling of orderly thoughts and organization. Above all, the assembly line should not take over the exhibits. They should be small, frequent, and meaningful.

## Must a Teacher Produce Creatively?

A work of art as a product of human spirit can be understood only when the driving forces that led to its creation are understood. These driving forces vary with the individual and his developmental stage; they are determined also by the culture in which the work is produced and the medium in which it is created. To motivate the student wisely, it is essential for the teacher not only to know these driving forces but to identify with the creator and to experience these forces as if they were part of his own experiences. The more complex these forces are, the more difficult it is for the teacher to understand, analyze, and identify with him. It might appear that the more primitive the creative product, the easier it is for the teacher to identify with the creator. This is not quite so, however, for primitiveness may be more remote from our thinking than is a generally accepted art expression. The two main sources of difficulty for a teacher in this process of self-identification with the creator are *a discrepancy between his own way of thinking and experiencing and that of his pupils* on the one hand and *a lack of skill in thinking and creating in the different media* on the other hand. The first is a matter of psychological understanding and insight, the latter is of a purely artistic nature.

## PSYCHOLOGICAL INSIGHT IN ART INSTRUCTION

In teaching situations the psychological insight and the ability to think in terms of different media cannot be separated. However, both attributes will vary in significance during different stages in human development. During childhood—that is, during the stage in which the child creates in an unaware, unconscious fashion—the handling of material, the thinking and creating in terms of different media, is done without premeditation. Thus, any influence by the teacher on the use of materials would only interfere with the child's individual approach. Thinking in terms of media is important for the understanding of artistic processes, but it is the *psychological insight* of the teacher that is of utmost significance for the young child and his creative activity. A child who cannot express himself freely will not gain freedom in his creative expression merely through technical aids. Since the young child is totally unaware of technical procedures, his inability to express himself is usually a sign of inhibitions or lack of self-confidence. It is this interference with the child's creative activity through giving technical advice that so often characterizes the instruction of artists or teachers who think for themselves in terms of creative use of media and who do not have the psychological insight necessary for properly motivating the child. If a child lacks confidence in expressing himself freely, the only way to remove his inhibitions is to find their cause. Usually this lies in the inability to establish a relationship between experiences and representation. If a child says, "I can't draw myself throwing a ball," an encouragement of technique in terms of drawing materials will not help him to establish more confidence. On the contrary, it may even widen the gap between his experience and the inability to express it. What the child needs is a boost in his experience. "Show me how *you* throw a ball. What did you do with your arms, your legs? Let's try it again. Now you threw it up high. What did you do with your hands? Where did you look?" and so on. Such questions will establish the child's confidence in relationship to his experience and will finally create the *urge* in him to express himself. *The "mastery" of a medium is only a result of the need for expression.* It is therefore of major importance to learn the child's needs. If these needs are understood, motivation becomes a simple procedure for the teacher.

Can the elementary school teacher profit through his *own* artistic achievements? Yes, by all means, for producing creatively is to a very great extent a matter of identification with the expressed experience. In fact, as it was discussed in the section on self-identification, no creative expression is possible without identification of the creator with his work. It is this ability of identification that the teacher has to use when properly motivating the child; with the young child this can be best achieved through psychological insight without direct reference to skills.

As the child grows, the final creative product becomes increasingly significant to him. With the shift from the emphasis on the working process to the final product, thinking in terms of art materials becomes a part of the creative process. It then becomes impossible for a teacher who has never gone through the experience of creating in a specific medium to understand the significance of thinking in terms of that medium, whether it is wood, clay, pencil, paint, plastic, or crayon. Nor will the study or the manipulation of design elements such as line, space, color, lights, darks, and textures be enough. The *real* experience with them is what counts. A teacher who has never experienced the qualities of wood—its grain and texture, its elasticity, its characteristics of splintering—will never be able to motivate and inspire the youth who has failed to solve a poorly conceived problem in working with wood. To think in terms of the material is an important part of the creative process, especially during the adolescent years, when the unity of concept, material, function, and purpose helps to encourage the youth in his desire to achieve a final product he can appreciate. If this final product does not grow out of organized thinking, a thinking in which medium and expression are unified, the result will express a chaos in which the medium fights the concept, in which materials have ceased to be a part of creative expression. It is understood, of course, that every teacher does not have to be practiced in all media in order to think creatively in terms of materials. It is rather the intense experience accompanying any creative occupation that is important for keeping alive the teacher's appreciation and understanding of creative experiences of the students.

## IDENTIFICATION OF THE TEACHER WITH THE CHILD

Both the mental act of self-identification with the intentions of the creator and the ability to think in terms of the medium in which his intentions are to be expressed are important prerequisites for good motivation in art teaching. To speak of an extreme case, a person who has been blind from birth could never be motivated in his desire for creative expression by referring to color, perspective, and other visual concepts. Color and visual perspective would be inconceivable to him. Being forced to express himself in these mediums would only be frustrating to him. A teacher who identifies with the intentions of his blind students would never do this. Although such extreme cases are rarely found in the average classroom, the principles involved in knowing the needs of the individual to be motivated are the same. Just as we would frustrate an individual who wants to express his inward feeling of a subjective relationship to his experiences by asking him to express merely visual relationships of objects in space, so a visually minded student would feel lost if he had to express himself subjectively or abstractly. While the first fact is becoming generally understood by teachers, there is a great danger in our progressive art schools that a modern standard is being created that excludes the visually minded individual from creative participation. Any rigid standard puts an end to creative production. The sincere desire of the teacher to identify with the creative intentions of his pupils will prevent him from adhering to such rigid principles, and his own experimentation in creative media may help him to refrain from setting up specific standards of "rightness."

## THE FLEXIBILITY OF THE TEACHER

There is still another important factor that makes creative activity necessary to a good art teacher. A work of art is not the representation of the thing; it is rather the representation of the experiences we have with the thing. These experiences change with our subjective relation to the environment as well as with the materials through which these relationships are expressed. This holds true for the design and execution of a chair as well as for the design and execution of a picture. Any form of art expression is therefore a dynamic, ever-changing process. It is this changing process that is of greatest educational significance, for through it the individual's mind remains flexible and adjustable. This is important not only for the student but even more so for the teacher, who needs this flexibility both to understand and motivate the individual and to be able to shift and adapt his thinking from individual to individual.

From what has been said, it is evident that the emphasis in this discussion is on the creative process and not on the final product. That the teacher of art sincerely experiments with the creative media in finding his own expression is, therefore, more significant for him than the final product he achieves. The most primitive and sincere outcome will be of greater value for his teaching than a brilliant technical performance that lacks the self-identification which is so vital a part of sound creative teaching.

## The Teacher's Need for Knowing Developmental Stages

As has been pointed out, the need for properly stimulating the child derives from the basic psychological connection between the child's emotional experience, his mental level, and his creative expression. It is this psychological connection that we have to study. Since subject matter in creative activity has such a different meaning from that in other fields, a thorough clarification of the relation between developmental stages and subject matter is necessary. In arithmetic, for instance, only a gradual increase in the difficulty and amount of subject matter will allow the child to grasp it properly. According to the child's mental development the amount and difficulty of subject matter is thoroughly balanced. The child starts by learning the single symbols for numbers. Then he learns to count, to add, to subtract, to multiply, and so forth.

How does subject matter relate to artistic expression and how is subject matter in creative activity related to the mental stages of the child? Before answering these important questions, it is necessary to clarify the meaning of subject matter in creative activity.

Whereas subject matter in other fields is almost exclusively related to content, in artistic expression it is quite different. The content, what we represent, is trees, houses, plants, flowers, men, and so forth. In creative activity there is no changing subject matter that must be taught, because the same subject matter is used in all the various age levels. There is no orderly sequence of subject matter, as in arithmetic or other fields. A man can be drawn by a five-year-old child or by a sixteen-year-old youth. What, then, can be expected to be the difference in teaching a five-year-old child or a sixteen-year-old youth? The difference in teaching arithmetic is evident. There, the child may first learn to distinguish between one and two and later he will study the higher forms of mathematics. Subject matter in creative art, as stated above, does not change during the different age levels. It is determined by "man and environment" throughout elementary school levels and beyond. Man and environment do not change. *What changes is our subjective relationship with man and environment.* It is this subjective relation between the world and ourselves that has to be studied in order to know how to stimulate a child properly according to his age level. A man to a five-year-old child means mainly the self, the ego, which needs a head for thinking and eating and two legs for running (head-feet representation). For a ten-year-old child a man still means mainly a projection of the self. However, consciously aware of the variety of man's actions, movements, and body parts, the ten-year-old represents man accordingly. A sixteen-year-old youth, however, has already discovered that man is a part of environment, and he represents man with conscious consideration of size and proportions in comparison to what surrounds him.

A tree also changes—for a five-year-old child the tree is something undifferentiated, a trunk and something indefinite on top; for a ten-year-old the tree is a trunk with branches to climb on; and for a sixteen-year-old youngster a tree is part of the environment, with which he is acquainted in detail. The subjective relation of these young people to the tree has changed entirely though it is still the same tree, the same subject matter. Thus it would be entirely wrong to teach *how* to draw a tree or a man. Moreover, it would be beyond the comprehension of a five-year-old child to perceive or understand a tree in all its details as a part of environment. He would not even be able to take in an explanation of the naturalistic meaning of a tree. Accordingly, a "perfect" drawing of a tree with all its details would be entirely out of place. "Perfect" is a relative value judgment, and in creative activity it means perfect in relation to the child's experience. "Perfect" for a five-year-old child is a representative symbol for tree. It would be unnatural if the child drew it naturalistically with all details. Hence, it is clear that subject matter must be confined more to the how than to the what. In creative activity subject matter is based upon *the subjective experience of man and environment according to the various mental levels.* A proper application of subject matter in creative activity requires the study of the change of the subjective relation of the child to man and environment throughout the mental levels. There is no subject matter tree, only the different ways a tree is experienced in the various years of life. However, since there are so many possible ways of drawing a tree in each school grade and since besides trees there are an almost unlimited number of things in the environment, it will be necessary to investigate the common base of children's experiences. This investigation will lead to the understanding of all various forms of expression used in their representations.

The answer to the question "What makes the child express one and the same thing differently at different mental levels" will be of essential importance for the understanding of the child's creative work. It also will be significant for the nature of motivation on the part of the teacher. What makes a child of four or five years express a man by drawing only a head and two legs? Does this really represent the child's knowledge of a human being? Certainly every four- or five-year-old child knows that we have fingernails if his attention is directed toward them. But no average child of this age would ever draw such details. *What the child draws is his subjective experience of what is important to him during the act of drawing.* Therefore, the child only draws what is actively in his mind. Thus in such a drawing of a man we get only a report of the *active knowledge* the child has of a man while he is drawing. In other words, *the drawing gives us an excellent record of the things that are of especial mental or emotional importance to the child.*

Still another factor has to be taken into consideration as an important means for the proper stimulation of a child's creative activity. The change of the child's *relationship* to environment involves *emotional* as well as *mental* growth. This is one of the most important facts in the child's emotional and social adjustment. The child, depending upon the help and care of others (at the beginning on the parents), does not feel the necessity of cooperating or collaborating with others. His most important experience is the experience of the self. That is why his spatial correlations are very indefinite in the beginning. The growing interdependence between the child and his environment is expressed in his drawings. If in this emotional experience the experience of perceiving environment sensually (bodily, kinesthetically, or visually) is included, the investigation of the child's relationship to what surrounds him is placed on a broader base. This investigation still lacks an important part if size, dimensions, distance, and relative proportions of the self to environment are not also included. The differences in the concept of size and distance of children and adults point clearly to the psychological importance of these questions. Distances and sizes that appeared large in childhood appear different to the adult. But since these psychological questions of the child's relationship to outside experiences can scarcely come under the heading "environment," all these experiences are put together under "space"—experiences in space or of space. To simplify matters, *all experiences that refer to things outside our body will be regarded as experiences of space.*

As a result of this discussion, it can be understood why no proper stimulation of the child's creative activity can be given without a thorough knowledge of what changes may be expected, at the various developmental stages in the child's subjective relation to man and environment.

## Classroom Procedures

Art is not a subject where there are specific answers, for here the teacher does not have the book with the right solution to every problem on her desk. In the usual academic subjects the teacher and the books are the authority. There may be many approaches to teaching academic subject matter, but the correct response to a multiplication problem, the exact date of some exploration, or the proper spelling of a particular word are all known by the teacher. In the area of artistic expression, however, the teacher neither knows nor is looking for right answers. Classroom procedures will be focused upon encouraging thinking, feeling, and perceiving for each child in his own very personal way. A teacher's function becomes one of developing children's self-discovery and stimulating a depth of expression.

The atmosphere that is conducive to artistic expression, the environment that will foster inventiveness and exploration, is not the same type of atmosphere that is favorable for memorizing arithmetic tables. In the latter activity the student must concentrate on areas outside himself; he is dependent upon the teacher for recognition of his efforts and he,

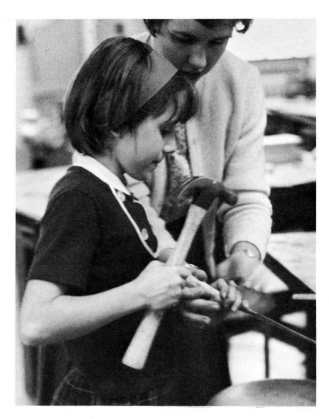

**Figure 16.** A warm, friendly teacher motivates and supports individual creative expression.

along with the rest of his classmates, must deny giving vent to his own feelings. Creative expression is the direct opposite of memorization. Where individual inventiveness, expression, and independence of thinking are crucial, an entirely different classroom atmosphere needs to be established.

A teacher who wants to foster individual expression in the classroom, who wants to encourage initiative and spontaneity, and who wants to have children motivated to produce freely will have to accept and reward creative behavior. Usually *good behavior* is thought to be synonymous with being quiet, polite, and retiring. Good behavior is too often considered the opposite of creative behavior, where a child may be full of curiosity, poke fun at himself and others, question the teacher's direction, and have original ideas of his own. Studies have shown that the creative child is usually not liked as well as he might be by his teachers.[12] Yet the child who looks upon learning as a self-initiated activity is the type of student we are trying to encourage, because he does the type of thinking that is so necessary in our society. This by no means should indicate that creativity and chaos go hand in hand. In fact, the very opposite may be true. Children who are personally involved in an activity may be oblivious to those around them and are not easily distracted. Certainly one of the first and foremost requirements for the development of an atmosphere conducive to artistic expression is the teacher's wholehearted support and belief in the necessity for such activities. Secondly, the teacher must provide the stimulation for individual thinking and remove any dependency upon himself as having the "right" answers. Third, the teacher needs to be warm and friendly (see Figure 16), for it has been found that pupils produce more work under warmth and friendliness than under aggressiveness or domination.[13]

If we look through the history of art, we find that those artists who are recognized as being great are often the ones who made changes in the accepted art of their times. Art has in the past, and must in the future, be considered an important force in developing creative thinking. The recent interest in the development of creativity in school children should give added support to the teacher for including a great variety of art activities within the school program. *The development of artistic ability and the development of creative thinking should be thought of as one and the same.*

There is some danger in encouraging students to think for themselves. But this danger exists only for the teacher who feels insecure within himself. An art class is often confusing to the outsider anyway, because of the problem of having numerous materials distributed and picked up. There is a great deal of responsibility assumed by children themselves in the handling of these materials, when what they are doing is important to them. In a teacher-dominated art lesson, these art materials may be looked upon as being a means of escape from the regimentation of folding paper just so or cutting the proper distance; the opportunity to drop the scissors or fold the paper into an airplane is too great a temptation for the creative child. If the project is developed through the child's own interest, even the folding of airplanes can become a creative undertaking: changes in the design of the folded paper, the adding of a paper clip to the nose, and the trying out of the folded airplane for greater distance in the hall can channel the energies and independent thinking of the creative child into a constructive artistic project. Frustrations that may come out in behavior behind the teacher's back can be channeled into art activities. Specific suggestions for motivating children to express the feelings and

**Figure 17.** Art expression thrives in a relaxed classroom.

emotions that may lie just beneath the surface will be included in the study of various developmental stages.

It goes without saying that the art program of a school will tend to be disruptive (see Figure 17) to the neat, orderly, quiet concept that many look upon as the ideal classroom setting. The art program should provide the stimulation for independent thinking and should encourage and reward curiosity, spontaneous thinking, and self-expression. This is especially important for those children who tend to be noncreative in their classroom behavior. Those children who have a good deal of energy and are freer in their responses need to have these energies channeled into artistic expression. Providing encouragement for creative behavior and rewarding independent thinking can go a long way toward developing an atmosphere of creativity.

## SOME COMMENTS ABOUT ART MATERIALS

Certain mechanical, routine methods of handling art materials make the art program much more effective. Children at all levels can take a great deal of responsibility for their own art materials. Occasionally a teacher will become so involved with the distribution and cleaning up process that he has little time to stimulate the children to a depth of expression. Having children take over some of this responsibility not only frees the teacher from the routine of passing out paper, distributing scissors, cleaning up paint brushes, but it also provides an opportunity for children to become more aware of an art activity as a total experience that is primarily theirs. A violin virtuoso handles his violin like something sacred not only because it is of material value but because it is the means by which he can express himself. A true artist develops a kinship to materials, and some of these feelings can certainly be developed within children.

Some materials should be placed where children can obtain them freely. Spontaneous drawing or painting should be encouraged, and the paper, crayons, or paints should be readily accessible not only for the kindergarten child but for all children through secondary school. The older child should be able to gather and put back materials without supervision. Although art materials in daily use should be left within easy reach of children, certain materials should be stored out of sight. These are not necessarily the expensive materials but rather those that can have special meaning at special times (styrofoam balls for mobiles, shiny paper for Christmas decorations) and those that are potentially dangerous (large glass jars, thin strands of wire, sets of cutting knives).

In no instance should the lack of materials stand in the way of a good art program. This is not to say that such basic materials as clay, tempera paint, and paper can be dispensed with. What is meant is that adding sheets of copper foil, gummed paper, clay glazes, and cans of spray paint do not in themselves insure a good art program. Often children can provide many inexpensive or free materials, such as old newspapers for making papier-mâché, cloth for making collages or banners, boxes for making animals or dragons, and of course bottle caps and straws for making decorations. The art materials are important to an art program, but they play a secondary role; the materials are not as important as the way in which they are used. Since children of each developmental level have different needs, and also have different capacities for using various media, specific suggestions for art materials will be included in each chapter.

One of the most precious parts in any art motivation is the moment of tension before the transition into expression. If this gets lost, we lose an important part of the creative atmosphere. How awful for a child who is stimulated in terms of shopping in the grocery store, and who is eager to portray his feelings about the canned goods stacked way above his head, the smell of the oranges, or the excitement about picking out his favorite cookies, to have to wait for six children in front of him to pass the paper back before he can get started. The materials should be ready for immediate use once the child is ready for them. Sometimes if the material would be a distraction, children can be gathered in a circle in a different part of the room for a discussion.

Although children should be given the feeling for the quality and wealth "buried" in every bit of material, no undue concern should be shown if the child uses this material in unexpected ways. If a second grader crumples his sheet of paper, do not condemn him to inactivity. A question like "Didn't you like that piece of paper?" may be better than trying to condemn his actions, and the child himself may not be able to understand why he felt like crumpling paper. A material like clay might be more appropriate, for it can be twisted and crushed without destroying the material itself. Every material should be thought of as meeting the needs of children and not as dictating a particular type of art lesson.

RELATED ACTIVITIES

1. Observe the changes that take place in art expression by collecting drawings from children from kindergarten through high school age. Trace the development of the representation of a single object, such as a tree. Notice how the subject matter (child's portrayal of his reaction to the environment) does not change, but the *manner* of representation changes as the child changes.
2. Observe in a classroom those children who look around, ask questions, and are easily distracted. Compare their products with those of children who are personally involved in portraying their experiences, noting stereotypes, simple objective reports, some inclusion of the self, complete self-identification with the product.
3. Collect the drawings from an elementary school class. Ask a teacher, an art teacher, a college student, and a child to grade these drawings, as for a

report card. Ask how these judges determined the best and poorest. How do the various ratings compare? Which, if any, seems to be the most valid approach? How does this compare with the discussion in the section "Grading the Child's Creative Product"?

4. Plan and display an exhibit of children's art work with a definite purpose. Organize the exhibit so that it presents a feeling of unity. Identify and label the specific age, grade level, medium, and subject matter or motivation.

5. Make a survey to determine what competitions are presently being sponsored in a local school in music, art, and so forth. Gather information from teachers and students and discuss the effects of these competitions upon the classroom behavior, the time consumed, and the results of the competitions.

6. Observe an elementary class for several sessions and list the number of opportunities for developing divergent thinking. Compare this with the number of times thinking is directed toward one "right" answer. Discuss the role of art in stimulating divergent thinking.

7. Collect drawings from a kindergarten class and list the various methods of portrayal of sensory experiences. Check especially for symbols for sounds and movements.

NOTES

1. See also Margaret Naumburg, "Studies of Free Art Expression of Behavior Problem Children and Adolescents As a Means of Diagnosis and Therapy," (*Nervous and Mental Disease Monographs,* No. 71 [New York: Coolidge Foundation, 1947]).

2. See also Edward Mattil, "A Study to Determine the Relationship Between the Creative Products of Children and Their Adjustment" (Unpublished doctoral dissertation, The Pennsylvania State University, 1953).

3. Florence Goodenough, *Draw a Man Test* (Worcester, Mass.: Clark University Press, 1931).

4. Calvin Countryman, "A Test on the Visualization of Tactile Sensations" (Unpublished doctoral dissertation, The Pennsylvania State University, 1955).

5. See Herbert Read, *Education Through Art* (London: Faber & Faber, Ltd., 1943), pp. 274, 275.

6. Midcentury White House Conference on Children and Youth, *Conference Findings* (Washington: G.P.O., 1950).

7. Edward Mattil, "A Study to Determine the Relationship Between the Creative Products of Children and Their Adjustment" (Unpublished doctoral dissertation, The Pennsylvania State University, 1953).

8. Read, *op. cit.,* p. 7.

9. Thomas Munro, "Creative Ability in Art and Its Educational Fostering," *The Fortieth Yearbook of the National Society for the Study of Education* (Bloomington, Ill.: Public School Publishing Co., 1941), pp. 289–322.

10. Munro, *op. cit.,* pp. 315–316.

11. John Michael, "The Effect of Award, Adult Standard, and Peer Standard Upon Creativeness in Art of High School Pupils," *Research in Art Education,* Ninth Yearbook (Kutztown, Pa.: National Art Education Association, 1959), pp. 98–104.

12. Jacob W. Getzels and Philip W. Jackson, *Creativity and Intelligence* (New York: John Wiley & Sons, Inc., 1962).

13. W. Lambert Brittain, "How Should an Art Teacher Behave?" *The Art Education Bulletin,* **XIX,** No. 4 (Apr. 1962), pp. 30–34.

4

# Beginnings of Self-expression: The Scribbling Stage, Two to Four Years

## The Importance of Scribbling

THE first drawing attempts of a child can be extremely important not only to the child himself as his first expressive symbol but also to the sensitive and aware adult who sees in these marks an individual's early efforts to express himself. It may be that these first marks and the way in which they are received by the adult world will have great importance to the child's continued growth. Adults usually pay little attention to children's early art attempts. The very word *scribble* may suggest a waste of time or at least a lack of content. In actuality the very opposite is true.

In order to understand the meaning of scribbling, it is necessary to know the significance of kinesthetic experiences in early infancy. These motions and movements that relate to the body can be either *passive* or *active*. The passive kinesthetic experiences are those in which the body is moved without engaging actively in movement, such as when the baby is rocked or is wheeled about in a carriage. The active kinesthetic experiences are those which the child originates, such as moving his arms or kicking his legs. These active and passive kinesthetic experiences have a strong influence as the baby develops; his body is very important in exploring, investigating, and in reacting to his surroundings.

At some point, usually at about two years of age, the child given a crayon will start to make marks on a piece of paper. Although scribbling may start earlier than this, a very young child will find a crayon more interesting to look at, feel, or taste. The first scribbles will be random marks; the child may even be looking elsewhere as he scribbles. Out of this he gains great satisfaction, for here he engages in an active kinesthetic experience, one of the first that allows a child to express himself outside of crying. All children in the world begin with scribbling, whether they are Chinese or Eskimos, Americans or Europeans, whether they have dark skin or light. So we can say that scribbling is a natural part of the total development of children and as such reflects their total physiological and psychological growth.

The average child, then, begins scribbling at about two years of age, although some children may start as early as eighteen months. These first marks are usually a haphazard array of lines; we can refer to this as the stage of disorderly scribbling. The crayon may be held upside down, or sideways, or be grasped with the fist, or even be held between clenched fingers. The child may be fascinated with this scribbling and get obvious enjoyment from it. However, he does not attempt to make any visual images with his marks but instead enjoys these motions as a kinesthetic activity.

The range and variety of scribbles is very great. Since the child is not trying to portray some visual object, the scribbles relate quite directly to the child's own development. It is fairly obvious that the only source of these scribbles is the child himself. The importance of understanding scribbles has been largely overlooked, although recently some work has been done in this area.[1] Parents may try to find something in the scribbling that they can recognize, or even attempt to draw something for the child to copy. At this point, drawing something "real" is inconceivable to the child. Such attempts would be similar to trying to teach a babbling baby to pronounce words correctly or to use them in sentences. Rarely would a parent ask a babbling child to repeat the Gettysburg Address, even though this may become important to a child when he reaches fifth grade. The stick figure or the apple drawn by an encouraging parent can be just as ridiculous. Such imposed ideas are far beyond the abilities of the child at this developmental stage and may be harmful to his future development. Thus it is clear that no child should ever be interrupted in his scribbling.

Since the child at this age has no visual control over his scribbling, parents (and teachers, too) should regard this as an indication that the child is not yet ready to perform tasks that require such control over his movements. He is going to be a sloppy eater, is going to have trouble with his buttons, and will not be able to follow visual directions. As long as the child has not yet reached the stage of scribbling where he has established visual control over his motions, it is both senseless and harmful to impose activities requiring such control.

## General Development of Scribbling

### DISORDERED SCRIBBLING

During the very early stages of scribbling the marks on the paper can go in many directions (see Figure 18). A lot depends upon whether the child is drawing on the floor or is standing and drawing on a low table. The way the crayon is held will also influence the type of marks that are put down. It is important to realize that the size of the motions shown on the paper is relative to the size of the child. If an adult swung his arm back and forth, he would cover an arc of about three feet; a child would tend to draw an arc only about twelve inches long. Since scribblers have not yet developed fine muscle control, usually only the larger sweeps will be repeated. We have to remember that the child scribbles with what are big motions for him, although to an adult the result may appear to be only a small drawing.

### CONTROLLED SCRIBBLING

At some point a child will discover that there is a connection between his motions and the marks on the paper. This may occur about six months or so after the child has started to scribble. This is a very important step, because now the child has discovered a visual control over the marks he is making. Although there is no difference in terms of the adult's casual inspection of these drawings, gaining control over his motions is a vital

**Figure 18.** This disordered scribble was made by a two-and-a-half-year-old child.

experience for the child. Now he experiences visually what he has done kinesthetically.

Most children approach scribbling at this stage with a great deal of enthusiasm, since this coordination between their visual and motor development is a very important achievement. Enjoyment of this new discovery stimulates the child to vary his motions. Repeated motions may indicate the establishment of control over certain motor movements. Lines

Figures 19 (above) and 20 (below). These are controlled scribbles by three-year-old children.

Figures 21 (above), 22 (right), and 23 (below). Scribbling is a serious, meaningful activity for young children.

can be drawn horizontally, vertically, and in circles (see Figures 19 and 20). Rarely do we find dots or small repeated patterns, because this means the child has to take his crayon off the page. Children can become very engrossed in this scribbling, sometimes with their noses practically glued to the paper (see Figures 21, 22, and 23).

We also find this new control having an effect upon the rest of the child's environment. The harried mother who six months earlier could not get the child to button his jacket now finds the same child insisting that he do it for himself. The child will understand and enjoy the practice of this newly won ability. Since motor coordination is one of the child's most important achievements, we can readily understand that any discouragement of scribbling at this stage could cause inhibitions. The child has no creative intentions other than to move his crayon over the paper. All his enjoyment is drawn from the kinesthetic sensation and its mastery.

## NAMING OF SCRIBBLING

This next step is a very important one in the development of the child. This is the stage when the child one day starts to name his scribbling. He may say, "This is Daddy," or, "I am running," although neither Daddy nor himself can be seen. This naming of scribbling is of the highest significance, for it is an indication that the child's thinking has changed (see Figure 24). Before this stage he was satisfied with the motions themselves, but now he has connected his motions to the world around him. He has changed from a kinesthetic thinking in terms of motions to an imaginative thinking in terms of pictures. The importance of this change can best be understood if we realize that as adults most of our thinking is done in terms of mental pictures. If we try to think back in our own memory as far as we can, our memory will carry us no further than the naming of scribbling stage. Therefore, when the child begins to think in terms of mental pictures, usually at about three and a half years of age, he has developed a basis for visual retention.

The drawings themselves have not changed remarkably from earlier scribbles. Although the child may start drawing with some mental picture, he is also affected by what he has drawn. So, as the child makes marks on the page, these marks may have a visual reference for him, and this in turn affects the drawings.

Some of the circular motions and longitudinal lines may now seem to tie together to make a person in a child's drawing, but adults should not try to find a visual reality there or try to read into scribbles their own

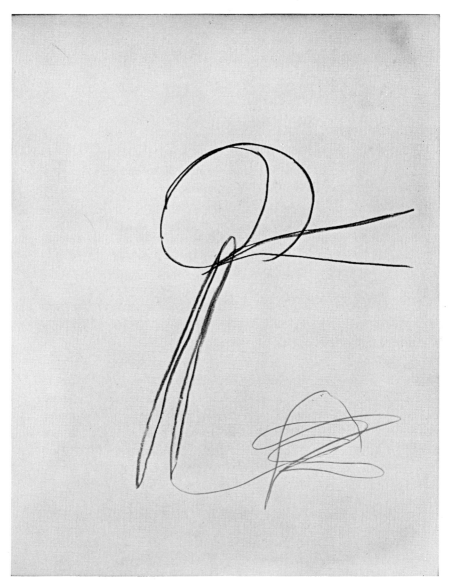

**Figure 24.** A four-year-old's drawing, which he called "Mother Goes Shopping," indicates that he is in the naming-of-scribbling stage.

interpretations of what the child was trying to draw. Most children are eager to show their picture of "Daddy" without interference. There may be real danger in parents' or teachers' pushing a child to find some name or excuse for what he has drawn. Rather, when this important stage in the mental growth of the child develops, we expect teachers to give confidence and encouragement in this new kind of thinking.

## The Meaning of Color

The experience of scribbling, then, is mainly one of motor activity. At first satisfaction is derived from the experience of kinesthetic motions, next from a visual control of these lines, and finally from the relationship of these lines to the outside world. Color, therefore, plays a decidedly subordinate role in the scribbling stage. This is particularly true in the first two levels when the child is establishing motor coordination. The choice of many colors, in fact, can sometimes divert the child from scribbling to the activity of playing with the colors. However, it is of great importance that the child be able to distinguish his marks from the rest of the page. Therefore, a strong contrast is important in the selection of the drawing materials. Black crayon on white paper or white chalk on a blackboard is much preferred over some colors that may not give this contrast.

The scribbling stages tend to last for a longer time when the child uses paint. This may be caused by the lack of control over a brush rather than by the color of the paint itself. We find this when the paint is too thin, and the child becomes confused with the running paint. This can be especially true when the painting is done at an easel, instead of flat on the floor or on a low table. A child who is attracted by color and finds that his marks on the paper are running together may have a fine time splashing his paint. Although this may release tensions, and therefore may be of some value, it should not become a habit and so stand in the way of the normal development of creative expression.

Changes in color can sometimes be significant in the naming of scribbling level, for here colors may have some meaning for the child. Colors can also be fun for the child to work with and to explore occasionally. However, it is of greater importance in the scribbling stages that the child first be given the opportunity to create lines and forms, to develop mastery of his coordination, and to begin his first pictorial relationships of his environment.

## Art Motivation

Usually in the first stages of scribbling no special motivation is needed except to provide the child with the proper materials and the encouragement to go ahead with the activity. Most children will eagerly cover two or three sheets of paper with scribbles. Do not expect the very young child to continue at this activity for more than a few minutes. The child of three may be involved for as long as fifteen minutes. The four-year-old child, if he has arrived at the naming of scribbling stage, or if he has been introduced to a new material, may keep at this activity for twenty to thirty minutes. However, no clock should dictate the length of time a child may spend in expressing himself on paper.

Scribbling should not be interfered with. Sometimes a nursery school teacher will see a child painting a picture that accidentally turns out to look quite like a piece of modern art. It is a great temptation to stop the child at this point and "save the picture". However, the child will not understand this interruption to his scribbling. The child himself should decide when a picture is completed. We have already mentioned the inhibiting effect of trying to see some representation in scribbles, for this may interrupt the normal growth of the child's motor activities at a time when he is developing visual control over his movements.

Occasionally one finds a child who seems to be afraid of scribbling. Certainly a parent or teacher should encourage this important developmental activity. There may be several reasons for this hesitancy to engage in a creative activity, from being told No by the parents when he has started to scribble in the past to a more deep-seated problem of anxiety or fear in a particular situation. Establishing mutual trust is important, and making the scribbling a tempting activity is sometimes necessary. "If you were in a large empty room, would you just stand in the corner? Or would it be fun to run all around the room? Do you think you would go out into the middle of the room and just sit? How do you suppose the crayon would feel if he had this large piece of paper to run in? Would he just stay down in one little corner? Show me how you think the crayon would behave in this large white space." Most children would scribble quite eagerly after such a motivation.

After a child has named his scribbling, we have, as mentioned earlier, a definite clue as to his thinking. This new direction, the relationship of his scribbles to the environment, should be stimulated. We are not talking about improving drawings now, for the drawings themselves do not look much different from earlier scribbles. We can, however, stimulate the child's thinking in the direction he has already indicated. For example, when the child says, "This is Daddy," it is possible to stimulate a greater awareness of Daddy. "Is your Daddy tall? Does he have big feet? Does he ever lift you up? Did you ever feel his whiskers? Do you like your Daddy?" The purpose here is to encourage imaginative thinking. We will be perfectly satisfied with the motions that are made on the paper, although they may not be recognizable to adults; additional lines may indeed give a feeling for lifting or texture of whiskers, or even be symbolic of being held. The inclusion of many senses is important. If the child says he is going shopping, such things as smells, sounds, personal involvement, the child's own part in the shopping experience, his likes and dislikes for this activity, can all be included in the stimulation. But the child should also feel free to ignore these comments and be satisfied with just the relationship between his scribble and his imaginative thinking.

During the very first stages of scribbling no particular motivation is

**Figure 25.** Fairly thick tempera paint is an excellent material for use with this age group.

necessary, whereas any topic the child suggests during the last stage of scribbling is suitable to extend his thinking process. Most important in all stages is the adult's understanding and encouragement.

## Art Materials

Any art material used with children must fit their needs. Since during scribbling the child needs to practice and experience kinesthetic sensations, the materials used should encourage free expression without the intrusion of technical difficulties. Water color, for example, is a very poor medium at this age because the colors tend to run and flow easily. The child is unable to gain control over his motions or to follow his motions on the paper and is therefore discouraged by the material. The usual type of pencil is also unsuitable for the scribbling child because sharp points prevent gliding along the paper, and of course the points break easily. There are numerous art materials that *do* lend themselves to the needs of the child at this stage. A big black unwrapped crayon is excellent and easily obtained. However, white chalk on a blackboard, or a felt pen with black ink, are also excellent materials. Any art material should facilitate expression rather than be a stumbling block, and at this age the need to control kinesthetic motions should be uppermost.

Because of some adults' feeling toward scribbling, we sometimes find that old newspapers, the back of wallpaper samples, or wrapping paper is used for the scribbling child. Although these materials may have a real place in the art program at a different developmental level, these materials have no place in the nursery school or in the kindergarten. Drawing a dark line over a printed news page is much too confusing, the back of old wallpaper tends to be rough and prevents the easy flow of the crayon, and wrapping paper does not provide good contrast with the drawing medium. A 12-by-18-inch size light colored or white paper is best for crayon; a larger 18-by-24-inch size is best if paint is going to be used.

Tempera or poster paint can be used to advantage with this age group (see Figure 25). This is especially true if the paint is mixed to a fairly thick consistency so that it does not dribble or run down the page. The opportunity to use paint can satisfy some of the emotional needs of the scribbler better than a crayon. The result is obvious joy in exploring a range of colors. We mentioned before that a flat surface was best for a child to paint on, since the problems of running paint are thus minimized and the child

**Figure 26.** Working with clay provides the opportunity for a child to experiment with a three-dimensional material.

can work from all sides of his paper. However, in situations where space is at a minimum, it is better to use an easel, or even to fasten paper on the wall, than not to give a painting experience at all. Large fairly absorbent paper, three-quarter-inch bristle brushes with the handle not too long, and some variety of thickly mixed tempera paint provide a wonderful opportunity for an emotional outlet and a truly artistic experience.

Clay is also an excellent material for this age (see Figure 26). Handling a three-dimensional material provides the opportunity for the child to use his fingers and muscles in a different way. Beating and pounding the clay without any visible purpose is a parallel stage to disordered scribbling. The forming of coils and balls without attempting any specific object is parallel to controlled scribbling. At some point the child may pick up a lump of clay and, perhaps with accompanying noises, call it an airplane or say, "This is a car." Psychologically, this is exactly the same change in the process of thinking as we discussed under "Naming of Scribbling." Also here, the child has changed his kinesthetic thinking to imaginative thinking. The clay should not be so hard as to be difficult to work with nor so thin that it sticks to the fingers. Clay of proper consistency can be stored in a plastic bag for an indefinite length of time. Since the scribbling child does not have good control over his small muscles, the clay chunk he works with should be large enough to be grasped with both hands. A grapefruit-sized piece of clay is probably adequate. Since the child is exploring and manipulating the material in a kinesthetic way, there is no need to let the clay harden or even to think of firing these products.

Providing an opportunity for children to become aware of color and texture by the handling of various collage materials may be of value (see Figure 27). Although it is interesting for the child to select some materials he enjoys, and then put these into some sort of assemblage, the continued use of collage materials may stand in the way of the development of motor-visual experiences. The occasional use of collage materials is certainly worthwhile for the scribbling child.

In some nursery schools and kindergartens finger paint is a favorite material. There is some real reason to doubt the advantages of using this medium with the scribbling child. Just as we would hesitate to have a very young infant handle and use a crayon, if the prime enjoyment from the crayon was scratching it or chewing on it, we should hesitate to use finger paint with the scribbling child who tends to be concerned with the sticky consistency. One of the great differences between men and animals is

**Figure 27.** A child enjoys exploring a box of materials of various colors and textures.

that men use tools and animals do not. If we think of art materials as primarily providing the opportunity for the expression of the child, then the misuse of materials may interfere with the activity for which the finger paint was originally planned. Instead of improving control over their muscular activities, children can become involved in the pastelike consistency. We also have evidence from experiments and direct observation that the young child may regress into an earlier stage of behavior. Finger paint, because of its very consistency, may remind children of these former stages and retard development temporarily. You may easily see this effect by watching your children. If they are more concerned with the sticky consistency and with smearing the paint all over than with using it for expression, then they are not using finger paint to satisfy the desire to control their kinesthetic movements. However, for tense, timid, or fearful children finger painting may provide an important outlet even when used in such a manner.

There is no place in the art program for those activities that do not have meaning to the scribbling child. Occasionally a nursery school or kindergarten teacher may plan certain art activities such as pasting, tracing, folding, or cutting; these are designed for a particular end product, such as May baskets, Pilgrim silhouettes, cute snowmen, or projects for Halloween, Christmas, or Mother's Day. Such activities are worthless and should never be included in a program planned for scribbling children, for such activities only point out the inability of the child to perform on a level foreign to his understanding and ability. Sometimes teachers have an interest in discovering new and novel activities for children. Any new material should be looked upon with a great deal of care to make sure that it can further the natural development of children. It must not obstruct the opportunity for the child to gain control over his material; rather, it should promote a closer relationship between his own creative expression and his environment.

## A Discussion of the Meaning of the Scribbling Stage

Growth tends to be an erratic process. This can be seen quite dramatically in the physical growth pattern of youngsters. Although we can say that children of a certain age have an average height of so many inches, we find great differences in individuals; sudden spurts of growth, especially during adolescence, make us realize that growth is not always a smooth continuous process. The same holds true for the development of the young child. We have said that art is a reflection of man's reaction to his environment; in the scribbling stage this is easily seen, as scribbling can be looked upon as a reflection of the physical and emotional development of children. As we find differences in growth, so we also find great individual differences in the scribbling of children.

To a great extent the differences as mentioned earlier in "Levels of Scribbling" reflect a biological change in the child. On the average we expect children to start scribbling at about the age of two and continue until about four years of age. If there is a marked discrepancy, the child is either above or below the average for his age. If we look at the scribble in the illustration in Figure 24 and are told that this was done by a child of three years of age who also said, "I am walking with my dog," as he drew, we recognize that the child is advanced for his age. If on the other hand we find that this is a drawing by a child of seven years who has never drawn other than scribbles, we assume that this child is below the average for his age. This is obviously not a lack of "talent."

The whole concept of intelligence as used within our society is essentially that of relating one child to the performances of others of his same chronological age. A child who performs tasks typical of an older age tends to be considered more intelligent. Since scribbling is a reflection of a child's total development, we then have here some indication of a child's intellectual growth, particularly at a time when the usual group-type intelligence tests do not function. Therefore, a kindergarten child who is still in the scribbling stage will not be able to perform at the level usually expected of kindergarten children. In first grade this same child could not, nor would he be biologically ready to, learn to read. It is obvious that the understanding of scribbling can help us understand children.

Teachers can look at the scribbles of children as being a part of the total child. There is some danger however in looking at scribbles from the point of view of making adult interpretations of them. That is, circles and vertical lines should be looked upon as being circles and vertical lines and not as being symbolic or having meaning other than scribbles. When adults look at an ink spot, each person can see within this ink spot certain figures or forms that remind him of certain aspects of his own life. Adults can also look at scribbles in the same way and see certain forms or shapes, but this has very little to do with the child's meaning or intent. We may get a better understanding of an adult, but little help in understanding children.

Some interesting work has been done in attempting to relate color and form to the personality of children of nursery school age. A well-known study by Alschuler and Hattwick attempts to relate the paintings of some one hundred and fifty nursery school children to certain of their behavioral characteristics.[2] In a two-volume report support is given to the assumption that children expose in painting their emotional experiences and adjustments. Those children who consistently painted in warm colors manifested free emotional behavior in warm affectionate relations, children who preferred blue tended to be more controlled in their behavior, and children who used black tended as a group to show a dearth of emotional behavior. More recent studies have raised questions about these conclusions, however. Corcoran found evidence that three-year-old children used colors in sequential order when painting at an easel.[3] That is, the colors were used from left to right or right to left on the easel tray, regardless of what the colors were. In a doctoral study by Biehler it appeared that nursery school children tended to apply colors in direct relationship to how they were placed on the easel tray.[4] This might indicate that painting at this level is more a mechanical approach than an emotional one. Although at this age scribbling tends to be primarily manipulative and striving for visual control, there are great individual differences. Color as part of the scribbling process in painting is mainly exploratory, and the use of particular colors may be related more closely to the physical arrangement of colors than to deep-seated emotional problems.

There is a direct relationship between how a child approaches scribbling and how he relates to the rest of his environment. His scribbles with crayon, paint, or clay exhibit the same type of characteristics the child exhibits in other situations. This can be readily observed. Children who tend to be delicate and timid usually have a similar approach to art materials. The scribbles themselves tend to reflect the delicate and timid personality of a child. A child who has lost confidence in his ability to adjust to new situations will tend to scribble in stereotyped repetitions (see Figure 28). Lack of confidence can be readily seen in these repeated

**Figure 28.** This scribble repeats stereotyped motions, showing a lack of self-confidence.

**Plate 1.** "Mommy and Daddy," painted by a four-year-old child. He has just left the scribbling stage, still employs a simple circular motion for heads, and has no desire as yet to establish color-object relationships.

Plate 2. "I Am in a Lightning Storm," painted by a six-year-old child. He has discovered his own relationship to color, which is not naturalistic. This discovery is a vital experience, satisfying the child's urge for expression.

patterns, which are drawn over and over again as a measure of security. This harmful security can inhibit the growth of a child, as it tends to block any further development. It is therefore important for the emotional growth of the child that he be encouraged to develop concepts and to realize the possibilities of scribbling.

It is very apparent that an adult artist uses his senses to acquaint himself with his surroundings and also to translate these reactions to his environment into paintings and constructions. The growth of sense apparatus is a vital necessity for everyone. We have already discussed the early development of an awareness of kinesthetic sensations. We also can encourage the development of tactile sensations at this age. The opportunity to examine common materials of our environment provides a variety of both kinesthetic and tactile experiences. By encouraging the exploration of a variety of tactile sensations, an adult can stimulate the child who approaches clay through the use of the finger tips only. A child who does not enjoy tactile sensations may avoid contact with different textures. Encouraging children to experience and become aware of a variety of tactile differences can help develop this area of perceptual growth. Noticing differences between hot and cold, hard and soft, or just enjoying the tactile differences between feathers and glass or between metal and velvet can be an exciting experience. The child who enjoys tactile sensations will become easily engrossed in working with clay.

Scribbling itself is primarily a kinesthetic activity, and the enjoyment of this activity is usually seen in the young child's drawings in the vigorous and large motions. However, it is important to point out that not all children have to make large motions. To force them upon a child is just as senseless as to try to change a delicate child into a robust one. Any imposition creates unhealthy reactions. Providing the encouragement and freedom to enjoy a variety of kinesthetic experiences can provide a firm foundation for future development.

Only when the child enters the stage of naming of scribbling does he have the desire to use different colors to designate different meanings. Color perception does not necessarily have to be connected with verbal recognition of color. One of the first stages of color perception is to merely distinguish between colors. This in no way indicates that a child should be expected to name colors, but rather that the child should be given the opportunity to have some choice of color at this stage.

Creative children scribble independently of outside influences. Even when they scribble in a group they seldom inquire, ask questions, or look at their neighbors' work. For them their own work provides all the necessary stimulation. But there are also children who constantly ask questions, wondering how to use the material, asking the way things should be done. They are also the ones who are easily influenced by the work of others. If one child starts with big round motions, they will start to imitate him. Lack of self-confidence and of independence in thinking are responsible for such easy influences. These are the children who lack confidence in their own creativeness. They are ready to imitate the works of others. They are the ones who most need a boost in their creativeness, and they are also the easy victims of coloring books and of people who promote the use of patterns. Especially when a child names his scribblings will his originality and creativeness become evident. He will develop his own stories and will not need the questions of adults. This in no way implies that the creative child is not influenced by things around him. Rather, the creative child is one who enjoys and gets satisfaction from his own work without the continuing approval of the teacher. Since scribbling is the beginning of creative expression, it is especially important at this time to develop self-confidence in the child and to give him the independence and responsibility for his own work. Ideally, each child should be self-motivated to express himself and to feel satisfaction with the process. It is sad but true that projects planned for the scribbling child occasionally undercut his confidence. Projects that develop dependence upon the adult, projects too difficult for a young child to accomplish by himself, projects conceived by and for adults—all tend to undercut the self-confidence of children in their own means of expression.

## Summary of Growth Characteristics Pertaining to the Scribbling Stage

For a better understanding of the child it is of great importance that scribbling be looked upon as part of the total growth pattern. A child at this age should reflect in his creative work his intellectual and emotional development. He should pursue his scribbles vigorously yet be flexible enough to change his movements whenever new experiences demand such changes. He should be responsible for what he is doing and relate the scribbles directly to himself. He should be able to enjoy his kinesthetic development through his scribbles and later gain visual control over these scribblings. Creatively, he should be independent and free from disturbing influences. He should feel free to explore his environment through a variety of senses and when he arrives at the naming of scribbling stage include some of these senses within his scribblings. The drawings themselves should have a healthy variety, starting at two years of age with a series of random markings, changing to continuous or controlled motions six months later, to much more complicated but varied scribbles when he begins to name what he has drawn. His work with paint will closely parallel the work with crayon, and he will particularly enjoy the use of a variety of colors when he begins to name his scribblings. He will also enjoy working with a range of three-dimensional materials, but no end product looking like something in nature will develop.

To provide the opportunity for a child to grow by means of his art experiences, to develop the confidence and sensitivity so important for self-expression, to provide a range of materials and the environmental setting so important for creative activities, to provide the stimulation and motivation for the developing awareness of his environment, and to provide the encouragement and approval for the creative act—all these responsibilities rest squarely upon the shoulders of the teacher.

### Related Activities

1. Collect examples of art work from a nursery school or preschool group of children. Observe the variety of expression. Try to classify the scribbles according to disordered, controlled, or naming of scribbling stage. Compare the drawings for use of space, control of line, boldness or timidity of motion.

2. Collect the scribbles of one child over a period of several months. Date each drawing and note any remarks the child made while drawing. Keep a notebook in which you record observations on length of attention span, materials used, amount of concentration or diversions, motions and technique used, and the emotional reactions of the child. Compare these notes with the child's motor coordination when eating, dressing, and so forth. Draw conclusions from the three sources of information (the scribbles, the notes, and the behavior) as to the child's growth during this time.

3. Find out the effectiveness of your motivation during the period of naming of scribbling by comparing one scribble done when the child was left completely alone with another made when you motivated the child in the direction of his thinking.

4. Observe children working with clay. See if those children who make forms or shapes also give these forms names. How does this relate to the scribbles of these same children?

5. Watch children paint at an easel several times. Make a list of the amount of paint used and the order of use. Shift the order of paints in the easel trough and see if there are any changes. Experiment with two or three different consistencies of paint each week. Repeat this for several weeks to see if children make any comments or if there is any relation between paint consistency and length of time spent in painting.

6. When a child starts to name his scribbling, does he introduce certain lines or motions for certain objects or experiences? Observe the development of a form for man. Collect scribbles and keep notes on the changes in the scribbles when naming begins.

## NOTES

1. Rhoda Kellogg, *What Children Scribble and Why* (Palo Alto, Calif.: The National Press, 1959).

2. Rose H. Alschuler and LaBerta Weiss Hattwick, *Painting and Personality* (Chicago: University of Chicago Press, 1947).

3. Ambrose L. Corcoran, "Color Usage in Nursery School Painting," *Child Development,* **XXV,** No. 2 (June 1954), p. 107 ff.

4. Robert F. Biehler, "An Analysis of Free Painting Procedures as Used with Preschool Children" (Unpublished doctoral dissertation, University of Minnesota, 1953).

# 5

# First Representational Attempts: The Preschematic Stage, Four to Seven Years

## Understanding the Preschematic Stage

A DIFFERENT mode of drawing has begun—the conscious creation of form! This stage grows directly out of the last stages of scribbling. Scribbling has lost more and more of its causal relationship between body movements and marks on the paper and now has made way for true representation, which is related to visual objects. In scribbling the child was mainly involved in a kinesthetic activity, but now he is involved with the establishment of a relationship to what he intends to represent. This relationship will create a great feeling of satisfaction; in the beginning the mere fact that a relationship with the visual world has been achieved will be of greater significance than will be the quality of that representation.

**Figure 29.** "A Man," drawn by a four-year-old child.
First representational attempts develop naturally
from the child's scribbles.

It is interesting to note how a child can reorganize his scribblings so
that circular motions and longitudinal motions now are brought into a
real functional relationship. These scribbles become recognizable both
to the child and to the observant adult as being a symbol for a man (see
Figure 29). A child's first representational attempts grow directly from
symbols the child was using in the scribbling stages. The fact that the
child is now able to represent on a two-dimensional surface a part of his
concept of the visual world is an exciting and satisfying experience. As
the child establishes this relationship to his world in his representation,
there is a need to enrich this newly won achievement.

Usually the first representational symbol achieved is a man. The man is
typically drawn with a circle for a head and two vertical lines usually
interpreted to be legs or body. These head-feet representations are common

for a five-year-old child (see Plate 1). It is not surprising that the first representation should be a person. The importance of people in children's drawings is quite evident throughout childhood. In fact, the head itself is continually drawn proportionately large. This head-feet representation, then, is the first step in establishing a relationship between the child's drawing and the most important parts of his external world. Additional lines will be placed upon this head-feet representation to further enrich it: the most common are arms, which are usually attached to the head itself, and some symbol for the eyes and other features. To what extent the child enriches this concept of a man depends upon many factors in his total growth.

During this stage of development the child is continually searching for new concepts, and his representational symbols change constantly. He represents a man today differently from the way he will draw a man tomorrow. We see at this stage the greatest variety of forms representing the same object. This constant searching for new concepts will gradually develop into a representative pattern for each child. This individual pattern, or schema, can be readily observed in drawings by the time a child is seven years old; however, before this individual pattern, or schema, is firmly established, we have a very flexible and, to some adults, the most exciting stage of development in children's drawings.

## General Development of Representative Symbols

The discovery that there is a relationship between his mental pictures and his drawings makes a great moment for Johnny. That these drawings can be shared with adults becomes of great importance, for here we find the first steps in graphic communication. The relationship between the drawing and Johnny's mental picture is not based on what he sees, because the child knows more of mother than just the fact that she has a head and two legs. The drawing depends upon the knowledge that Johnny has readily available and that becomes important and meaningful during the act of drawing. Johnny knows much more than he draws for he can name various parts of the body if these are pointed out to him.

The child discovers that there is a relationship between his drawings and outside experiences; and the drawing of this relationship is a process of translation into a new realization of what the child actually knows and sees. This translation we can call a *concept*. The concept the child draws depends upon his mental understanding of past experiences with some object or other stimulus. A *percept,* on the other hand, is a sensory activity, and is done with the eyes and other senses. A child in this preschematic stage is involved in portraying his concepts or his own mental translations of what he has perceived in the past into some new formation or symbol. Since this symbol in art represents something, we shall call the concept in art a representative symbol. By looking at some drawings of a child of this age we can readily differentiate between the understanding of a concept and a percept. Let us look at the drawing in Figure 30. This is obviously a concept. The child thinks that this is a man; a man has a head, two legs, and two feet. "My drawing has a head, two legs, and two feet; therefore, my drawing is a man." If we were to subtract the head from the rest of the drawing, we could not be sure that this was indeed a head. This is very obvious if we try to take away one of the legs. The leg might look like some letter or possibly just a musical note, but it is quite clear that it would not be a leg. Therefore, we have here a concept that deals with the mental understanding and thinking process of the child. What he knows and what he perceives is much more than what is actively in his mind as he is drawing. One can readily tell if a child is still in the preschematic stage by seeing if the parts of the drawing lose their meaning when separated from the whole.

Herbert Read has made an important and extensive study of the significance of the lines in drawing in relationship to the emotions and character of the creator.[1] Since the development of the representative symbol has its origin in scribbling, we can readily understand that in it are reflected some of the personal and even body characteristics of the child. The earliest representational attempts of children continue to be closely tied up with the individual's development.

## Meaning of Space

The representation of space in drawings or paintings by adult artists differs widely, depending not only upon the individual artist but also upon the culture in which he finds himself. Our own society tends to look upon the representation of space as being appropriately shown by the use of perspective, a mechanical perspective with vanishing points and horizon lines. However, this has not been true for other times or other cultures; for example, an oriental concept of space shows objects in the

**Figure 30.** "I Am on the Street," painted by a five-and-a-half-year-old child. Notice the ambulance and airplanes. Space and objects are conceived to be revolving around the child.

distance drawn higher on the page. Many contemporary artists have rejected mechanical perspective of space in favor of placing subject matter honestly on a two-dimensional surface. It can be readily seen, then, that there is no right or wrong way to portray space in a drawing.

The drawings of a child in the first representational level show a concept of space quite different from that of an adult. At first glance, objects in space tend to be put down in a somewhat random order. However, closer inspection will show that the child conceives of space as that which is around him. That is, objects will appear above, below, or beside each other in the way the child understands them. He does not see himself standing on the ground with other objects also on the ground beside him. Possibly this could be better understood if we were to quickly look around the room and list the things we have seen. "There is a table, there is a light, here is a chair, and I am in the middle." No spatial relationship has been established outside the child's concept of himself. Space, therefore, is conceived of as revolving around the child. A boy of five and one-half years drew the picture in Figure 30. Here he thinks, "There am I. There is an ambulance. There are airplanes. There is the sky." No relationship between the objects has been established. The child did not think, "I am standing on the street. The ambulance comes along the street. Above, there is the sky. The airplanes fly in the air." Notice the four wheels on the ambulance.

Since experiencing one's self as part of the environment is one of the most important assumptions for cooperation and for visual coordination, the child's inability to relate things to each other in space, outside the self, is a clear indication that he is not ready to cooperate socially and he does not have the ability to relate letters to each other or to learn to read. A kindergarten teacher can readily tell from a child's drawings whether the child is ready to participate in tasks that require spatial coordination. Forcing a child too early into tasks he is not yet ready for may lead to undesirable actions and attitudes, which may last longer and be more important than doing the task at the moment. Since the child sees himself as the center of his environment, in what might be called a stage of egotism, experiences that are directly related to himself become the most meaningful. A child's conception of his world may be so bound up with himself that he may confuse his own thoughts and feelings with those things around him. If a chair falls over, he is concerned about the chair's being hurt. It is almost as though he, too, were the chair. We can say, therefore, that the child at this stage is emotionally involved in his spatial relationships. The size of objects and the subject matter he selects from his environment, and the way in which these are placed in this early stage, are to a large degree conditioned by value judgments. We can see that the way in which a child portrays space is intimately tied up with his whole thinking process. To teach an adult's concept of space to children at this age not only would be most confusing but might actually damage the self-confidence of the child in his own creative work.

## The Significance of Color

During the child's first representational attempts, more interest and excitement are stimulated through the relationship of a drawing to an object than between the color and those objects. It has been shown that a child of this age discriminates differences in form before differences in color.[2] Therefore, we often find little relationship between the colors selected at this age and the objects represented. A man might be red, blue, green, or yellow, depending upon how the different colors appeal to the child. We discussed earlier some of the findings about the meaning of color in the scribbling stage. Although color can be looked upon as more a mechanical selection at that level, during these first representational attempts a child will often select a color because of its particular appeal. There are surely deeper psychological meanings in the choice of color, but these meanings tend to be highly individualized. It is not strange to think of a child's liking red, and it seems to make sense that when a child is drawing or painting his mother, he will want to select his favorite color for drawing her (see Plate 2). The first relationships of color therefore are determined primarily by their emotional qualities.

The use of color at this age can be an exciting experience. Although the child has no desire for "direct" color relationship, he can and does enjoy the use of color for its own sake. Criticizing a child's use of color, or pointing out the "correct" color for objects at this age would be interfering with the child's own expressions. Ample opportunity should be provided for the child to discover his own relationships with color, for it is through the continued experimentation with color that a child establishes a sensitive relationship between his own emotional involvement with color and a harmonious organization of color on the page.

## Art Motivation

Any art motivation should stimulate a child's thinking, feeling, and perceiving. To be successful, the motivation should make the art experience much more than just an activity; it should stimulate a child's awareness of his environment and make him feel that the art activity is extremely vital and more important than anything else. A teacher, too, must feel that this is an important activity, and he himself must be a part of the motivation and identify with it. As long as the adult remains outside the motivation and merely directs an art activity, we should not expect children to be "with it." To merely follow an adult's instructions for working with materials, or to be handed paper and told, "Draw what you want," or even to have a range of material and activities to do over a period of time—this can result in busyness but can fail miserably in being a meaningful learning experience. One cannot expect a child to gain in his knowledge and confidence and in his sensitivity toward his environment if there is a barrier between adult and child. The teacher

**Figure 31.** The child's concept of the world may be puzzling to the adult, but obviously these forms have significance of an intensely personal nature.

as well as the child needs to feel that this is an important, meaningful, and stimulating experience.

A child should become involved in, and identified with, his art experiences. Since we have discovered that all contact or communication with the environment is established through the self, it is of great importance to stimulate the sensitivity toward the self. Therefore, any art motivation at this age should start directly with the child himself. We know that a child's development in art follows general growth patterns. He has certain needs, which should be considered in any good motivation. First of all we know the child needs to discover a relationship between his own marks and the outside world. Now for the first time he relates to his own work and to his concept of his environment (see Figure 31). These concepts deal directly with the child himself and therefore we know that they are always related to the "I" and "my." In order to do justice at this age level and to make a meaningful experience for the child, these needs must be carefully considered. Ideas imposed by adults and activities not meaningful to the child, which do not stimulate his relationship to his own environment, should be discarded.

One of the best means of stimulating the child's relationship to things around him is to start with the function of the various body parts. This stimulation of a child's concept of his body parts will show readily in the drawings of children at this age. For example, a class of first graders who draw only a line for a mouth can be motivated to include teeth and other facial features by stimulating an awareness of teeth in a topic such as "Brushing Your Teeth in the Morning."

"When do you get up in the morning, children? When do you get up? What, at seven? How long does it take you to get dressed? Does your mother call you? Do you have an alarm clock? How long does it take you to get dressed then? Does your mother have to help you? Do you have to catch a bus? Where do you have your bedroom? On the second floor? Why? All by yourself? After you are dressed are you ready to catch the bus? No? Oh, you haven't eaten your breakfast yet? But you forgot! You went to breakfast without brushing your teeth! Oh, you brush your teeth after breakfast? Don't you have to hurry? Especially if it's raining? Oh, you brush your teeth anyway! Why? You mean it's bad to leave all that food in between your teeth all day? Do you brush your teeth every morning, Johnny? How do you hold your toothbrush? With just two fingers? Oh, you hold it this way! Do you brush your teeth back and forth? Oh, no; you mean you do it up and down? Why? Did you ever get your toothbrush caught in between your teeth? Does it hurt? You have to be a little careful when you brush your teeth, don't you! But, Johnny, did you forget the tooth paste? Some people don't use tooth paste! Do you? Let's think of how we brush our teeth! Let's really brush them good and clean! Now are we all set to go to school? Oh, no; not with all that toothpaste still there!

"Now, children, we are going to paint how we get up in the morning and go to the bathroom and brush our teeth."

Every child should now have a feeling for brushing his teeth, and one may even have a pain where he got his toothbrush caught between his teeth. But every child will be conscious of his teeth, and each drawing will include teeth as an active part of the child's awareness. We can compare former drawings with those drawn after the motivation; if an enrichment of the form concept has taken place, the teacher was successful. In this topic, "Brushing Our Teeth," an enrichment of the form concept of mouth and a closer coordination between mouth and arm may be expected.

In some cases the motivation for a lesson such as the one above can be done by actively engaging the child in an actual experience. One example might be to pass out a bag of candy for the children to munch on. "Is it hard? Do you really have to bite with your teeth?" Actual experiences are sometimes very helpful. However, the activating of the child's knowledge of himself in his immediate environment, to develop his concept of the environment through his own body self, is what is important. Any such motivation should include as many senses and sensory experiences as possible, and should include the total child in terms of his thinking, feeling, and perceiving.

The length of motivation may depend upon several factors. If the children have just engaged in an actual experience, a short discussion may be quite sufficient. However, in some cases the motivation may take longer than the actual drawing or painting experience. Discussing how a child feels in the rain, how the rain feels on his face, or what clothes the child has to put on, and stimulating an awareness of the sensations of walking with boots on or even how his feet feel if they are wet inside his boots, may take a longer time.

In some cases the motivation may be concerned primarily with the material itself. When first working with clay or collage material, the experience with the actual qualities of the material will be most important. "How does the clay feel? Is it hot or cold? Can you push your finger into it? Does it bend easily?" This type of question may be the only motivation necessary to stimulate a child to a greater awareness of his own senses and to help him to identify directly with what he is doing.

A motivation based primarily upon recall of something in which the children have all been involved, should provide the opportunity for each child to express his own feelings and emotions in his own individual way. No attempt should be made to censor the child's creative expression, but rather we should try to stimulate the greatest variety of responses. The general atmosphere for the particular topic should be generally established by a discussion of the *where* and *when*. "Where do you go to school? What time do you go to school? Do you walk?" The *what* should always follow. In this case it might be catching the bus. After a discussion of catching the bus the motivation should culminate in a thorough discussion of *how*. "How do you get on the bus? Do you hold on to the door when you climb in? Is the first step a high one?" Every topic for motivation should therefore include first the *where* and *when,* second the *what,* and third the *how.*

## Subject Matter

The most important consideration in the selection of topics for children in these first representational attempts should be the meaning of the activity for the children. *The more involved the child becomes in the art activity, the more he identifies with what he is doing, the more he is actively using his senses, the more the project is really his own, the more meaningful it becomes for him.* At this age it is particularly important that any motivation or any subject matter be related directly through the child himself. To emphasize this, the following topics are characterized by the words *I* and *my.*

"I and My Mother" (sizes)
"I and My Family" (sizes)
"I and My House" (sizes)
"I Am Brushing My Teeth" (teeth)
"I Am Drinking My Milk" (mouth)
"I Am Blowing My Nose" (nose)
"I Hurt My Knee" (knee)
"I Am at the Dentist" (teeth)
"I Am Picking Flowers" (hand, arms)
"I Am Eating Breakfast" (mouth)
"I Am on the Swing" (body)
"I Have a Stomach Ache" (body)
"I and My Doll" (emotional relationship)
"I Get a Birthday Present" (emotional relationship)
"I and My Pet" (emotional relationship)

Children often have subject matter within themselves, requiring no motivation or further encouragement for it to spill out. Every kindergarten and first grade teacher realizes that if Johnny's cat has had kittens, this news will come out in arithmetic class, during social studies, or maybe when the child bursts into the room first thing in the morning. Ample opportunity should be given children to express on paper their feelings and emotions. Some of these feelings will be very apparent to any adult. Such topics as "The First Snowfall," "The Storm," "An Approaching Holiday," "A Community Celebration," "A Big Fire" are all subject matter that cannot be ignored. However, some subject matter will be a great deal more personal to the individual child. Such topics as "My New Baby Sister," "I Got Hit by a Car," "I Got Lost in the Store," "My House Caught on Fire," or "I Have a New Dress" all make appropriate subject matter for any age. The child who produced Figure 32 eagerly explained that his teacher, represented by an armless figure, watched while he played in the kindergarten play yard. When the child is eager for expression, art should certainly not be limited to a specific time of the day nor regimented to a particular topic.

Another topic area that is suitable for subject matter during these first representational attempts is an art material itself. Any art material should play a subordinate role in an art experience, and the child's own expression should be of greatest importance. However, at this age children have been exposed to a limited number of art materials, and in some cases

**Figure 32.** "I Am Playing in the School Yard," drawn in chalk by a five-year-old boy. Apparently the teacher only watches while the youngster plays on the slide, for the child has drawn the teacher without arms.

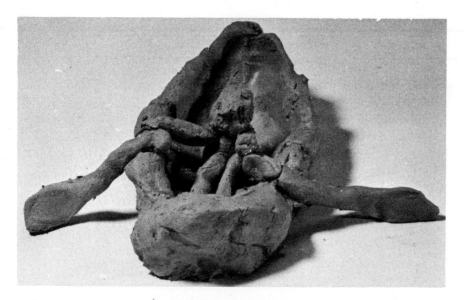

**Figure 33.** "I Am Rowing the Boat," modeled in clay, shows how exploration of a three-dimensional material may provide new spatial concepts and understanding.

the experience with these materials may have been limited to a restricted use. The prime reason, then, for using an art material for subject matter is to provide the child with a positive attitude toward these materials and to insure the greatest amount of exploration and flexibility in its use. Such experimentations with art materials should be related directly to the child himself (see Figure 33) and should not be concerned with any adult consideration of "artistic qualities." The use of an art material as a subject matter should therefore take the form of "How I Explore and Experiment with the Various Qualities of Clay," or "How I Find Out About the Qualities of Tempera Paint."

Any topic for art expression, whether it is an experiment with art materials or an expression of a real or vicarious experience, should not only be tied closely to the child's body self but should also provide the opportunity for the child to establish a relationship between his drawing and his own environment.

## Art Materials

Since the child at this age is excited by his ability to represent what is meaningful to him, any art experience should provide the opportunity for developing mastery of the material itself. Since the process of creating is of greater significance than the final product, an art material should be selected that meets the need of the age group for which it was planned. Constantly introducing or changing art materials may actually stand in the way of a child's mastering the material enough to express his own feelings, his own reactions to his sensory processes and his own intellectual concepts of his environment.

Another consideration is that any art material should be a true art material. That is, expression itself is not limited to any age group, and any material used with children should be of such a nature that a child may use this material throughout his life. There should be no "cute" art materials for kindergarten children to use, since they provide no opportunity for continued growth.

For developing great freedom, a bristle brush, tempera paint thickly prepared, on a somewhat absorbent large sheet of paper are best materials for this age level. Absorbent paper (about 18 by 24 inches) is recommended because it prevents the paint from running. A low flat table provides the best surface on which to paint; the floor can also be successfully used. If the limitations of space do not allow painting on a flat surface, easels or a bulletin board can be used. Here, however, the paint should be of thick enough consistency so that the child can control his painting without the frustration of dripping accidents.

Good quality colored crayons and smaller sheets of paper (12 by 18 inches) are excellent materials. The quality of the crayon can be determined by the amount of surplus wax that can easily be scratched off the paper. The more surplus there is, the poorer the quality of the crayon. The crayon should be large and unwrapped. Too often a new set of wrapped, sharply pointed crayons is looked upon as a treasure to keep rather than a material to use. Unwrapped crayons can be used on the sides and ends, and their use is less likely to be confused with the function of a pencil.

Clay is an excellent three-dimensional material for the preschematic stage. As in drawings we find a search for a definite concept of form; in clay this search is seen in a constant change of modes of representation and in the representations themselves. Both pulling out from the lump of clay all meaningful parts and adding parts together to make a form can be observed. Moist clay can be easily stored in plastic bags, and water can be added as needed to maintain the proper consistency. Plasticine, which is essentially clay with an oil base, is much more expensive than clay and the consistency cannot be altered.

**Figure 34.** "Indians," drawn with a felt-tipped pen by a seven-year-old girl. This material lends itself to a bold, direct presentation of thought. Every art material has its own characteristics and specific values.

In addition to these basic materials there is a range of other materials that are quite suitable for this developmental level. These include colored chalk, felt tipped pens (see the Indians in Figure 34), colored papers, collage materials, and other materials that truly give the child an opportunity to explore and manipulate his environment and provide for a flexible development of his concepts. Cute or tricky use of materials should be avoided, such as dripping paint, pasting cereals, printing or using stencils, or using materials in methods foreign to the child's own intentions. Purposely, no decorative techniques have been suggested, as on this level no child feels the conscious need for decoration. As long as the desire to search for a concept of form and space is predominant, the desire for decoration generally does not develop.

There is no place at this age level for cutting out paper flying angels or Pilgrim hats. A kindergarten or first grade teacher should not be concerned with mass-producing little stereotypes for holidays or seasonal events, since such activities can only make the child feel inadequate and tend to reduce his confidence in his own means of expression.

## A Discussion of the Meaning of the Preschematic Stage

It is important to remember that a child's art is a reflection of himself. A child cannot, nor should he be expected to, draw or paint like someone else. Although this may seem like an obvious statement, it is well to keep this firmly in mind. There are great individual differences in children just as there are great individual differences in children's drawings. Children also have some general growth characteristics that are common to their developmental level and we find this also true in their art work. In talking about the child's developing concepts, we have of course been talking about his thought processes. The development of these concepts in art and their relationship to reality can help us understand the total thinking processes of these children. Since this is an age where we find great flexibility and change in drawings, it is also an age at which we find rapid changes in mode of thinking. We are not discussing thinking as only the quiet contemplation of a problem but rather considering the total intellectual development, which at this age is nicely confused with fantasy, reality, and biological responses to the environment.

A child who has reached the chronological age of four or five and who still thinks in terms of motions has not advanced intellectually to an average stage of growth. In looking over a series of drawings by a five-year-old child, we would normally expect some representational attempts. The more differentiated these attempts are, the higher the intellectual processes have been developed. Generally, the more details included in a drawing, the more aware the child is of those things around him. Our whole concept of intelligence is based primarily upon this assumption. The more a person knows about his environment—the more he is actively aware of and can utilize the various factors within his environment —the more intellectually developed he is. It is fairly obvious, then, that the child who has not yet developed concepts of his environment at the age of five is retarded, and one reason for this retardation might be retardation in his intellectual growth.

We find some of the same characteristics of development in looking at clay. Here also it is of prime significance for the intellectual advancement

**Figure 35.** "Walking in the Grass After the Rain," drawn by a six-year-old boy. The picture shows the intense feeling of wetness from the grass on the boy's toes.

of the child to see if his creative concepts are already concerned with imaginative projections. Children at this age may model by starting with details, bringing the different parts into their consciousness and relating them to each other. Children who model by starting with the whole lump of clay usually do not go into detailed expression but rather remain with the whole.

One of the most important indications of this preschematic stage is the flexibility of the child. This can best be seen in the frequent changes in the child's concepts. The significance of stereotyped repetitions as an escape mechanism and as an indication of an emotional block has been discussed previously. During the preschematic stage these stereotyped repetitions are usually seen as merely repetitions of the same symbol without any deviations. A child who finds a symbol to hide behind, will exhibit in other behavior a tendency to withdraw or to hide behind social stereotypes. However, a child who reacts toward meaningful experiences in an emotionally sensitive way will show this emotional sensitivity in his art work. In his drawings he will exaggerate those things or parts with which he has become emotionally involved. For example, in Figure 35, John walked barefoot in the grass after the rain; the obvious delight of this kinesthetic experience shows in his emphasized toes, almost to the extent that we, too, can feel our toes in the cool grass. An oversensitive child who becomes too bound up with one part of his drawing may easily lose connections with the rest of his subject matter. This can sometimes be seen in greatly overexaggerated details.

It has been demonstrated by several investigators that continuous exaggerations or omissions of the same body parts usually point toward a defect or abnormality of this particular body part.[3] Blind individuals quite commonly exaggerate the eyes in their creative works. A child with a deformed foot continually omitted the foot. Another child who was hard of hearing continually emphasized the ears in his creative work. We not only find that the exaggerations or omissions can be of importance to a child within one particular drawing but we also find that the continued exaggeration or omission can point to possible deviations in a child's physical growth.

Of particular interest is the meaning of the child's spatial concepts at this age. He conceives space as being primarily related to himself and his own body. This is sometimes referred to as *body space*. We will later see how the concept of space changes in his drawings to what is sometimes termed *object space*. We find that children's drawings show markedly different spatial organization from that usually conceived of as being correct from an adult point of view. Just as children draw what is around them in an apparently random fashion, their comments tend to be loose-jointed and disconnected. If a child of five is asked what he did at a birthday party, his reply does not follow any logical sequence. In fact, the importance of his remarks may be more closely tied up with their emotional significance to him, rather than to any orderly array of events. As long as a child is still in the preschematic stage, there is no advantage in trying to teach this child how to read, or in getting him to reason in an abstract way the logical relationships of numbers. Although children can learn early how to count or to recognize a word or so, there is no genuine understanding of content.

The first requisite for any degree of awareness of the responsibility for social functions is the ability to face one's own experiences and identify with them. It is therefore of immediate significance for the proper social functioning of an individual whether he has the desire to relate his experiences to his creative work. A drawing of an environment in which the child has included himself as in Figure 32 shows the first steps toward social cooperation and awareness of others within this environment.

The mere presence of objects in drawings is not an indication of perception, but may indicate conceptual knowledge or emotional relationships. However, the way things are represented is an indication of the type of experiences the child has had with them. We will find a development of perceptual growth starting at this age. That is, the image a person has of himself and of the things around him will change as he becomes more aware of the significant characteristics of these objects. *Perception* means more than just the visual appearance of objects; it includes the awareness of all of the senses, such as kinesthetic or auditory experiences. We have already discussed the fact that most representations during this stage are only of a conceptual nature. However, as soon as a child establishes more than the mere meaning of an object by visually relating his drawings to objects, visual perception will begin and a child will now use lines other than mere geometric ones.

By way of comparison look at the drawing in Figure 35; we find that only geometric lines are used. All details would lose their meanings when separated from the whole. The same relationship exists in color at this age. Looking at Plate 1 and Plate 2 we find that a child's use of color is for the sake of color itself. It does not relate to the subject matter. We can see here purple rain and a green body and head that obviously express very little of a visual percept.

There will be differences in perceptual sensitivity between children at any age; also, some children will be more aware of sound or touch whereas another child may be more sensitive to visual stimulation. Since we acquaint ourselves with our environment only through our senses, the development and cultivation of perception are of prime concern in art education.

One of the most vital areas of growth with which we should be concerned is the area of creative growth. Although it reveals itself in many characteristics, creative growth itself is seen in the independence of approach. During the first representational attempts, the creative child will develop independent relationships to things that are expressed in independent concepts. The creative child will never ask how to draw a mouth or a nose. He will without hesitancy draw his own concepts. The child's own concepts can readily be distinguished from those taken from other sources by the free and flexible use and frequent changes that he applies to his own concepts. Foreign or copied symbols are usually repeated in a stiff and inflexible fashion. In a group the creative child remains completely uninfluenced in his own concept by what he sees around him, although he may show interest in what others are doing. The creative child spontaneously paints or draws or manipulates materials and does not create only when motivated. The development of creative growth within the context of art education is one of the prime considerations and justifications for inclusion of art experiences for any age group. A creative first grade girl was stimulated by the Christmas Story to paint the manger scene in Figure 36. Notice how she has shown the top view of the basket so we can look inside but has shown the side view of the stable. That's an angel just arriving on the scene from the left, carrying the star. At the level of first representations early patterns are established by which a child can develop into a creative adult or by which he can develop a dependence in thinking. It is essential, therefore, that at this crucial time great consideration be given to the creative development of children.

## Summary of Growth Characteristics of the Preschematic Stage

The art of children in the stages of first representation can be seen as a direct reflection of the child himself. Not only are the drawing and painting of a child a record of his concepts, feelings, and perceptions of his environment, but these drawings and paintings also provide the sensitively aware adult with the means for a better understanding of the child. In our discussion of the intellectual growth, the emotional growth, the social growth, the perceptual growth, and the creative growth of children our concern has been primarily to see art as one of the essential components in a child's total development.

The art of children provides us not only with the understanding of a child but also with an opportunity to develop growth patterns through the area of art education. Here we mean something a great deal more significant than changing the outward appearance of the drawings themselves; we are concerned with the total process of creating. We cannot positively affect a child's behavior by providing him with patterns or procedures to follow in order to achieve a "better-looking" product. The change in the product itself should come about through the changes in a child's thinking, feeling, and perceiving. It is through the *process* that changes in behavior or changes in growth patterns develop. It is also through the process that meaningful changes take place in the product itself.

The art motivation for this particular age group concentrates upon the experiences the child himself has had, either in his own physical self, or in fantasy, or in vicarious experiences. Since we are all composed of both hereditary and environmental factors, and since we can do little about the heredity of those children with whom we are working, we must concentrate upon the environmental factors within a learning situation. Art can play a tremendous role in providing the environment in which the various growth patterns can develop. Art plays a crucial part in our educational system, particularly in the area of perceptual growth, the developing awareness toward those things around us through all of the senses; through creative growth, the development of characteristics of flexibility, imaginative thinking, originality, and fluency of thinking; and also through emotional growth, the ability to face new situations, the ability to express both pleasant and unpleasant feelings. Of course to a

**Figure 36.** Plan and elevation are combined in this drawing of the manger scene by a six-and-a-half-year-old girl.

lesser extent at this age art also provides the opportunity for growth in the intellectual, social, and aesthetic areas.

The majority of children who are beginning to attend public school will be in the stages of first representational attempts. It is therefore crucial that their introduction to art experiences be a meaningful one. A great deal of what goes on within school is dictated by the adult society in which we live; however, as we have discovered, the child is not a miniature adult nor does he think in adult terms. Art can provide not only the opportunity for growth in several vital areas but also the opportunity for a child to investigate, invent, explore, make mistakes, have feelings of fear and hate, love and joy. Most essential, he should have all these experiences of living for himself, for himself as an entity—an individual who can, should, and will think for himself.

RELATED ACTIVITIES

1. Collect drawings over a period of time from a child who is scribbling, and trace the evolution of the first representational symbols. Check to see which technique (drawing, painting, or modeling) is the most satisfactory for this development.
2. Collect drawings that include symbols for the mouth. Stimulate these children by a motivation built around chewing peanuts. Compare the drawings done before and after the motivation to see what changes, if any, have taken place in the symbol for the mouth.
3. Observe the activity of a group of kindergarten children during their free play and during organized games. Relate the amount of parallel play to the preceding discussion of the use of space in drawings. What are the differences or similarities between these two segments of a child's growth?
4. Compare the development of representational symbols in drawings with symbols in clay. Photograph the clay products to keep a record of the development in clay to compare with the drawings.
5. Compile a list of the various art materials used in several kindergarten classes. Rank these in order of value for the child. Are there any materials used that cannot be justified as being of value for development? Explain your reasons.
6. Observe a child who is making his first representational symbols. Keep a verbatim record of his comments for several different fifteen-minute periods. What relationship is there between his verbal and his graphic expression?
7. From a collection of paintings by five-year-olds list the objects that are painted with a visibly established color-object relationship. List those objects

that are painted with *no* visually established color-object relationship. What might cause some of these choices of color?

NOTES

1. Herbert Read, *Education Through Art* (London: Faber & Faber, Ltd., 1943), p. 320.
2. Jerome Kagan and Judith Lemkin, "Form, Color, and Size in Children's Conceptual Behavior," *Child Development,* **XXXII,** No. 1 (1961), pp. 25–28.
3. Read, *op. cit.;* Walter Kroetsch, *Rhythmus und Form in der freien Kinderzeichnung* (Leipzig: Dürr, 1917); Ludwig Munz and Viktor Lowenfeld, *Plastische Arbeiten Blinder* (Brünn: Rohrer, 1934); Viktor Lowenfeld, *The Nature of Creative Activity* (London: Routledge and Kegan Paul, Ltd., 1952).

# 6

# The Achievement of a Form Concept: The Schematic Stage, Seven to Nine Years

### The Schema in Drawings by Children

THE importance of the schema can only be fully realized when we understand the child's desire, after much experimentation, for a definite concept of man and his environment. Although any drawing could be called a schema, or symbol, of a real object, here we will refer to schema as the concept at which a child has arrived and which he repeats again and again whenever no intentional experience influences him to change this concept. These concepts are highly individualized. For some children the schema can be a very rich concept, but for other children the schema can be a fairly meager symbol. Differences in schemata depend upon many things, but just as no two children are the same, we find that no schemata are identical; rather they depend upon personality differences and upon

138

the degree to which a teacher was able to activate the child's passive knowledge while he was forming his concepts. Although there is no magical time for the formation of a schema, most children arrive at this stage at about seven years of age.

We find a pure schema in a child's drawing whenever a child's representation confines itself to the object. "This is a tree." "This a man." However, when intentions are present that alter the forms, we can no longer speak of a pure schema. Thus, a pure schema, or schematic representation, is a representation with no intentional experiences represented. When intentional experiences are represented, or when there are modifications of the schema, we know that the child has portrayed something of importance to him. A study of the kinds of modification undergone by the schema allows us to understand the intention underlying the representation. This is of special importance to the teacher who may study the effects of his teaching by comparing the schema with its deviations.

The schema of an object is the concept at which the child has finally arrived, and it represents the child's active knowledge of the object. The schema also refers to space and figures as it refers to objects. For example, a child might usually draw a house with roof and windows only. For a particular experience the door might be of special significance; he would then change his schema and add the door. Through this deviation of the schema the child has manifested his particular experience.

### HUMAN SCHEMA

We use the term *human schema* to describe the concept of a figure at which the child has arrived after much experimentation. Younger children in their first representational attempts drew the human figure in many different ways, and one child's drawing of a man changed from one day to the next. As a child gets closer to the achievement of a form concept, he gradually achieves a symbol for a man that is repeated again and again, as long as he has no particular experience to influence him to change this concept. Each child's schema of a man will be quite different from any other child's.[1] They consist of highly individualized form symbols.

At about the age of seven the drawing of a human figure by a child should be a readily recognizable symbol. Not only should there be a head, body, arms, and legs but also some active knowledge of the various features. The eyes should be different from the nose, the symbol for nose should be different from that for the mouth, and there should be hair

**Figure 38.** "My Family," drawn by a seven-year-old boy. Here a schema is repeated for each member of the family.

and even an awareness of neck. Usually, the child includes separate symbols for hands and even fingers, and of course a different symbol for feet. Often clothing is drawn instead of the body, but the average schema for a seven-year-old should include most of these items. The schema still consists of geometric lines—lines which when separated from the whole lose their meaning. Sometimes ovals, triangles, squares, circles, rectangles, or irregular shapes are used as schema for the body, though all kinds of shapes are used for legs, arms, clothes, and so forth. In Figure 38, "My Family," notice how the boy repeats his schema for each member of his family. It is quite clear in the human schema that a child is not attempting to copy a visual form, but rather the child's concept is arrived at by a combination of many factors: his process of thinking, his awareness of his own feelings, and his development of perceptual sensitivities. The human schema is therefore highly individualized and can be looked at as a reflection of the development of an individual.

## SPACE SCHEMA

The great discovery during this age level is that there is a definite order in space relationships. The child no longer thinks, "There is a tree, there is a man, there is a car," without relating them to one another as he has done during the preschematic stage. A child now thinks, "I am on the ground, the car is on the ground, the grass grows on the ground, mud is on the ground, we are all on the ground." This first conscious awareness that a child is part of his environment is expressed by a symbol which we shall call *base line*. From now on this consciousness, which includes all objects in a common space relationship, is expressed by putting everything on this important base line (see Figure 39).

We can speak of a schema when the representation of an object or of space has become established through repetition. What we have discussed about the human figure is very largely true of the schematic representation of objects and space. The schema can originate in visual or in nonvisual experiences. In other words, the schema might be determined by how a child sees something, the emotional significance he attaches to it, his kinesthetic experience with or touch impression of the object, or how the object functions or behaves. It is important to keep in mind that we speak of a space schema when space is represented by some signs or other which, through repetition, assume a consistent meaning in the draw-

**Figure 39.** "Picking Flowers." The importance of the hands is stressed. Notice how everything is organized along a base line.

**Plate 3.** "I Am Standing in My Back Yard," painted by a six-and-a-half-year-old girl. Notice the first signs of color-object relationships. The child has painted herself much larger than the tree. The relative sizes show the importance of the ego at this stage of development.

**Plate 4.** "Lightning and Rain," drawn by a seven-year-old girl. The color-object relationship is so firmly established that the sky remains blue in spite of the rain. See how the exaggerated hands grasp the umbrella, and that it remains dry underneath.

ings of a child. At this stage of development the child has not developed an awareness of the representation of a three-dimensional quality of space. We find, therefore, that the schema is usually a representation of two dimensions. Occasionally some abstract lines are substituted for depth, but the biggest discovery is that there is a definite order in spatial relationships. It is quite clear that the space schema is almost entirely abstract and has only an indirect connection with nature as adults know it.

## Deviations from the Schema—Expression of Subjective Experiences

If we accept the schema as the concept of man and environment at which the child has arrived, then every deviation has special importance according to its origin and its meaning. From an understanding of the origin and meaning of the deviations in their various forms we can gain insights into the child's experience. Three principal forms of deviations can be noticed in children's drawings: (1) exaggeration of important parts, (2) neglect or omission of unimportant or suppressed parts, and (3) change of symbols for emotionally significant parts. It should be understood that exaggeration and neglect refer to size only, whereas the change of symbols refers to their shapes. Needless to say, all these characteristics refer to the way in which adults see them. Children are not conscious of these exaggerations, for as Barkan says, "Children do not overstate; rather they create size relationships which are 'real' to them."[2] The origin of such deviations lies either in autoplastic experiences (that is, the feelings of the bodily self or muscular sensations), in the relative importance of specific parts, or in the emotional significance the particular part has for the child.

An interesting piece of work that displays many types of deviations in a single drawing is shown in Figure 40*a*. Here we see a schematic representation of a man that the child drew when simply asked to draw a man. Thus, in this drawing no intentional experiences are represented; rather, it is the form concept of a man at which the child has arrived and which he repeats again and again whenever he is asked to draw a man. In comparing this schema with the drawing "Searching for the Lost Pencil" (Figure 40*b*), we see clearly the deviations and the experiences these deviations express. In this lower picture the arms and the hands are the main vehicles of expression, and by means of them the theme is symbolized. The intense experience of searching and of groping about after the pencil is expressed by the different emphasis and exaggeration of the arm, and by changes in the shape of the symbol for hand. The enormously lengthened groping arm in the first figure shows how the representation has been modified by the experience of reaching. "With this hand I have just found the pencil." The arms show a double line indicating their special functional importance. Compare this with the schema in the picture above. Notice, too, the enormously exaggerated pencil, showing the emotional importance it had for the child when he found it.

"With this hand I put it in my pocket," the child says, and points to one of the arms of the second figure which, in fact, represents the same figure as the first one. The arm putting the pencil into the pocket is now far less emphasized and is represented by a single line only; the second arm of the figure, no longer having a function, has shriveled to a mere stump. The pencil has been reduced in size now that it has been found and has lost its special significance.

Another experience originating in bodily sensations is also quite obviously shown. The left figure in the lower drawing is supposed to be bent forward, and this is expressed by means of shorter legs and a lowered head. But when the head is bent forward, blood accumulates in it, and we become more intensely aware of it. This is expressed in the drawing by an exaggeration of the size of the bent head. The figure on the right is standing upright while putting the pencil in his pocket, and since the sensation of bending down is no longer important, the head and the neck diminish in size and the figure looks more like the schema represented above. We might also speculate that the introduction of a base line in the lower drawing might be caused because of the awareness that the pencil is on the floor and therefore a representation of the floor becomes important.

We have here an example of a very natural form of expression at this age. Although the child has arrived at a definite schema for a person, this schema is transformed in the act of creation. Furthermore, it shows that disproportions nearly always result from some definite intention or experience, though this does not mean that the experience is necessarily conscious. We therefore have no right to speak of "false proportions," since such a judgment is determined by an adult visual attitude, the attitude of objectively representing the environment. On the contrary, it is only when we understand the reasons for these apparent disproportions that

**Figure 40a.** "A Man." **Figure 40b.** "Searching for the Lost Pencil." Figure 40*a* is the child's schema, used when no particular experience was portrayed. In Figure 40*b*, notice how the schema has been changed to show how the child looked for and found the pencil.

we are able to penetrate into the true basis of creativeness. Since the child is not aware of making exaggerations or omitting parts, correcting such expression would only mean changing a true and sincere feeling to an imposed rigid form. Measuring and comparing the size of body parts is obviously meaningless to the child. Naturalistic tendencies and conceptions, therefore, have little place in children's drawings. The child is intimately bound up with the experience of the self, and he experiences his world subjectively.

## The Psychological Importance of the Schema

We have said that the drawing reflects the child's total being; the emergence of a definite schema has many implications and can give an understanding adult some valuable insights into the child's development. The child no longer represents objects in relation to himself but now begins to represent objects in some logical relationship one to another. A child of five will draw a house or a tree or a toy in juxtaposition without any objective order. Now, however, the child includes himself in his concept in the same way he includes the tree, the house, or the whole environment. This first common experience of space—"I am on the street, the house is on the street, John is on the street"—is sometimes a most decisive factor in the psychological development of the child. His attitude now changes from a completely egocentric attitude, and this is reflected not only in his drawings but also in his total development. The child seeks to find order in his environment and to develop formulas for proper behavior.[3] These often make no sense to an adult but often become very important in a child's life. Most of us can remember some of these laws governing our behavior at this age, such as avoiding stepping on the crack in the sidewalk for fear of dire consequences, or performing some private ritual if two children said the same thing at the same time, or touching every desk in the row before sitting down, to insure good luck. These laws and rules for behavior make a schema of sorts in another area of the child's development.

The development of the schema also signifies a change from a completely egocentric attitude to a more cooperative attitude. The differences between these two stages can easily be seen by observing children in a kindergarten and then comparing their behavior with children in second grade. Kindergarten children play and work together only when urged to do so. In freedom they will generally follow their own directions. One child will be going in one direction imitating a train, another child will be sitting self-concerned in a chair, whereas a third will be playing in the sand, scarcely noticing the others. Their conversation will also be ego-involved. Although they apparently will be talking to one another, they neither listen to, nor apparently expect a reply from, those near them. Their talk is usually tied up with their own play and seems to be more concerned with explaining what is going on to themselves rather than to others. This is clearly indicated, as we have seen, in the spatial concept of children during this age. However, when the schema develops and we see a definite order in space, the child begins to relate to others, and sees himself as part of the environment. It is fairly obvious that before the development of the schema is not a time for cooperative games, and an awareness of others and others' feelings will not be understood. It may be that a tremendous amount of time is wasted at the kindergarten level in trying to maintain order and quiet, since true learning is apparently taking place when a child is expressing himself, whether others are listening or not. At this egocentric age it is most important to converse with one's self and with one's own expression, whereas during the schematic stage the ability to share and understand others' feelings is beginning to develop.

The introduction of the base line in the schema has other important implications for the understanding of children. Since a child can now see logical relationships between objects in his environment, it is possible to begin to think of a meaningful reading program. For instance, in reading, this very same correlation is necessary in relating letters to one another in order to form a word symbol. Pushing a child into a reading program before he is ready may build negative attitudes toward reading; these are difficult to erase and cannot be counterbalanced by any advantage in making a child conform to an arbitrary time schedule. His thought processes at this time are also less ego-involved, and he is therefore ready to accept and be curious about meanings of objects and words outside himself.

The child's particular schema is uniquely his. We can readily tell the drawings of one child from those of another just by looking at the schematic representations. One child may have a very meager schema while another child may have a rich concept of his environment. Observing these differences can provide us a deeper understanding of a child's sensitivity to, and awareness of, his environment. As we have said before, the type of representation a child achieves depends largely upon psychological, biological, and environmental factors, and the stimulation the child has received. It is then possible to assume that a child with a rich schema will be one who has developed a greater active awareness and a greater interaction with his surroundings. Hopefully, this is an area in which art education can play an important role; we will discuss this at greater length later in this chapter. The opinion that the profile represents a more advanced stage in a child's creative concept is, according to experiments, incorrect. Apparently, for some children the symmetry of the body, the two arms, the two legs, the two eyes, the two ears, is of most importance. In some cases the side-view, or profile, concept is the first schema. As we see in Figure 40, some schemata can have a mixed profile and front view, which includes a representation of two eyes and profile nose. The schema still consists of geometric lines, which when separated from the whole, lose their meaning. It becomes obvious that during this mental age the child derives his schema from many sources, with visual experiences playing a minor role.

## The Origin of the Base Line

The base line is a very interesting phenomenon in children's drawings, and since it is universal, it can be considered as much a part of the natural development of children as learning to run or skip. The base line appears as an indication of the child's conscious relationship between himself and environment. He places everything on this base line; this line can apparently represent not only the ground on which objects stand but can represent a floor, street, or any base upon which a child is standing.

It is quite obvious that in nature neither objects nor persons standing on the ground are in actuality standing upon a line. That is why we can state that a base line cannot have its origin in visual experiences. When questioned, children invariably identify this base line as being the ground. A counterpart to the base line appears in drawings as a sky line. This is usually drawn at the top of the page and the space between this and the base line is identified by children as being air (see Figure 39). As adults we usually think of the sky in pictures as coming down to ground level; however, this is actually an optical illusion. Not only does the sky never actually meet the ground, but of course there is no tangible sky, only an accumulation of air over a dark background. The concept of the sky above, ground below, and air between is just as valid as our concept that the sky and ground meet. Both are illusions.

In creative products of primitive stages of mankind we often see the base line used as a means of indicating motion. Australian drawings made on the bark of trees or drawings by arctic tribes use the base line to indicate motion. It may be that the origin of the base line is the kinesthetic experience of moving along a line. The use of the base line is very apparent in the art of more advanced cultures, such as in the carvings on the tombs in ancient Egypt, or on the vase decorations in ancient Greece. In the latter two instances pictorial matter was arranged on a line in a storytelling fashion. If children use their art as communication, it may be natural to think of objects coming one after another on a line. From the play of our early childhood we know, too, that we frequently connect the experience of moving with the thought of going along a line.

### THE BASE LINE AS PART OF THE LANDSCAPE

When a child is drawing or painting an outdoor picture, the base line is used at one time to symbolize the base on which things stand and at another time to characterize the surface of the landscape. In the painting in Figure 41 one base line symbolizes the level ground while another base

**Figure 41.** "I Am Climbing a Hill," painted by a seven-year-old boy. The upper base line is bent, representing the experience of walking up and down the hill.

**Figure 42.** "Fruit Harvest." The child has used two base lines to represent the orchard.

represents the mountain. Apparently the child wishes to indicate that this second base line is elevated over the plain and represents the surface character of the landscape. It can readily be seen that the mountain is still meant as a base line from the fact that the flowers stand perpendicularly to the mountain. Even the figure is bound to its base line. We can realize this experience most clearly if we consider the base line to be a length of wire, a straight wire with flowers attached to it. If we bend the wire according to the kinesthetic experience of going up and down, the flowers attached to the wire stand out perpendicularly as we see them in this drawing. Clearly, it is not the shape of the mountain that is of significance but the line itself, which goes up and down.

If we look at the illustration in Figure 42, entitled "Fruit Harvest," we will see two base lines representing an orchard. The child himself is shown on the lower part of the paper picking apples off a tree. Above him is the sky and above that another base line upon which his father appears driving a wagon full of apples. Notice the schema the child has for apple tree. Notice also the size of the apples on the tree as compared to the size of the apples in the basket. This becomes almost a poetic form of expression: the things the child longs for loom large in his mind, and the apples take on great importance on the tree, but once they are in the basket they become less important. One can get a real feeling for the freshness of children's expression from this, and it is this freshness many adult artists strive to achieve. The bird in the upper corner becomes important, too, for apples pecked by a bird must be discarded. The showing of two base lines is a later development, and is a step toward perspective as we know it in drawings. However, this is strictly a two-dimensional representation, as can clearly be seen by the fact that the sky is represented in both halves of the painting. Children rarely draw anything that is not directly related to this base line, even if two or more base lines appear in one picture. A better understanding of "Fruit Harvest" may be had by seeing the top portion as a more distant row of trees in the orchard, beyond the lower or closer trees. In this picture everything functions and has meaning. The child wanted to say, "There is an orchard," therefore he is not satisfied by merely drawing one tree. "The apples on the tree are the most beautiful ones, because I want them, but I have picked some into the basket. I am just now reaching for one. Those in the basket are no longer single apples, they are the dozens of apples I have collected. Daddy is carrying them to town. He is going away, therefore he needs a distance. Birds are pecking on the apples. We don't want the birds." All this gives the whole story of the feeling of the child. We can also see how the child related himself actively to his environment. He is on the ground, the basket is on the ground, the apples are in the basket, the tree is on the ground; and farther away, the wagon is on the ground, the horse is on the ground, and the bird is in the air with the sky above. The consciousness that signifies the child's understanding not only of himself but also the significance the environment has for him is the awakening of the total being.

## Other Means of Space Representation

Although the base line is the most common means used by children to represent space in their drawings and paintings, occasionally an emotional experience forces a child to deviate from this type of schema. We shall refer to these as subjective space representations. The frequently used process of folding over belongs to this category of subjective space representations. By *folding over* we mean the process of creating a space

**Figure 43.** "Norfolk Ferry," painted by an eight-year-old boy. This painting is an example of representing space by "folding over."

concept by drawing objects perpendicularly to the base line, even when these objects appear to be drawn upside down.

The illustration in Figure 43 is a typical painting by a child which shows the process of folding over. Here we see that the child has depicted himself as waving to the ferry. After the child drew himself waving with his handkerchief, standing on one side of the bay, he decided to draw the boat. "What kind of nonsense is this? This child cannot be normal, he drew the boat upside down." It isn't upside down; indeed not. This child was leaning on the floor and after drawing himself on one side of the base line, he walked around his paper and drew the other side of the bay and the ferryboat. You can even see where the ferryboat is landing. This concept can best be understood if we fold the paper along the base line on which the boy is standing. We then get the experience of the child standing upright and facing the boat. If we fold the other side of the bay upright also, we get a model of the scene and we suddenly realize the interesting concept of the two skies, one at the bottom and the other at the top of the paper. Now both skies are folded up. This type of representation might be what we would do if we were asked to make a diagram of both sides of a room. On this side there are four windows and so we draw them, and then for the other side of the room we diagram the wall on the bottom of the page. Actually this is a very valid concept, since the child wanted to draw both sides of the bay simultaneously because both sides have significance for his concept. Basically, the subjective experience of a child was that of being in the center of the scene, seeing one shore to the left and the other to the right. This experience shows very clearly that it is of great advantage to have children work on the floor or on low tables, on which the drawing or painting can be approached from all directions. In Figure 44, "I Say 'Hello' to My Friend on the Other Side of the Street," this principle of folding over is used to show the opposite sides of the street. This was drawn by a nine-year-old partially blind boy.

**Figure 44.** "I Say 'Hello' to My Friend on the Other Side of the Street." The children often called to each other at the street crossing. Here the base lines are at the edges of the paper, in contrast with their location in Figure 43.

**Figure 45.** "On the Seesaw," painted by a nine-year-old boy. The kinesthetic experience of going up and down determined the spatial concept.

Another type of deviation is when a child who usually uses the base line drops the lines altogether. As we said before, the emotional experience can be so strong it overpowers the feeling of being connected with the ground. The painting in Figure 45, "On the Seesaw," is a typical example of such a drawing, in which the child's feeling of being a part of the environment was overpowered by his emotional feeling of swinging up and down. The sensation of this kinesthetic experience determined the spatial concept. The boy shows himself way up near the sky and sun. His emotions are visibly expressed by the exaggerated size of his body as well as by his facial expression; the mouth is wide open. "My older sister lifted me up so high," he said. Although this indicates that his older sister was at least heavy enough to lift him up high, because of his own subjective experience he has exaggerated his own size and made his sister seem much smaller. Since the sister was sitting opposite, the boy painted her seemingly upside down. In reality this is his subjective view and can be better understood if we fold the representation of the boy and his sister up so that they appear to be sitting on the ends of the seesaw itself. We then again realize what a marvelous space concept the child has created through the power of his subjective feelings.

Another important aspect of subjective space experiences results in drawings with a mixture of plan and elevation. The painting "Playing Checkers" in Figure 46, by a seven-year-old boy, shows the checkerboard

**Figure 46.** "Playing Checkers," painted by a seven-year-old boy. The checkerboard is shown in top view because of its significance.

**Figure 47.** "Amusement Island," drawn by an eight-year-old boy. The boy had gone around the island in a rowboat.

folded over because of its significance. Since the child was emotionally bound up with the playing of checkers, he had to show the full checkerboard. The table, however, would not be a table if it did not have legs. So the child drew a table with legs and, when necessary, folded over the top of the table to show its significance, thus mixing plan and elevation in one drawing. Another drawing of great interest, which shows the same type of experience, is "Amusement Island" (see Figure 47). The child visited an island on which were all types of amusement, people playing cards, hot-dog stands, and so forth. There were boats for rent, and in such a boat the child took a ride around the island. The drawing shows a top view of the island, since it was important to show that water surrounds the land. Everything is standing out of the island; that is why all objects on the island are represented in side view. Since the child took a ride around the island in a boat, it was important that this be portrayed. Here it seems as if the four edges of the paper have become four separate base lines. It is not unusual to see all four sides of a house portrayed at one time, nor to see all four wheels drawn on an automobile. It is quite clear that a child can include a great deal within his paintings, which are a direct reflection of his subjective experiences. There is obviously nothing wrong with these representations. We should appreciate them and their poetic quality, for the sensitive adult can gain great insight and understanding about the child's relationship to his world by becoming more involved in the meaning of his creative expression.

## SPACE AND TIME REPRESENTATIONS

By *space and time representations* we mean the inclusion in one drawing of different time sequences or of spatially distinct impressions. Just as a child has his own way of showing two- and three-dimensional objects, sometimes by using plan and elevation at the same time, so he has his own way of showing events that occur in different time sequences. Apparently children have two different reasons for developing these space and time representations, and an understanding of these is important because they can provide a rich source for motivation.

One method of space-time representation arises out of the urge for communication. A child likes to listen to and tell stories. This is one reason why we find different episodes represented by different pictures in one sequence of drawings. The pictures may be separate, like those in a comic book, although they may not be divided by a line. Journeys, trips, travel episodes, or other events that require a sequence of time belong in this type of representation. In such topics usually the most important events are described. Separate pictures characterize a complex event, so the topic of the series is usually the same.

Another manner of space-time representation has its origin in the emotional involvement with the representation and in the act of drawing itself. Here we see distinct actions that have taken place at various times but are represented within one drawing space. This does not spring from the desire to communicate something but from the importance of the action itself. This emotional involvement diminishes the child's consciousness of time to such an extent that he is not aware of representing different time phases in one drawing. He is concerned only with expressing within one drawing what he considers most characteristic about the action, in much the same way as alternations between plan and elevation are used to express what is most characteristic about an object. In the one case distinct time spaces, in the other distinct spatial impressions, are fused and used for characterization. In Figure 48 we see a boy in his house, supposedly upstairs getting ready for school. One drawer in the dresser must have special meaning, for it has been drawn darker. Notice the stairs going down to the dining room; they are drawn as he experienced them and not in the usual adult side-view representation. The breakfast bowls are on the table downstairs and have been folded up so that we can look into them. Turning back to Figure 38 and comparing the human schema, we can easily see that these drawings were made by the same boy, although actually several weeks apart. (An ironic note is the rubber stamp of a dog under the drawing of the boy himself. Apparently these stamps were available in the classroom for the less "artistic" youngsters to use.)

It is important to realize that in these space and time representations the picture is confined to a single sequence of action or sequence of movements. Placing the various aspects next to one another in one space is merely a method of portraying the distinctive qualities of a particular experience. For a typical example of this type of expression refer again to Figure 40, the drawing entitled "Searching for the Lost Pencil." We are referring now only to the content of this drawing, which deals with the expression of different time sequences within one space. The figure

**Figure 48.** In "Getting Ready for School," what appears to be a bent ladder is the stairway connecting the bedroom with the dining room, so that upstairs and downstairs appear to be on the same level.

on the left both is looking for and has found the pencil. The child used the next figure to express putting the pencil into his pocket with one hand, and the other hand shows clearly that it no longer has any function. In other words, by means of two figures he represented four different time phases. In a sense he could have given one figure four arms, as has been done in medieval manuscripts, but this would have contradicted his concept of a man. He was emotionally so tied up with the content that it overpowered his feeling for reality. The experience he had with all the phases—searching for the pencil, finding the pencil, picking it up, and putting it in his pocket—made him draw all these aspects.

In the section on motivation we shall see that we can use our understanding about the origins of space and time representations to great advantage in education.

## X-RAY PICTURES

A child uses another most interesting nonvisual way of representation to show different views that could not possibly be perceived visually at the same time. He depicts the inside and outside of a building or other enclosure simultaneously. This can be seen whenever the inside is of greater importance for the child than is the outside of the structure. In the very same way as the child depicts plan and elevation at the same time to show significant "views," while apparently unaware of the impossibility of such a visual concept, he mixes up the inside and outside concepts within his drawing. Sometimes if the child becomes so bound up with the inside, he will completely "forget" that there is an outside and drop this outside altogether. Frequently, however, part of the inside and part of the outside are shown together as if the outside were transparent.

The child reacts in his drawings more toward the self-involvement in what is being portrayed than toward the visual characteristics of his subject matter. This is extremely important for education. It shows very definitely that the adult concept of surface phenomena is not the concept of a child. Educationally, we can then understand what stands out in the child's thinking, and we have a great opportunity to utilize this knowledge in integrating other fields into creative activities.

A group of children visited a factory in which they were shown the manufacture of a product from a raw material kept in the basement to the finished product on the upper floor. When the children were asked to draw this experience, most of them developed a complete "plan" of the factory. The front wall was eliminated and the views of the different

**Figure 49.** "Coal Mine," painted by a nine-year-old girl. This X-ray picture shows both inside and outside representations.

floors showed the different important working stages, which had been discussed and experienced. Since the front of the building stood in the way of communicating its function as a factory, it was eliminated. The working stages, now actively in the minds of the children, had become a part of each child's knowledge and experience and could readily be observed.

In Figure 49 the illustration "Coal Mine" shows an X-ray representation in which the inside and outside are shown according to their significance. The child realized the significance of the mine shaft and tunnels. She became absorbed in the interior of the mine and how the coal is produced. It is interesting to note that the mountain surface is treated like a bent base line, with the house and trees placed perpendicularly to it. It is not surprising to find that the child was a daughter of a coal miner and that she lived in a company house near the mine. This expression of inside and outside is the mixing of two distinct impressions, which are expressed in one space.

We have seen how the pictorial representations of children follow laws of their own that have nothing to do with "naturalistic" laws. An awareness of the variety and an understanding of the meanings of these deviations give us a greater sensitivity to the inner thought processes of children. In some cases the subjective space representations may look confusing or incomprehensible. Although a child should never be expected to justify or interpret a painting, most children are more than eager to discuss their involvement in the experience that motivated the picture. A sympathetic and understanding adult can learn a great deal about the meaningfulness of these activities by showing an interest in how and what a child thinks.

## The Meaning of Color

The child naturally discovers that there is a relationship between color and object. It is no longer his subjective experience, or emotional relationship, that determines color. In all spheres of the child's development we see the awakening process of such a consciousness. In the drawing of the human figure the child has arrived at a definite concept, crystalized in the schema. In representing space, the child has experienced himself as part of the environment, and has developed definite space relationships. Also in color the child has discovered such a definite relationship. A new awareness of the relationship of man to his environment makes the child realize that there is a relationship between color and object. Just as the child repeats again and again his schema for a man, or for space, he also repeats the same colors for the same objects.

We should understand that the establishment of a definite color for an object and its constant repetition is a direct reflection of the continuing development of the child's thinking processes. The child has begun to think in abstract terms, and to be able to formulate and generalize. "What color is the sky?" "Why, the sky is blue!" "What color is grass?" "Why, the grass is green!" To the visually aware adult the answers might be quite different, depending upon whether it is a hazy day or a stormy sky, or whether the grass is dry and brittle or fresh from a spring rain. To the child, however, the mere establishment of a definite relationship between color and object is a satisfying experience. He has begun to find some logical order in the world and is establishing concrete relationships with things around him (see Plate 3).

It is important to realize that although there are common colors used by most children for particular objects, each child has developed his own color relationships. The origin of the individual's color schema might be found in a visual or emotional concept of color. Apparently the first meaningful relationship that the child has with an object can determine his color schema. If the child's relationship to the ground was first established on a muddy back yard, and through repetition this space experience has become firmly established, then ground will be brown, regardless of whether there is grass over it or not. This established color schema will not change unless the child becomes personally involved in an experience in which a change in color becomes important. Therefore, in the same way as we have seen deviations in space or deviations in form concepts, changes in the color schema will give us insight into the meaningful experiences of the child.

In looking at Plate 3, "I Am Standing in My Back Yard," we can see that the child has established definite color-object relationships. Notice that the eyes, lips, hair, and also the grass, tree, and sky have been painted in a very direct bold color that seems to indicate that the child "knows" the color of these objects. Plate 4, "Lightning and Rain," is drawn with crayon. Notice that the sky retains its blue color although it is raining. Criticism of the use of color in these two pictures would only be upsetting to the children. Also a happy accident that may stimulate an adult to see new color forms where colors accidentally run into one another can be very frustrating to a child who is establishing definite color relationships. Not only is the child unable to capitalize on these accidental happenings, but he does not have the need or observational powers to relate these interesting color patterns to color patterns one might see in the sky, for example. For the child such accidental happenings are just mistakes. Once we have understood the important meaning of repetition within the psychological development of the child, we can then understand why the establishment of a definite color for definite objects is so important.

## The Meaning of Design

From our discussion we realize that a child has no concern for any formal aspects of art. Art for him is chiefly a means of self-expression; he is not aware of the beauty in what he does, nor does he spontaneously decorate an object. However, adults can see many design qualities in what a child of this age paints or draws. A conscious approach, or the teaching of "fundamentals of design" during this period, would not only be an artificial adult imposition but could, under certain circumstances, destroy the spontaneous creativity. Or, as D'Amico says, one "factor responsible for weakening the child's native sense of design is the nature of teaching design, the imposing of fixed formulas on the child, now in general practice."[4]

How does this native or innate sense of design show itself? Often adults show a great deal of interest in this natural sense of the child, although this was not true one hundred years ago. Today it is obvious that a new freshness and directness in expression has become important in the adult art world, and the same freshness and directness can be seen in the drawings of children during this schematic stage. One of the important attributes of design is rhythm, and this rhythm is often seen in children's paintings in the repetition of form. Looking over drawings or paintings by children of this age will quickly show that the way children deal with space contributes greatly to this achievement of "design." Yet all this is natural to the child as part of his development. It is his innate space concept and his innate desire for repeating forms or schemata that makes the child an "innate designer." Surely an adult can be an intuitive artist without knowing it. The child is such an intuitive designer; but the difference lies in the fact that the artist may gain through a conscious approach and the child can only be disturbed through it, because this consciousness is something strange to him, something that lies beyond his comprehension. The teaching of formal aspects of proportion would be detrimental to the spontaneity and freedom typical of children's drawings, because they would interfere with the innate urge for expression. Formal elements like balance and rhythm, if used as a guide or as a motivation, miss the purpose. Although an adult may get satisfaction in teaching design qualities, so as to develop beautiful drawings, it is quite apparent that this would be most harmful to the free development of a child.

## The Importance of Clay

Clay is not just another material. Since it is three-dimensional, it stimulates another kind of thinking. A material is wisely used only if it fulfills the purpose for which it is intended. As long as the same thing can be done better in a different medium, then this particular material is not the best one. Thus, nothing should be done in clay if it could better be painted, and nothing should be painted if it could be done better in clay; nothing should be done in clay or paint if it could best be done with

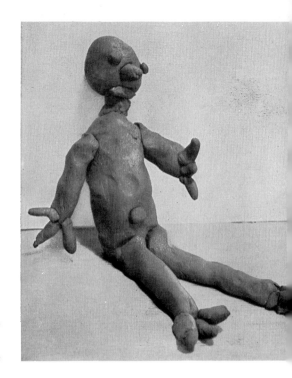

**Figure 50.** In the synthetic method of modeling (left), single pieces are put together. In the analytic method of modeling (right), single parts are pulled out from the whole form.

wood. Therefore, it is important that the material selected suit the type of expression.

The real nature of clay is its plasticity. Because of this plasticity clay can be used most advantageously with children who have developed concepts, for the very nature of the material will necessitate the flexible use of these concepts. The function of a three-dimensional plastic material lies in its adaptability to a constant and continual changing of form. Whereas a drawing demands a simultaneous concept of one event (with the exception of the space-time representations), the process of modeling with clay permits a constant change. Figures can be added or taken away or changed in their position and shape. This is the big advantage in using clay. Therefore, it is important that this opportunity to include action within the art experience be included in any motivation. Of course, these actions should be related directly to the child's experience. Environment should be avoided because it has the same three-dimensional quality as the material itself. Distance and space in nature would compete with distance and space in clay, the result of which would be small scale models of objects, and the child's own feeling and reactions to his environment would not be stimulated. The making of small models is not a creative

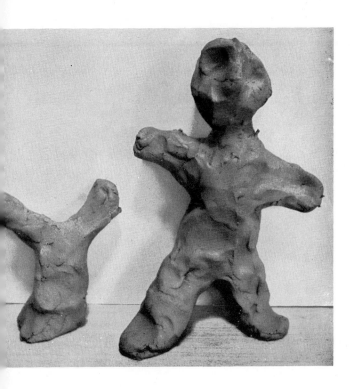

activity but the development of a technical skill and has no place at this age level. However, objects of the immediate environment that have significance to the child may at times be included spontaneously. An example of this might be a child who models a picnic scene and actually develops the effect of visitors coming and sitting down by moving the figures and bending them in the sitting position until the final expression is achieved. Or children sometimes actually move an arm up to the position of eating when this is the desired representation.

Two different modes of expression can be observed, each of which exists in its own right. One is that of "pulling out from the whole" and the other is that of "putting single representative symbols together into a whole." In Figure 50 we have two examples of work in clay showing these two different modes of expression. Since both methods reveal different kinds of thinking, it would be disturbing and of the greatest disadvantage to a child to be diverted from his own method of thinking. Pulling the clay out from the whole means to have a concept of the total, however vague, from which details will be developed. This method of pulling out the single details from the whole is called the *analytic method*. Since this type of thinking is psychologically the same as that applied when observing or seeing things, we can assume that the thinking under-lying this method is basically visual, although at this stage this type of thinking is not applied on a conscious level. That is why the creative product is still made up of representative symbols, form symbols that lose their significance when detached from the whole.

The other method of expression described as putting single representa-tive symbols together into a whole means that the child is building up a synthesis out of partial impressions. Because the child arrives at a synthesis by putting single details together, we call this method the *synthetic method*. Since this type of thinking does not refer to observation, we assume that this type of thinking derives from nonvisual experiences. These nonvisual experiences can be of many different origins. They can refer to body experiences as well as to the activation of passive knowledge. Pulling out or putting together is not merely a superficial means of achieving a form, but is deeply rooted in the child's thinking. We shall go into a discussion of these two types of thinking in a later chapter. However, it is important at this point to state that no change should be made in the child's normal mode of expression, for although few children think in a completely analytic or synthetic fashion, any diversion from one method to another may only block the child's thinking.

## Art Motivation

The kind and type of motivation a teacher should use during the dif-ferent age levels grows out of the need of the children during each par-ticular stage of development. We have seen that, during the schematic stage, the child has formed a definite concept of man, space, color, and objects in all areas of art expression and in his psychological development as a whole. This definite concept, through repetition, has become the schema.

The task of the teacher is to give the child an opportunity to use these concepts, not as rigid form symbols but as living experiences. Our motiva-tion must create an atmosphere in which the child's consciousness of being a part of the environment is stimulated. In the same way we need to stimulate a greater awareness of the actions and functions of the human figure. The inclusion of actions in an orderly space concept will therefore be of greatest significance. Our motivations could be characterized by the words *we* (stimulating the consciousness of I and somebody else), *action* (meaning what we are doing), and *where* (referring to the actual description of the place, restricted to the characteristics only and not to depth or distance).

Knowing that it lies in the child's thinking to fuse time and space, it will be educationally and psychologically of advantage to use time and space stimuli. The motivation for these time and space representations should be concerned with subjective experiences such as hikes, trips, or personal experiences that include different time sequences. Later, there should be added stimulations that refer to objective reports, such as "How the Firemen Prepare for a Fire," or "How I Come to School," or "Our Trip to the Bakery." There are many topics appropriate for X-ray representations. Both the inside and the outside should be stressed in any motivation in this area.

Of greatest importance, however, is the need for creating an atmosphere that is strong and tense, and open and flexible to any suggestions from the child. Rigidity is the death of any creative method. Any motivation should make the child more sensitively aware of himself and of his environment, should develop and stimulate an intense desire to paint a meaningful picture, and should encourage the child to be flexible in his approach to both materials and subject matter. Every motivation should have an introduction, a point of culmination, and a concluding summary statement. So, when we introduce a topic such as "We Are Playing on the School Ground," we would begin with a general introduction.

"When do you play? Didn't I just see you playing outside a short time ago? When do you usually play on the school grounds? When? Oh, during recess; oh, I see. Where do you play? Do you use the whole playground? What do you play? Do you just stand out there and look at each other? Oh, you play tag! Yes, I have played tag, too. How do you play this game? You have to run! Do you run fast? Do you keep yourself nice and straight and tall? You mean you can't run fast that way? Oh, you have to bend forward when you run; why do you bend forward? If you run fast you would fall on your back if you didn't lean forward? Johnny, show me how you run fast! Yes, you really do have to lean forward! If you leaned too far, what would happen? You would fall on your knee! Oh, some of the gravel even got stuck in your knee once—that made it all bloody; yes, I know it hurts. Sometimes your body wants to go faster than your legs can. If you didn't bend forward at all, you would fall backward and hurt your head. . . . I guess it is better to hurt your knee than your head! How about your legs? Do you have both legs in front at the same time? No, that could only be a rabbit! You are right, we cannot jump like rabbits and go very fast. Couldn't both legs be on the ground at the same time? What happens when you run? Oh, one leg is in the air. Isn't that funny! One leg is in the air, did you ever think of that?" (In stimulating a greater awareness of the child's own actions you have also developed a flexibility within his schema for a man. The child can actually sense his legs and feet on the ground, so he has become personally involved in the motivation.) "Does everyone know how to play tag? Oh, we have all played tag! Let's paint how we play on the school grounds."

It is important in any motivation such as this to be sure that each child is personally involved. However, there should be a wide range of topics so that the child has the opportunity to identify with his own particular interests. At this age we begin to find differences in the subjects drawn by boys and girls. Boys begin to show an interest in mechanical and vehicle representation (see Figure 51) while girls tend to develop interests in houses and animals. Each child should feel that the motivation was planned just for him.

**Figure 51.** Mechanical features are often of great interest to boys at this stage of development.

## Subject Matter in Art

The following suggested topics are presented only as a means of showing the direction our thinking should take when motivating children at this level. By no means are these topics to replace an exciting and intense motivation, but rather they are suggested as areas for this motivation. The more emotionally interested and involved the child becomes in any experience, the better will be the development of his work. The following subject areas are divided into groups to point out some of the types of stimulation that are meaningful and educationally valuable to children at this developmental level.

This first group is designed to make the child's form concepts functional. Action and the awareness of action will stress a flexible use of the schema. The *we, action, where* should be an essential part of these topics.

**"Playing with My Friends on the School Ground"**
**"Jumping over a Rope Held by Bob and John"**
**"Pulling Myself High on the Playground Rings"**
**"Playing Ball with My Friends"**
**"Going to Church with Mother and Dad"**
**"We Are Climbing a Mountain"**
**"Doing an Errand for Mother"**
**"Helping Plant a Garden"**
**"We Are Sledding down a Hill"**
**"We Are Skating on the Pond"**
**"Climbing a Tree"**
**"Saying Goodbye As I Go to School"**

The following group of topics provides an opportunity for using profile and front view.

**"Holding onto the Rope While Swinging"**
**"Playing Checkers with My Friend"**
**"Talking with My Mother and Father"**
**"Eating Breakfast Across the Table from My Brother"**
**"Holding an Umbrella in One Hand and My Books in the Other"**
**"Watching a Parade Go By"**

The following group provides stimulation for a variety of space-time representations.

"How I Come to School"
"We Eat in the School Cafeteria"
"Our Trip to the Police Department"
"When We Went to Visit the Farm"
"We Helped Bake Bread"

The following may give some suggestions for X-ray pictures. Again we need to remember that stimulations for topics of this nature should be characterized by the *we, action, where.*

"My Parents and I Stay in a Hotel"
"We Visit Different Floors of a Factory"
"My Friends and I Explore a Cave"
"My Stay in the Hospital"
"We Visit a Cow-Barn and See the Hay Stored"
"My Father and I Go Shopping in the Hardware Store"

Just as we are interested in developing a flexible, functional use of the schema in terms of form, we are also interested in developing a flexible approach to color. Although it is obvious that some of these topic areas overlap, the following list may give some suggestions for particular reference to color concepts. It is interesting to see how effective a motivation is by comparing the use of color after a particular motivation with the use of color before such motivation.

"We Find Bright Colors in the Fall"
"We Like to Play in the Rain"
"The Workmen Are Painting Our House"
"The New Grass in the Yard Is Beginning to Grow"
"We Got Our New Shoes Covered with Mud"

Another area of importance to consider for subject matter, is the private world of the child. This includes topics that have emotional significance to the child in the area of fantasy and dreams. When a child paints what is of deep concern to him, or reveals certain desires and conflicts, it should be remembered that any subject matter is acceptable. Although the teacher may show interest in the representations, under no conditions should any moral judgment be made about the content of these pictures.

**"The Time I Was Most Afraid"**
**"Once I Had a Horrible Dream"**
**"If I Could Do Anything I Wanted to Do for One Day"**
**"I Make Believe I Am an Animal"**
**"If I Were Teacher"**

One other area of subject matter that should be considered is the topic of the particular material itself. The principal reason for concentrating on the material itself is to insure that the child uses materials in a flexible fashion and has an opportunity to investigate their possibilities. Occasionally some children will use this nonrepresentational theme as a means of retreating from a creative expressive experience. This lack of involvement can be seen when children too often hide behind the phrase "I am just making a design."

**"Painting in Light and Dark Colors"**
**"Making a Collage"**
**"Making Tall Things with Holes out of Clay"**
**"Making Things from Boxes and Colored Paper"**
**"Using Crayons in Different Ways"**
**"A Rough and Smooth Picture"**

## Art Materials

The selection of an art material, its relevance to a particular group of children and their needs at a particular time, and its preparation and handling are all important considerations. Any art material should facilitate the self-expression of children and not be a stumbling block. When children have become eager to create after a meaningful motivation, the art materials should be ready for their use. How frustrating to get all excited about painting "How I Broke My Leg While Sledding" and then have to stand in line waiting for paints! Often the material can be prepared and distributed with the help of the children, and then the motivation can take place in another part of the room.

Three things are important with regard to developing techniques or methods of working with materials. First, the teacher should know that each child must develop his own techniques and that every "help" from the teacher in showing the child a "correct" technique will only mean restricting the child's individual approach. There are many ways of working with art materials; and, as mentioned above, time should be taken to explore many different ways of working with art materials. No child should be stopped in the middle of his expression to show him the "proper" way to hold a brush, use a crayon, or fill his paper. The teacher's job is to introduce the appropriate material at a time when a child is most ready to use it.

Secondly, every material or technique must make its own contribution. If a task can be done in a different art material with a better effect, the wrong material has been used. Therefore, it is important that the teacher know the qualities of the material being used so that the best material will be used for any particular expression.

Finally, the teacher should develop economy in the use of art materials. In some books on art education we find that many materials are introduced and used from the very beginning of childhood. At a time when the child is overwhelmed by his own creativity, when he is full of intuitive power, too many different media may not only be wasteful but often prove distracting as well.

The child at the age level from seven to nine years is not concerned with the representation of depth. What is most characteristic of this mental level is that the child has found a form, space, and color concept, which through repetition develops into his schema. At times these repetitions develop a designlike quality. It is of great importance that the child repeat the same colors for the same objects whenever he wishes to do so. An art material that does not afford the child the opportunity of experiencing mastery or self-assurance is not a good medium for this developmental stage. The consistency and texture of poster paint or tempera serve this purpose best, but crayon or colored chalk can also be used successfully.

There is no reason whatsoever for introducing water color at this stage. Water color is transparent, runs, and at times introduces many happy accidents. The transparency of water color serves best to paint atmosphere and landscape, but does not lend itself to repetition or to painting the designlike qualities so typical of this age. Since the child in his painting is more concerned with expressing his own ideas then with visual stimuli, these "happy accidents" turn into "sad disappointments." The child is striving for order and attempting to categorize his knowledge into a working form for functional patterning. Since we consider this feeling of mastery of prime importance for the psychological development of the child, we must not sacrifice these important gains to some happy incidents, regardless of their beauty to adults. We shall see that at older age levels, when the urge for repetition is not important, water color will serve to inspire the child. It is quite apparent, then, that an art material should be selected because it is closely connected with the child's development, and should not be introduced merely for the purpose of changing a material.

Larger paper can be used at this age, to give the child more freedom than smaller sheets provide. Since he has developed better coordination, and his arms have grown longer, the larger sheets may fit his needs better. Also, hair brushes can now be used along with bristle, since children have developed a greater awareness of detail. As has been said before, clay is an excellent means for three-dimensional expression. You may at some time hear that it is wise to discourage modeling by the "synthetic method" of putting details together, because such modeling cannot be fired in the kiln. Since we know that the process of creating is of greater importance than the final product, changing the creative concept of the child by discouraging his own method of working cannot be justified. It is true that such pieces cannot be fired easily because of the danger of air bubbles and because the parts may separate in the firing process, but it is absolutely an adult's concept that clay products made by children should be fired. Unless some adult has influenced a child's thinking, there will be no request for firing these clay products. As our earlier discussion suggested, the two modes of modeling express a different kind of thinking. Changing the technique from synthetic to analytic work therefore means restricting the child in freedom of expression.

There are, of course, a number of materials in addition to those mentioned above, that can meet the needs of this age group. Colored paper, collage materials, paste and scissors, many natural materials such as twigs or pebbles, and even a large, fat, soft pencil can be used to advantage. *Care should be taken to insure that the child has an opportunity for a depth of art experience and that new materials are not introduced just to stimulate the teacher.* Ideally, art materials should provide the opportunity for both a variety of experience and a depth of expression.

# A Discussion of the Meaning
## of the Schematic Stage

Within any classroom we find a large range of individual differences. For example, it is not unusual in the area of intellectual development to have a second grade class composed of children whose intellectual quotient may range from 75 to 125. This means essentially that the mental age of these children will range from the six-year level to the ten-year level. We would also find a large range in physical differences. In looking at the drawings by children in this same second grade, we can also expect to find a comparable range of individual differences. A few drawings and paintings may be more typical of a ten-year-old. We have come to expect the child who is more developed intellectually to be in general more developed physically. Since art is a reflection of a child's total development, we can expect his artistic achievements to follow the same general pattern.

One of the indications for the child's growing intellect is his understanding of the world that surrounds him. This world may range from meaningful to meaningless for the child, depending upon his emotional relationship to it and his intellectual comprehension of it. Whether or not the world has become meaningful to the child partially depends upon the degree to which he has formulated his concepts. It is to be expected, then, that the child will express in his drawings a definite concept or schema for the things he repeatedly represents. The difference between the repeated use of a schema and the use of stereotyped repetitions is that a schema is flexible and undergoes many deviations and changes while stereotyped repetitions always remain the same. If we look at the drawing of the children playing checkers in Figure 46, we can see where the child repeated his schema of a man for both figures. However, the sizes as well as the motions of the figures differ, but the child's concepts are not clear. Notice, for example, that the nose as well as the eyes is expressed with the same symbol, just a dot. Yet obviously these parts have different functional characteristics.

Intelligent children are never satisfied with generalizations. The inquiring spirit often goes deeply into details. The "active knowledge" of the child reveals his understanding and interest in the world about him, and this is what is expressed in his drawings. The degree to which a child tends to differentiate his schema, that is, the extent that he is not satisfied with generalizations and wants to find more detailed characteristics, is a clear expression of his inquiring spirit. Our checker-playing youngster shows little awareness of these details. His eyes have no eyebrows, lids, or

**Plate 5.** "We Are Playing on the Playground," drawn by an eight-year-old girl. There is a schema for running and a separate one for standing. The children standing in a circle are represented according to the child's experience of a circle, rather than perceived visually.

**Plate 6.** "We Are Exploring the Surface of Venus," a four-by-eight-foot wall mural painted by a group of ten-year-old boys. In a project such as this, where imaginative subject matter is used, diverse ideas are welcomed by the group.

any other details, nor is the nose or the mouth indicated by more than a mere generalization. The only concept that shows some of the detail is the concept for hand. It consists of the palm and five fingers.

Of course, our checker player may not have been very involved in this particular picture; several drawings would be important to help us understand him better. However, the field of art can contribute a great deal to a child's growth by stimulating an awareness of those things around him. "Do you have to watch the moves carefully in checkers? Are you hoping your partner will not notice that he can jump you? Do you keep track of how many men you have left?" The clarifications of concepts and the stimulation of an awareness toward details can be a big step toward developing a greater awareness of eyes. Since children are a product of their heredity and of their environment, we should strive to make their environment as rich and stimulating as possible in order to develop the child to his fullest capacities. Figure 52 was drawn by a boy after a trip to a firehouse. He not only remembered the rubber boots and pole but became very involved with the fire truck, and was particularly interested in the hose and ladder. The overlapping is unusual for this age. Certainly art can contribute much to a child's intellectual eagerness by developing his *active knowledge*.

The area of emotional growth can often be neglected in a classroom. A child who has hurt his finger usually gets immediate attention from the teacher and often from a nurse or even a physician. A child with hurt feelings, however, usually has no one to whom to turn for help in patching up his wounds. However, it has been fairly well established that a child's emotions, feelings, and attitudes can affect the learning situation. Art can certainly contribute much to the area of emotional growth. The opportunity to express in socially acceptable fashion the feelings of anger, fear, and even hatred, not only produces a release of tensions but also provides the opportunity for the child to discover that constructive use can be made of one's emotional involvement.

When a schema is used in a rigid fashion, it may actually be an escape from facing one's own feelings and emotions. The flexible use of the schema is the most important requisite for true self-expression. The very nature of the schema, that it is the concept of the child that he uses over and over again whenever he needs it, provides a danger of becoming a stereotype that is repeated without any personal involvement. Flexibility is therefore the most important attribute of emotional growth to which special attention should be given during this period. Usually many changes and deviations in the schema can be observed, especially if the child is

**Figure 52.** "At the Firehouse." The boy felt as if he were a fireman. At the left is the fire truck with its hose and ladder.

free to express his own reactions without the concern of being censored. When the schema is used too rigidly, a child may hide behind these stereotypes; such hiding can readily be observed by noticing day-by-day changes or consistencies in the schema itself. Another form of flexibility in response can be seen in the variation in the sizes of the represented objects. With such variaitons the child may indicate the significance various objects have to him. Changes in the sizes of objects indicate the particular emotional value these objects have to the child. Exaggerations, neglect, or omissions, which indicate a child's emotional relationship to his environment, are not only typical of this age but are indicative of a child's healthy emotional reactions to his environment.

If a child becomes bound up with one part of a drawing by losing all ties with the rest of it, the response of the child is no longer emotionally normal. He then continues to draw the one part of the figure to such an extent that the main part appears only an as appendage. Children who frequently draw such pathological exaggerations may be emotionally maladjusted. Continued and extremely distorted exaggerations are quite rare, however. A child who continuously uses the process of folding over habitually considers himself the center. Such ego-involved reaction to the environment is not to be confused with the occasional use of folding over, which is typical of this age.

It is quite apparent, then, that *art can not only provide an opportunity for the release of emotions but can also provide the child with an opportunity to use these emotions constructively*. Schools have to limit the degree of emotional outbursts that can be accepted within the society of a classroom. Outbursts of anger, frustration, envy, and sheer joy are usually not tolerated. However, the usual classroom goes far beyond this and strives to make an emotionless environment in which only the intellectual pursuits are worthy of consideration. Art then can provide a place for emotional growth, and should encourage a greater emotional involvement in a healthy tension-free environment.

The social growth of children can also be seen in their creative productions. The presence of the schema itself indicates that the child no longer thinks of himself as the center of his environment. Most important, he has become less ego-involved and more aware of himself in an objective way. The child's putting himself on a base line signifies that he is beginning to view himself in relation to others.

The self-identification of a child with his own experiences in his creative work is one of the prerequisites for the establishment of a desire for some contacts outside the self. It is necessary to identify one's own actions and to feel responsible for, and to have some control over, these actions before the development of a greater group consciousness. For example, in Figure 46 our checker-playing friend wanted to show us how he plays checkers by folding over his checkerboard. He also went beyond the immediate self by properly establishing contact with the rest of his environment. Note also that the table, chairs, and children are all in relation to the base line. Other parts of his environment are also noted. The awareness of things around the self, having no immediate relationship to the central experience, shows a high level of social growth. It seems that in this particular drawing the child was not personally aware of which room he was in or of the particular characteristics of the lamp or the window, which he did include.

Related here is the child's development in perceptual growth. The mere portrayal of a symbolic form of an object connotes little that indicates the development of a perceptual awareness. Since we know that perception includes many of the ways in which a child acquaints himself with his environment, the development of growth in perception is of prime importance in the field of art. The awareness of textures, sounds, smells, tastes, and visual shapes and forms can all be shown in a variety of ways in drawings. Developing a sensitive perceptual awareness becomes crucial when we realize that it is the interaction between a child and his environment that can establish the amount or kind of learning that takes place. We have seen that color follows the same schematic patterns as form and space at this age. A child who has not yet established color-object relationships throughout his drawings has not developed perceptually as much as the child who is already aware that objects in the distance tend to become smaller. This does not mean that under the guise of developing perceptual growth, teachers should stress "proper" colors for objects or teach rules of perspective; rather, any motivation that attempts to focus upon perceptual growth should concentrate upon developing a more meaningful relationship between the child and what he is portraying. The products should be looked upon as a record of a child's growth rather than something to "correct."

To some extent even physical growth can be seen in the productions of children. A child who is physically active is much more likely to give his figures movement and action than a child who lacks physical energies. As has been said previously, continuous exaggeration of the same body parts may indicate some defect. The reader might be interested in the fact that the child who drew our friends playing checkers was hard of hearing. He continuously exaggerated or at least emphasized the ears, as we can see in Figure 46. Certainly we can see the continuing development of coordination by the greater control children exhibit in the use of their materials during this age. Providing a range of sizes in brushes allows the child to progress at his own rate of growth.

Aesthetic growth does not start at any particular age. Whenever objects or forms are seen in harmonious relationship to each other, and where we have an integration of thinking, feeling, and perceiving, we have developed either consciously or unconsciously an aesthetic awareness. The lack of aesthetic growth can be seen in pictorial representations that are disorganized either in thought and feeling or in the lack of awareness of any harmonious organization. We have already discussed the fact that rhythm, one of the basic elements of design, consists mainly of repetition, a natural type of expression during this schematic stage. Some children, especially those whose aesthetic growth is more developed, utilize this repetition in an unconscious way for decorative purposes. The bold and direct use of color, so typical of this age, adds to its decorative quality. However, we must remember that this is a natural outgrowth of the development of a child and is not subject to the same awareness of which an adult would be conscious. No dogma regarding rhythm, balance, or harmony will ever have anything but a negative effect upon a child's natural growth pattern. *It is the effect of art experiences and processes upon the individual, and not the final product, that is the true meaning of aesthetic growth.*

If a child casually starts somewhere and either does not have enough space to place everything he wants to draw or discovers he has nothing to add and too much blank space left, the child obviously lacks a sensitive awareness of the relationship between his paper and what he is expressing. To develop those senses, we need to involve the whole child. "Imagine your paper is a treasure map of a large island. You will need to have an X marked where the treasure is. What else will you need on this map? Harbor? Boats? Trees? Mountains? Swamps? Lakes? Streams? Graveyard? Stockade?" Here the emotional and perceptual relationship to the use of the total paper may have become more sensitive. Certainly a motivation that makes the child more sensitively aware of his personal relationship with those things around him—particularly in terms of form, size, and texture—cannot help providing a product that is more developed along these lines. It must be stressed, however, that there are no set rules that can be applied to any individual. What is harmoniously right for one child may not be right for another. Just as we have large differences in the design characteristics of modern artists, we should also expect and encourage large differences in children's work.

As has been stressed before, creativity can be seen in the flexibility of thinking and the originality of approach. To some extent the products of this schematic stage appear more rigid than the drawings and paintings of younger children. However, we realize that the child is structuring his environment in such a way that he can begin to organize and see relationships in his thinking processes. Rather than being a step backward, the child is beginning to organize the structure of his drawings and paintings in such a way that he can have some basis for change and reorganization. That is, creative thinking is not disorganized thinking, but rather is the ability to redefine and reorganize in a flexible manner those forms and elements with which we are familiar. Abstract thinking is based entirely upon symbols, and during this stage of development we can see the child's first steps toward structuring and organizing his environment.

It is essential that a child be given constant encouragement to explore and investigate new ways and methods. Occasionally children will try to copy each other, particularly if one child has just received praise and another wishes that he could have this praise too. Putting a positive emphasis upon differences, and praising nonconformity and experimentation, will encourage creative thinking. A child's *own* creative effort should be accepted regardless of how meager the product appears. Ideally, each child should be eager to create, with the teacher's role being primarily that of encouraging depth of expression and a meaningful experience. The child who clings too closely to stereotypes, or repeats too often a particular schema, or is constantly looking for suggestions, is the one who needs the attention and special guidance of the teacher to bolster his own self-confidence and to provide him positive experiences in self-expression. At this age the opportunity to establish the self as an acceptable being, who thinks for himself and is able to express these thoughts, whatever they are, becomes very important. Since the child is searching for a pattern or structure within the environment, his concept of himself that is developed at this time may be an important factor in his relationships with learning abilities and with people. To develop a positive image of one's self, to encourage confidence in one's own means of expression, to provide the opportunity for constructive divergent thinking, should certainly be basic aims of the art program.

RELATED ACTIVITIES

1. Collect drawings of a man, done by a second grade class. Find how many different symbols are used for nose, mouth, body, arms, and so forth. What percentage of these children are using geometric lines for their expression? Compare with drawings done by a third grade, to see if the percentages change.

2. Find one child's schema for man. See how this is repeated over a period of several weeks. After a strong motivation centered upon some physical activity, notice the deviations in his schema. A week later, has he reverted to his usual schema?

3. In observing the behavior of children of this age, outside the classroom, can you detect any social schemata? Are there fixed rules for games? Are there set patterns for certain activities? Are there set songs or chants for such games as jump-rope? Is there any evidence of adults' pressure for these patterns, or do they come from the children themselves?

4. How many children in a first grade use the base line in their representations? Compare the percentage with a second grade class.

5. Collect examples of X-ray drawings, folding over, and space-time representations. Why were these subjective representations important to the child's expression? How would adults portray the same event? Which is the most adequate?

6. In examining children's drawings and paintings, show how the use of color parallels the establishment of a schema in form. What are some of the differences found in color schemata for common objects?

7. Keep a list of the different reasons for exaggerations, omissions, or neglect of parts as shown in drawings. Illustrate each, from examples of children's work.

NOTES

1. For a variety of schemata see Florence L. Goodenough, *Measurement of Intelligence by Drawings* (Yonkers, N.Y.: World Book Company, 1926).

2. Manuel Barkan, *A Foundation for Art Education* (New York: Ronald Press Co., 1955), p. 117.

3. For a discussion of this development outside the field of art see Jean Piaget, *Judgment and Reasoning in the Child* (Paterson, N.J.: Littlefield, Adams and Co., 1959).

4. Victor D'Amico, *Creative Teaching in Art,* rev. ed. (Scranton, Pa.: International Textbook Co., 1953).

# 7

# The Dawning Realism:
# The Gang Age,
# Nine to Eleven Years

ONE of the outstanding characteristics of this age of development is the child's discovery that he is a member of society—a society of his peers. It is during this time that children lay the groundwork for the ability to work in groups and to cooperate in adult life. The discovery of having similar interests, of sharing secrets, of the pleasure of doing things together, are all very fundamental. There is a growing awareness that one can do more in a group than alone and that the group is more powerful than a single person. This age is the time for group friendships and peer groups or gangs. The word *gang* has taken on some negative connotations within today's society, but we as adults may have some very happy memories of the gang of kids we went around with at school. This age shows an increasing development of "social independence" from adult domination, a learning about social structures in a personal way. This is a fundamental part of the developmental process and is an important step in social interaction.

Because of the different interests of boys and girls in our society, and because of real differences in development, the groups or gangs are commonly of the same sex. Boys often ignore girls, and girls despise boys. It is a time when boys prefer camping, belong to groups that have rules of their own, take great interest in group sports, build elaborate hideouts from boxes or stray pieces of lumber, and not infrequently lead wars against girls. Girls, on the other hand, are more eager to dress, enjoy parties, sit with their own group to watch a love movie, invent their own secret codes or languages, and not infrequently lead wars against boys of their own age, although often secretly admiring an older junior-high-school lad.

These important feelings of an awakened social independence are often in direct conflict with the desires of parents or adults who do not want to give up the close supervision and guidance of their children. It is mostly for this reason that adults consider this stage of development undesirable and often interfering with their own lives. Needless to say, teachers who are unaware of the important implications of group activities often find themselves the uncomfortable target of secret groups. Instead of giving support to this awakening feeling for group cooperation and the discovery of social independence, parents and teachers often counteract it by prolonging close dependency by authoritarian means. Instead of showing their sympathetic and warm feelings and interest for the desires of their children for group life, they often oppose it, not knowing that with such actions they only drive their children into secrecy. This may be one reason why cooperation with adults reaches an apparent low point, and it is interesting to note that "the peak of the delinquent period is usually said to coincide with the peak of the gang age at 10 or 11 years."[1] The attitudes of adults may be in part responsible for some of the factors involved in delinquency.

For the child, however, this age may be a most dramatic and healthy period of discoveries, as can be clearly seen in the child's creative work.

## The Greater Awareness of the Self

During this stage a child begins to develop a greater awareness of, and sensitivity to, his environment. He has come to wonder about why things work the way they do, and about his own being. He may now raise questions about areas that not very long ago he looked upon as unquestionable. He is becoming increasingly critical of others and of himself, and some children will begin to hide their drawings from an inquisitive adult or make some disparaging remark about their efforts. Children of this age also develop a sense of justice and may object violently to actions that "aren't fair." There is also an increasing concern with sex differences; although publicly the opposite sex is treated with a great deal of disdain, privately there are the awakenings of feelings of curiosity and affection. A child of ten has gained a fair amount of information about the workings of the world, both natural and social. However, to a great extent this tends to be isolated, concrete learning, and therefore much of the information that has been drilled into him in the classroom tends to be meaningless. The fact that the Pilgrims landed in 1620 is readily repeated on a test, but whether 1620 was before or after the last ice age is not clear. Some of the concepts children develop by this time continue with them through adult life. This is even true of their drawing characteristics. Studies have shown that there is surprising similarity between drawings of children during this stage and the drawings of adults who have had no formal art training.

## The Concept of Realism

There is sometimes confusion in the use of the term *realism,* even with art educators. Often it is confused with the term *naturalism*. However, these terms can be self-explanatory as long as we remember that *naturalism* refers directly to nature and *realism* refers to what is real. Nature can be looked upon by many people. Their backgrounds, reactions, or emotions do not affect what is there. Nature may be snow on the ground, a hot summer day, or any part of the environment—it is this way whether we look at it or not. What is real, however, is firmly rooted within us. We can be inspired by the beauty in nature, be disgusted with the selfishness of man, or be full of hope for the future, and all of these are very real. A question might arise whether it is desirable from the viewpoint of modern art education to stress the naturalistic tendencies. Although the imaginative and realistic tendencies are important, it would be a complete misunderstanding of modern art education to deny tendencies that lie sincerely in the development of a child. It would be a misconception to say there are no naturalistic tendencies in the child. We shall see that a visual concept of their environment is deeply rooted in a large number of growing adolescent children. However, a work of art is not the representation of an object itself; rather, it is the representation of the experience we have with the particular object. A mere photographic imitation of his environment is not expressive of a child's individual relationship to what he perceives. The question, then, is not whether the child should draw in a photographic way or be forced to rely upon imaginative patterns, but whether the art experience provides the opportunity for a child to identify with his own experience and encourages him in his own personal, sensitive artistic creation.

## The Representation of the Human Figure

The schema is no longer adequate to represent the human figure during the gang age. The concept of the human figure as expressed during the schematic stage is by its nature a generalized expression of man. At a later stage where the child is eager to express characteristics of sex, as boys with trousers and girls with dresses, the schematic generalization cannot suffice. We have discussed the greater awareness of this age; the modes of expression of the preceding stage are no longer suitable to express this increasing awareness.

We found in earlier stages of drawing that the separate parts of these drawings were not self-explanatory, but rather were composed of geometric shapes and geometric lines. That is, a part when removed from the whole lost its meaning. Now, however, geometric lines no longer suffice. The child moves to a form of expression that relates more closely to nature. But the child is still far from a visual representation. For example, girls in their drawings do not yet "see" that their dresses have folds or wrinkles, or that the hem is uneven when they walk. The hemline itself is always drawn straight across, even during this period. This shows clearly that the drawing is not an outcome of the child's visual observation, but rather that the child is eager to characterize girls as girls or boys as boys. We find that the child gains a feeling for details but often loses a feeling for action. Indeed, we see a greater stiffness in the representations of the human figure in drawings of children of this age. It is significant that henceforth every part has its meaning and retains this meaning even when separated from the whole.

**Figure 53.** This drawing of a farm shows a meager development of visual concepts, but has an interesting space interpretation. Two base lines are used, the upper with barn and trees and the lower with a tree and horses.

## The Representation of Space

In the same way as the greater awareness of the self and of the environment led a child to realize that geometric lines and forms are inadequate expression for the human figure, we also see in the representation of space a change from the symbolic expression, as seen in the base line concept, to a more naturalistic representation. As a result of this growing visual awareness, the child discovers that the space between base lines becomes meaningful and the plane is discovered.

The change from a single base line to the discovery of the plane is usually a fairly rapid one. The stage of transition can be seen in drawings that include several base lines; we find the space between these base lines being filled in. An example of this appears in Figure 53. We can only speculate that the child himself may physically discover the plane by his increased physical activity and developing curiosity. One can almost picture a first grader walking to school along his prescribed route. Compare this with a fourth grader who acts as if the sidewalk were there to ignore;

he is much more interested in walking on the wrong side of the hedge, kicking a can in the gutter, or going around in back of some of the houses to make sure that nothing interesting is happening. At any rate, the base line begins to disappear, and trees and houses no longer stand only on the edge of this line. Although for some children the base line representation remains in frequent use, the space below the base line now takes on the meaning of ground.

We also find that the sky line is no longer drawn across the top of the page but now extends all the way down to what at the beginning may be a base line but gradually assumes the significance of the horizon. At this time, however, the child has not yet become aware of the meaning of the horizon. He has not yet developed a conscious visual percept of depth, but he has taken the first steps toward such an awareness. With the sky all the way down the child soon realizes that a tree growing from the ground will partially cover the sky. Hence, he becomes conscious of

**Figure 54.** The beginnings of overlapping may be seen in this drawing of a car with buildings in the background.

overlapping, and another step toward a more naturalistic representation has been perceived, as seen in the buildings behind the car in Figure 54. This can be a very real discovery. That it is possible for objects to overlap can be an exciting experience; this awareness can be utilized by the sensitive teacher, as we shall discuss later. That one object can cover another is an important fact, because it implies an awareness of the existence of the other object. It is especially at this period that cooperation with adults is at a low point, although the support and acceptance of the child's peers is considered essential. We have not seen the development of this awareness in earlier stages.

## The Changing Mode of Expression

Since the child is developing a greater visual awareness, he no longer uses exaggerations, omissions, or other deviations in expressing his emotions. Although at the age of nine most children still exaggerate size relationships, particularly of the human figure, studies have shown that this exaggeration tends to disappear during this stage of development.[2] The child now begins to substitute other means of expression to show emphasis. We commonly see an accumulation of details on those parts that are emotionally significant.

We have discussed the fact that geometric lines are no longer adequate for expression, but the greater awareness and concern for detail at this stage of development can even extend to making a left hand quite different from the right. This concern for proper detail can occasionally make the total look distorted. Sometimes this concern for detail will even make a child exclaim that he has "goofed" if he has not drawn the proper number of buttons on his shirt. This dawning awareness of the visual appearance of objects has nothing to do with true naturalistic tendencies. This can be readily seen in these drawings and paintings, since there is no attempt at showing the light or shade, the effect of motion or any folds or wrinkles; rather, the child is characterizing his environment. His drawings have taken on a certain stiffness and formality.

The X-ray drawing and drawings using folding over are now criticized by children as being unnatural. Since this type of representation is primarily subjective, children who are becoming more aware of nature no longer look upon this mode of organization as being appropriate.

## The Use of Color

There is a great unity in the way in which children change in their means of expression. In color the child moves from a rigid color-object relationship to a characterization of color. Now he distinguishes between a bluish-red sweater and a yellowish-red sweater. This greater awareness of color differences can not be called a true visual perception. This is because he does not indicate the changing effects of colors in light and shade, or the effect of atmosphere upon color. Some children will find that the sky has a different blue from the blue of the river or the lake, and some will find that the tree is a different green from the green of the grass. If a child in this stage of development still uses rigid color-object relationships, he is slow to develop in his color relationships. This is not because he does not use new colors (this would be a very superficial answer) but because in his visual perception the child has not yet refined his sensitivity toward seeing differences that distinguish a green shrub from a green lawn. We shall discuss the methods of developing a greater sensitivity to those things around us. A refined perception can add a great richness to our lives, without which we pass the beauties in life like animals.

The more a child moves toward the establishment of a visual relationship between color and object, the more teachers are tempted to misuse this dawning sense for "realistic" colors by teaching the child how to use and apply color. There is no place in the elementary school for the teaching of color theories by means of color wheels or other "helps." Such teaching would only destroy the child's spontaneous approach and would make him insecure in his own developing sense of color relationships. The only way a child can be made more color-conscious is through the emphasis of the child's own reactions to color. The more meaningful the interaction between child and color, the deeper will be the experience.

How should we stimulate a greater awareness of color? Although there may be many techniques in stimulating a greater awareness of color, the basic underlying philosophy should be that the child himself becomes aware of the significance of color through his own experiences and achievements. An example might be a visit to a slum area, and upon return a discussion about the unpainted houses, the shattered windows replaced by wooden boards, the yards filled with junk, and a discussion about the people who live there. After consideration of these living conditions and their social implications, the children could paint "How It Would Be to Live in the Slums." Another time a trip to some well-designed and nicely kept homes would provide contrast. A discussion of the use of paint, the amount of light, the well-kept lawns, and the greater amount of space would be background for a picture of "The House in Which I Wish to Live." It is easily understood that the comparison of the dull atmosphere of the slums with the bright and joyous treatment of the house in which the child wished to live could give many opportunities to talk of dull and bright colors—in an abstract way, but in connection with an experience. Other sensitivity to color such as warm and cool colors could be experienced in the same way. A child is especially ready at this period for deviations from a former rigid color schema, and he will usually use such meaningful stimulations most willingly.

The impressionistic, or visual, color scale is the last and most complex to experience. We will discuss this in a later chapter. At this stage, the nine-to-eleven-year-old child's use of color is related to his subjective re-

**Figure 55.** Toads, beetles, rocks, and other natural objects are fascinating and inspiring to children of this age.

actions. The child enjoys colors and is now capable of being much more sensitive toward differences and similarities, and his eager explorations through fall leaves, or his sudden realization of the constantly changing sky colors, should certainly be encouraged. Any discussion of color, therefore, should focus upon the experience and not upon the "proper" use of color in a particular painting.

## The Meaning of Design and Crafts

As children now discover the meaningfulness of their environment and begin to relate this closely to themselves, it becomes most important for education to give them a feeling for what is sincere in our environment and what is insincere. One of the main functions of design can be the establishment of harmonious relationships. At this age, then, it is important that we stimulate children's thinking and provide opportunities for discoveries that relate to the natural beauty of materials as they are found unspoiled within our environment. This means developing a feeling for differences in rocks, pebbles, shells, barks, moss—this wealth we can find in nature. Children of this age are normally collecting a variety of objects anyway, from bits of string to toads, as any mother of a nine-year-old can testify (see Figure 55). A collection of a pile of pebbles in a classroom can actually be very exciting. A discussion of the different shapes and different colors, noticing how the water has worn down some edges, or seeing how the light tries to shine through some varieties but not others— all of this can be real discovery and can awaken perceptual sensitivity. Such explorations take a relaxed atmosphere, for such learning cannot be rushed.

We need not be limited to discovering the beauty of natural materials in just woods and streams. Even scrap material can have beauty hidden in it. Certainly rusty iron, or wrinkled paper, or even mold and mildew can be pleasing to look at if we can redefine our values and not think of them as being discarded and rejected parts of our sometimes too-sterile environment.

The sincerity of beauty as found in nature should be stressed, since this is a natural extension of the child's own direction at this age. Occasionally children will enjoy putting these collections into some form, such as putting the pebbles into a little sand in a box and pouring plaster over the back of them to make a mosaic, or putting scrap material into a collage

**Figure 56.** Holes and textures were of prime concern in this collage.

(see Figure 56). Becoming sensitive to the qualities of a material is of great importance, and children should be given an opportunity to improvise on their own account combinations of materials that need not necessarily serve a useful purpose. Getting acquainted with the different functions and qualities of materials is the main aim.

From our discussion it may seem as if emphasis is being placed upon a knowledge and understanding of materials, whereas the area of design may be bypassed. However, there should be no separation between the material and its function or between crafts and design. Rather, from the very beginning, inspirations for working with materials should come from the structure and nature of the material itself. The results of such relationships between a child and the materials will be crucial in enabling the child to adapt intuitively the qualities inherent in materials to any design in later years. In our greatest cultures skill, design, and workmanship were inseparable. Today we are again beginning to see some glimmer of a closer relationship between the craftsman, the material, and the function or design.

In the drawings and paintings of children in this stage of development we begin to see a conscious awareness of decoration. Girls more and more frequently begin putting patterns on their dresses. Boys become more aware of the plaid of their flannel shirts. This developing awareness of pattern and decoration within our environment is no excuse for the formal teaching of design. We certainly would not begin to teach the formal elements of grammar to a two-year-old child who has discovered that he can make his needs known through speech, nor would we teach the formal problems of balance, rhythm, or half-drop repeats to a child who is beginning to discover these patterns within his environment. A project such as designing a decorative border for a tea towel has little meaning, and it is entirely unsuitable to plan a design carefully on paper for possible transfer to some other material with which the child is not involved. However, simple potato, eraser, or spool prints may give a sense of an understanding of repetition as part of the principles of design. This is feasible only when the material and the design itself have a function in the life of the child. Such repeating patterns, although looking primitive to adults, will give an understanding of the nature of repetitions, and the folds in such material will show how the pattern can become dynamic through the nature of the material. To identify with the needs of the materials, that is, to learn their behavior, is important not only educationally but also ethically, as it will promote a feeling for sincerity and truth in design.

It is of course entirely possible to stimulate a greater sensitivity toward common materials within the usual classroom setting. For example, a common material like paper can be looked upon as having many possibilities. "What can paper do? How does it feel? Is it smooth or rough? Can you fold it or crease it? How does it look when it is crumpled? Notice how it tears. Can you make it turn or bend so that it looks happy? Can you make it feel sad?" Other materials can be treated in somewhat the same way, with the emphasis being upon the process of manipulation and exploring the material and not upon achieving a "nice-looking" finished product. There is no reason to think that all children need be equally occupied and interested in the same materials. Boys at this age often develop great interest in working with wood. If simple tools are available, a great deal of interest can be generated in discovering the qualities of wood, and the physical exertion of hammering and sawing and nailing often gives positive release to bottled-up energies (see Figure 57).

A word should be said here about exposing insincerity in the use of art materials. We constantly see around us examples of sham and falsehood in

**Figure 57.** These ten-year-old boys enjoy the experience of building their own projects in wood.

the use of materials. There is so much in the way of natural beauty for children of this age to discover, that exposing for what they are the false flowers, the imitation stone floors, the false chimneys, should be a part of the awareness of these children. To a great extent children accept the things around them as appropriate, and unconsciously we may go on living in an insincere environment. If we would live in a more truthful society, it is not too soon to stress the sincerity of design.

Clay continues to be an excellent material for three-dimensional expression. However, sometimes clay is used as a craft material to make such things as plaques and ash trays. Unless these objects have a real need in the life of children, and not very many children between nine and eleven smoke cigarettes, these projects will be mere busy-work. Pressing various textures into clay, or exploring the possibility of space and form such as holes in clay, or repeating a pattern of lines in a clay batt may have some utilitarian value if the clay pieces are fired. However, the teacher must not put the emphasis upon the preservation of the final product. If the child can participate in the total process—seeing the clay in its natural state to watching it come fired from the kiln—this is a very worthwhile experience. Occasionally, however, teachers remove the clay pieces and have them fired. Then the finished product has no relationship to the child who made it; the color, texture, and consistency have been so altered that the child can no longer identify with the object. Under such conditions it is better to leave the clay piece unfired. Clay that has been modeled or made to represent some object, person, or animal is usually not fired anyway. This is merely because the experience has been expressed in the process itself, and the procedure of firing can often cause these pieces to break apart. Most of the synthetically modeled pieces (those put together from single details) would not be able to stand firing. As has been said before, it is not worthwhile to sacrifice the child's individual thinking to conform to mere procedure.

Since the child has developed an interest in the possibilities of working with a variety of materials, he is also a "pushover" for a range of non-creative craft projects to be found on the market. Such items as precut leather tooling kits, easy-to-glue-together plastic objects, or mosaic kits that "anybody can put together" can be a real menace to his normal curiosity and development. It certainly rests with the teacher to point out that making a boat from scrap wood can be a much more enjoyable activity than trying to fit together some adult's preconceived plastic model. If a child can get satisfaction from working with a range of common materials, and if misguided parents stop praising products instead of children, the precut already-thought-out "easy projects" companies will be out of business.

## Art Motivation

Adults often have pleasant memories of childhood; however, most of these memories are of happenings and situations outside of school. Probably each of us has particular memories of the time when we were either nine, ten, or eleven. One adult remembering back to this stage had the following to say.

"If I remember back at my childhood—now, you see if I remember back at this stage, it must have made a very distinct impression on me, but I remember very distinctly how we converted a small, little, oh, island into something, into a wonderland. When I was a child we were in a gang—a wonderful gang—and we would sit on a footbridge over a small stream, I am quite sure it was not larger than a few feet, but when we went over this bridge it appeared to us like, oh, miles long you know, going over the bridge and entering our land which no one knew. This was fascinating. We made a building there at the highest point—there was a little hill, and we made our own money, of course, we collected the money, you know, for entrance into this island. I can still remember that we had pockets full of paper money which we ourselves printed. And we had there, we found bones of a dead animal and made a little sign saying, 'These are the bones discovered of an animal two thousand years ago,' and we really looked at it as we put it there in a certain order, and you know, this was something magic to us. And another place was the Snake Point where we had spread out a dead snake which we found, and when we went there we really got goose pimples. This was the Snake Point, let's go to the Snake Point, and then you know we collected gravel and built little paths, and these were then real paths, you know. We had a hideout when it rained, so this island was really something magic."

Imagine if we could promote in school these same intense experiences. All too often school is looked upon as being a place to "behave," a place to suffer through because of the misfortune to have been born young. But there is no reason why school should not be a stimulating, exciting place, where the natural drives of children are not only accepted but developed into meaningful stimulating education.

Motivation during this period must stress the newly discovered social independence in order to give the child a feeling of self-esteem. An art experience must give him an opportunity to express the growing awareness of sex, to develop a greater awareness of self, and to satisfy a new curiosity for the environment. It must also inspire the child to use the newly found methods of group cooperation as beneficial means for achieving results.

To inspire cooperation, two means can successfully be used: first, the *subjective* method of cooperation, which deals with representations of individual experiences of cooperation or the representations of scenes in which cooperation is important. However, it is vital for the teacher to know that much depends upon the way such motivation is presented to the group. The atmosphere the teacher develops during the motivation

**Figure 58.** "A City Picture," drawn by a nine-year-old boy. The boy identifies with the traffic-directing policeman, who is symbolic of order in our society.

contributes greatly to its success. Such topics as "Helping the Flood Victims" or "Cleaning Up After the Storm" can be presented very dramatically. Whenever the child can identify with a larger undertaking in which the individual feels that the group effort can not be successful without his contribution, such a topic will inspire cooperation. It continues to be important that each motivation be stimulating and develop a greater awareness of the possibilities in the subject matter. Such motivation should include a discussion and a point of culmination. The implications of being a flood victim are important considerations. "Whose house is under water? No one's? Suppose you were living there and we could watch how the water rises and rises! How would we feel?" The putting of one's self into the place of those for whom we do the group work is, of course, most important in motivating effective cooperation. Further areas might include the identification of the self with those people who are responsible for the social welfare. Such activities as drawing the firemen during the big fire or the policeman during the evening rush hour can also effectively stimulate a greater social cooperation (see Figure 58).

The second method, the *objective* method of cooperation, deals more directly with group work itself: a whole group works on one project (see

**Figure 59.** Every child must feel that his contribution is important to the success of the group effort. Here youngsters paint their mural on the floor.

Figure 59). Here also the kind of motivation is vital for its success. The group work can be quite simple in its planning, such as having each child make a fierce animal of clay and then assembling these animals into a large zoo. Straws or sticks can serve as bars, and the children will enjoy making signs for the various parts of the zoo. Group work can get quite elaborate, with a class dividing up into several working units. An example might be making a mural of a city.

"What makes a city? Yes, houses and stores and factories. But we cannot have them all mixed up together! How would you like to live right next to a factory! Yes, we need to have some zoning laws. We will certainly need the residential district. How many children would like to work on the residential section of our city? You will have to work hard because there are so many different kinds of buildings that people live in! Now we have the industrial area for our factories. How many would like to work on this section? And, yes, the shopping area, too. But there are more than just stores in the shopping section! What other districts do we have? Oh, yes, playground and recreation area, fine! Does everyone know what section he is going to be working on? You had better pick a leader to help your group decide what kind of buildings you are going to need. You say we still need a school district? Oh, I think the residential area committee should worry about that. Why, John and Joseph, you are not on any committee! Would you like to plan the background for our city? Should we have a stream or river near the city? Do you think we should have some mountains, fields, or forest land around?"

Probably a material such as colored paper would be quite suitable for this topic. A large background paper or board would be essential. It is not expected that a cooperative enterprise like this would be a smooth, quiet operation. Democratic action may not be easily learned, but it is an essential part of our way of life. When the various committees of the city have completed their districts, the city can be assembled. A lack of trees may be very apparent, or some small houses may be needed, and "someone had better cut out some gray smoke to go on the factory chimneys; and, oh, we forgot all about making cars and trucks for our streets." In such a way all children become involved in the activities. It is probably best to staple or tack the various buildings in place so that these buildings can be readily moved from one spot to another. There may be a sudden cry of dismay as Johnny finds that someone has placed a church right over his house. This provides a fine opportunity for some explanation of the meaning of overlapping, especially at the time when overlapping becomes meaningful. "Did you ever go to a movie and find a nice seat where you could see the screen, and right in front of you a lady with a big hat sits down and now you can see nothing? Is that good? Would it be all right if a little boy sat in front of you? It wouldn't matter if a little boy sat in front because you could still see and people could still see you. Overlapping is fine, but one should not completely cover the other. Maybe the small house can go in front of the church since the church could still be seen. And look, a tree can go in front of the house." The child has developed a fair amount of understanding when he can accept a minor role for one of his buildings, but maybe can feel better when his tree goes over someone else's building. Every individual, every child in the class, should think, "I could not have accomplished by myself what the whole group has done." This is a main part of cooperation.

As we can see, the teacher's role was a subordinate one in this activity. Her main role was to act as a catalyst. It is a much more difficult task to stimulate and encourage children to learn, produce, and explore on their own. An easier method of producing products would be to authoritatively assign projects and have the "best" method for achieving results already worked out beforehand. To provide a rich meaningful experience for children, such authoritarian methods must be discarded. It is much more important to increase the interest of children in the materials of expression, it is much more important to give a sense of discovery, it is much more important to give the child an opportunity to determine his own relationships with the world, than to worry about how "artistic" a particular product looks.

Care should be taken in any art motivation to insure that the individual has ample opportunity to develop his own means of expression. As we have seen, there is a need for group activities, but these group activities should never be accompanied by pressure for conformity to the norm.

## Subject Matter in Art

Subject matter throughout the grades is determined by the subjective relationship of man to his environment. As the child changes, so does his expression. The following suggestions for subject matter are based upon the particular characteristics of the developmental level as previously discussed. These topics are only meant to be suggestions; it is assumed that they will always be adjusted and subordinated to the particular classroom situation and to the particular group of children involved. It is important that the teacher become involved and excited about the content of art expression. The following topics, then, are not to be considered as assignments but as areas of interest, which can be pursued with enthusiasm.

To stimulate subjective cooperation and to encourage children to identify with group activities the following topics are suggested.

**"Picking Up After the Storm"**
**"Helping After the Flood"**
**"Gathering Wood for Our Campfire"**
**"Building a Clubhouse with My Friends"**

It is also important to stimulate cooperation through the identification of a child with the forces of social preservation and maintenance. Such topics as the following might be appropriate.

**"A Policeman in Five-o'clock Traffic"**
**"Repairing the Broken Water Main"**
**"A Nurse Taking Care of the Sick"**

There are of course many ways in which a group can work objectively together for group cooperation. We have already discussed a few possibilities, but there are many more. There should be opportunity for small groups of children to work together on such a project, and the final product should be large enough and complex enough so that each child can contribute in his own way and so that no one child could possibly do the whole project alone. The following are some suggestions for group projects.

**"We Are All Making a Circus"**
**"We Are Making Our Own County Fair"**
**"We Are All Making a Farm"**
**"We Are Exploring the Surface of Venus"** (See Plate 6.)

We have discussed the disappearance of the base line at this age, and ample opportunity should be given children to explore the possibilities of using the plane. Since there is an increasing awareness of differences

**Figure 60.** Cardboard boxes are the material from which this animal grows. Many materials can be manipulated and transformed into objects with real meaning to the creator.

in sex and a greater attention to detail, ample opportunity should be allowed to explore and express subject matter that will provide for these tendencies. It should be stressed that all subject matter should have meaning for the child and not be removed from his own experiences. Suitable topics for this age might include:

"Sitting Around a Table for Supper"
"Planting a Garden in the Spring"
"Watching the Parade Come down the Street"
"Skating on the Pond in the Woods"

**"Playing Baseball on the School Grounds"**

One of the characteristics of this age is the beginning awareness of over-lapping. We have discussed some of the possibilities in this area, and it is to be expected that discussions will arise normally from the painting procedures. However, some specific topics to stimulate thinking in this area might include:

**"Looking out the Window of the School Bus"**
**"Sitting in the Movie Theater"**
**"Looking at Clothes in the Store Window"**
**"Singing for the School Assembly"**

There is another large area of subject matter in art that is related more to the development of skills and the increased familiarity with the nature of materials. Although these experiences with different materials may not have a specific subject or topic to represent, the purpose and reason behind each of the activities should be made quite clear to the youngsters. Since children of this age are becoming more outspoken about themselves and about adults, these children should have a knowledge and understanding of the purposes of any project. A number of craft activities can be included under this heading, although care should be taken to insure that the direction and planning rests with the children involved. This would mean that activities such as those that are preplanned by the teacher or those that are "cute" or "tricky" would be discarded. Some suggestions for projects in this general area follow.

**"Geometric Potato Printing on Textiles"**
**"Making a Collage for Our Fingers to Feel"**
**"Making a Funny Animal in Papier-Mâché" (See Figure 60.)**
**"Making Some Prints for a Christmas Card"**
**"Putting Together an Object from Wood"**
**"Making a Mosaic from Pebbles and Plaster"**
**"Some Imaginative Animals in Clay"**
**"Using Shiny Paper for Decorations"**

There is one very important subject matter area in art that should never be overlooked. This is the subject matter that is within each child. In some cases this subject matter may be very apparent, such as a boy's love for working with tools; however, sometimes this subject matter can be hidden beneath the surface, as in a quiet girl's feelings of rejection. There should be ample opportunity for these extremes to be expressed. That is, both the joy and pleasure of creating should be given free rein, but also deeper emotional feelings and subconscious drives should be given an opportunity to be expressed. Some materials lend themselves to the expression of the inner self better than others. Finger paint provides a direct release for such feelings; working in clay can provide the opportunity for frustrations to be eased. Ideally, every child would express himself freely. In some cases the understanding support of a sensitive teacher is necessary to put strong feelings and emotions into artistically constructive channels.

## Art Materials

The child has advanced beyond the use of geometric lines and base line representations in their linear meaning. With the discovery of the plane he now feels the need of filling in spaces, as for example in the representation of the sky, which is now usually painted down to the horizon. Although crayons can be used on their sides to fill large areas, the best material for this purpose is poster or tempera paint. Since the child now has greater control over the paint, it is no longer as necessary to have the paint mixed to a thick consistency. In fact, the child himself can now add water to the paints to make them the consistency that he himself likes, and he can also be responsible for refilling his own paint container.

We have found that children during this stage of development are more concerned with detail than formerly. Therefore, some children will want to use a hair brush in addition to the bristle brush. Although children at this age differentiate their color-object relationships, using different greens for grass and trees, it is not necessary to increase the number of colors the child has available. Actually, a limited number of paints encourages a child to creatively mix his colors himself (see Figure 61). Good crayons also mix, but this is even more true with poster paint. If you give children a limited scale of colors, you encourage them to invent their colors if they feel the desire, and if they don't feel the desire for greater color differentiation, it is of no use to give them a larger color scale anyway, because they won't use it except as a matter of multiple

**Figure 61.** Mixing their own paints gives these girls an opportunity to enjoy and explore the possibilities of color.

choice. Actively engaging in mixing colors for a particular reason is much more desirable than providing a variety of hues that the child passively accepts.

As we have said before, a material is good only if it contributes to the child's needs and helps him to express what is in his mind. Although there are unlimited materials for the use of children, care should be taken that these materials lend themselves to expression rather than restrict children's originality. If a material is by its very nature restrictive or inhibiting, it should be discarded. Some strange creations have resulted from some misguided "arty" programs. Such things as marshmallows and toothpicks, wilted phonograph records, decorated light bulbs, or lamps made from old ginger ale bottles can make a mockery of an art program.

Colored paper is a basic material at this age. It provides a natural means of overlapping and is an appropriate material for the early stages of cooperation through projects. Another essential material is pottery clay, which can be used for many three-dimensional projects. This clay can be easily stored in plastic bags, and of course it can be used again and again. There are certain advantages to using materials that are considered adult art materials, and clay is certainly one of these.

Finger paint is a material that we have not considered to any degree before this stage. Now, however, it can be used for expression without the concern that children will be too involved with its textural consistencies. Needless to say, there should also be a good supply of basic equipment. This includes scissors, a stapler, paste, cellophane tape, and some woodworking tools.

For craft work many materials can be used, such as wood, papier-mâché, wire, cloth, and of course a scrap container with a wide range of straws, buttons, boxes, colored cellophane, and anything else that looks interesting. Of course, children themselves will collect barks, rocks, pieces of wood, feathers, or whatever happens to attract them. Although some care should be taken to insure the safety of the children from such things as broken glass or sharp points, undue concern for sanitation and cleanliness may stand in the way of a child developing skill in hammering or cutting, or of digging up a particularly pleasing pebble.

## A Discussion of the Art of the Gang Age

As has been said before, one of the outstanding characteristics of this age is that the child discovers his social independence. He has discovered

**Plate 7.** "Standing in the Rain," drawn by an eleven-year-old girl. Color, use of space, and wealth of detail combine to give an aesthetically pleasing whole. Here we see a growing visual awareness coupled with a child's directness and freshness.

**Plate 8.** "Barns," painted in watercolor by a preadolescent girl. Her direct expression shows her developing aesthetic awareness. Such decorative and pleasing preadolescent art should be valued for its own sake. It should not have to conform to adult standards, to inflexible rules of perspective and proportion, or to arbitrary principles of design.

that he can have actions and thoughts quite independent of adults. He has developed a feeling for himself as a member of a group. He has also become more aware of the details of his environment. His drawings are no longer composed of a schema for people, but rather his concept of people has altered so that the schema is no longer adequate. How much he has departed from schematic representation and how much he feels the need to characterize particular objects, figures, and his environment is indicative of his intellectual growth. It can be easily understood that a child of low mentality neither becomes aware of his changing environment nor discovers those characteristics that allow him to individualize objects or figures.

The ability to break away from the schema and to recognize particular details connected with the self and with the environment is one of the characteristics of this age. We have also seen that children between the ages of nine and eleven are much more observant about their environment, and their interest in discovering the details of nature can be seen in the variety of collections made by boys and girls. To a great extent, however, these children do not remove themselves from their own observations. That is, their drawings and paintings show quite clearly that they see things through their own experiences, and assume that this "reality" is the way things really are. Children can sometimes be critical of the drawings of others and even their own drawings if these do not live up to their own interpretation of what is "real." We can see that naturalism is not the ultimate goal at this age, because there is usually no attempt at showing light and shade, atmospheric effects, or even color reflections or folds in cloth. The child then has left the stage of schemata and laws for behavior behind him, has developed a curiosity about himself and those things around him, but has not achieved an objective naturalistic viewpoint. In a later chapter we shall discuss the fact that for some people this stage may never come.

It should be emphasized at this point that there is no value judgment implied in the various stages of children's development. Our concern here is merely to understand these differences and to become more sensitive to the great variety of artistic expression.

If we look at Plate 7, "Standing in the Rain," we can relate our discussion to a particular drawing. This picture was done by an eleven-year-old girl using crayons. The schema has practically disappeared except for some facial features. Notice, for example, the repeated symbol for the nose in the central three figures and the sharp nose form in the rest of the figures. One of the distinguishing characteristics of this stage is the

**Figure 62.** "Man with Umbrella," painted by a ten-year-old boy. For some children, the base line and the exaggeration of meaningful parts, such as the enlargement of the hand holding the umbrella, continue at this age.

fact that parts of a drawing can now be subtracted from the total without losing their meaning. No longer do geometric lines suffice. It can be noticed in "Standing in the Rain" that the feet or facial features would remain as recognizable parts even though they were removed from the context of the drawing. It is also very apparent that the child has departed from his base line representation and has a distinct feeling for the plane. The inclusion of such details as puddles, houses with windows, raincoats with buttons and belts, boots of various colors, and umbrellas of various patterns clearly shows that this child is very aware of her environment. It can be easily understood, then, that a child of lower mentality would draw quite a different picture. Notice for comparison the drawing "Man with Umbrella" in Figure 62, where awareness of detail is much less.

The question may be raised whether intelligence alone might cause such differences in representation. Comparing "Standing in the Rain" with "Man with Umbrella," might not lack of motivation be a real consideration? We have said before that a closer look at children's drawings can give us a better understanding of children and some insight into their thinking processes. Indeed, yes; lack of motivation may cause great differences in drawings. However, we are dealing with functional intelligence, that is, how one actually acts and performs within the environment. In some cases a potentially brilliant person may go to his grave without ever being motivated to utilize this potential. One of the important roles of the teacher is to motivate and excite children to utilize their potential to fullest capacity. We might be a little more exact in saying that these two children have differences in their functional intelligence that may be caused by several unknowns. However, for the teacher it is quite clear that promoting in the child a greater sensitivity to his changing environment and awareness of his own thinking, feeling, and perceiving will help to develop him to his fullest potential.

Within the framework of art experiences we have the opportunity to provide for the development of emotional growth. Within our society too often children's emotions and feelings are squelched. This is particularly true of boys who are at an early age told not to be sissies. Even within a group of age-mates a boy usually has to conceal his true feelings in order to remain "manly." For the opportunity to express emotional content and to develop in emotional growth, children need to identify with their own experiences in their art. Children who constantly hide behind stereotypes or who are unable to paint their own relationships with their environment are not able to express their true feelings.

Children now usually refrain from using as much exaggeration as they did earlier. We find that there is a more naturalistic proportion. One of the characteristics of emotional interest in a particular part of a drawing or a painting is the accumulation of details in this particular part. This can be easily understood, for the child uses more affection to characterize a part that is of emotional significance to him.

Social growth, during this period, is one of the outstanding factors of development. This is the time when the child discovers his social independence, when he recognizes that he has more power in a group than as an individual. Yet when something interferes with this new feeling of social belonging, the child may withdraw and remain an outsider. Whether or not a child identifies himself with a group can be recognized by two factors from his creative work: (1) from the content of the work, (2) from the participation in group work. Since we have mentioned "Standing in the Rain" in Plate 7, we shall look at this illustration for content indicating group identification. It seems obvious that this child is aware of people, and since she makes the children different sizes, she is aware of group differences. However, every figure is looking straight forward and seems to have little relationship with the others. The figures appear more like a group of individuals who happen to be standing next to each other. To a great extent, however, the topic may have been responsible for this lack of common feeling of participation. There are two methods of group identification, the one being involved with the event or action, the other being the representation of group interaction. The illustration indicates that the child has identified strongly with the scene and with the people involved but has not shown much interaction within the group. This child is obviously socially conscious of the environment, for not only is the particular setting portrayed but also we see differences in clothes, an awareness of everyone's being in the rain, and also the rain, boots, and puddles indicate an awareness of the child's relationship to his environment.

The ability of children to participate in group activities can readily be seen when children work on such topics as "We Are Making a Dairy Farm." We mentioned that children of this age have the urge to work in group activities, but the child who withdraws from such activities may need this social experience the most. To a great extent democracy is based upon social action. A child who avoids the group and who is unable to relate to his own experiences in his drawings may need to have some support from the teacher in order to develop a greater social growth. Such experience as being in charge of a section of a mural may be of value. Certainly the individual's contribution to the group should be recognized, and a sensitive teacher can insure that each child is able to participate. It is very apparent that changes in drawing and painting will come about naturally when a child has experienced greater interaction in group activities. Pointing out that his figures do not relate one to another, would only make the child unsure of his own creative abilities and would be absolutely against the basic premises of art education. It is only through the child himself and the interaction with the environment and with people that significant changes will take place in creative productions.

The child who painted Plate 7 ranks high in perceptual growth. The child's growing visual awareness and her beginning feelings for nature are part of her perceptual growth. One of the first indications of a child's visual awareness is expressed by the inclusion of the horizon line and the painting of the sky to meet this line. Here, we can see that the child has become very aware of depth, even though no sky is indicated. Another aspect of visual perception is expressed by the child's awareness of overlappings, and here we see not only overlapping of people but overlapping of objects. There is also a visual awareness of differences in color, although as we might expect during this age, there is no particular awareness of light and shade. Also the hemline continues to remain straight, at least in this particular illustration. The child has an advanced awareness of detail, which can be observed in the raincoats and in the background houses. Certainly the encouragement of perceptual sensitivity is a vital part of any art experience.

There are also indications of aesthetic growth in this picture. Notice the conscious awareness of design in the umbrellas. Not only are these interesting in themselves, but they nicely repeat colors that are used elsewhere in the drawing. Aesthetic growth can also be seen in the way children relate the material to the subject matter; that is, how sensitive are they to the qualities of the material with which they are working, and to what extent does the subject matter reflect this awareness? Children of this age are now a great deal more aware of the nature of the clay, paint, or crayon with which they are working. Using a material to its fullest extent and utilizing its intrinsic qualities is a characteristic of aesthetic sensitivity. Children who work with clay as a flat drawing material are not aware of the distinctive qualities of clay. Apparently our artist who drew "Standing in the Rain" was very aware of the possibilities crayon could afford.

Certainly one of the most important areas of growth to which art can contribute is that of creative growth. During this stage of development there is a great deal of pressure put upon children to conform not only to the wishes of adults but also to the demands of the group. To function creatively, however, one must be able to function as an individual. This means that imitation and conformity to patterns outside the self must be discouraged. The encouragement of the individual child's own approach to working out problems is vital in this area. To what extent a child is creative at this age can be seen by the desire shown for experimentation, exploration, and invention. A child who is rigid or does not utilize material in new ways needs to be encouraged in his flexibility. Encouraging new and different ways to use materials and rewarding the interesting stipple or the effect of one color being placed over another will be a positive step in the direction of supporting creative growth.

# Summary of the Art of the Gang Age

During the schematic stage we noticed that children had the need to repeat the same symbol again and again. Now, however, the repetition of form should gradually disappear, and there should be a greater development of new forms or shapes that are not constantly repeated. Working in unfamiliar materials can often have a positive effect upon drawings and paintings. Children who have worked in collage materials may become much more aware of a variety of texture and forms and be able to transfer this awareness into a painting medium. Art should certainly give support for individual expression and creative thinking.

In summarizing this stage, it appears obvious that art can contribute to total development. One of the greatest needs of children during this period is to find themselves, to realize their own power, and to develop their own relationships within their own group. Second is the need for the child to discover his own sincere relationship to his environment and to objects and materials that make up this environment as we have discussed them. There are no short cuts to the development of perceptual abilities or creative growth. Although the range of individual differences can be very great, the end product should be viewed only as an indication of individual development. Standards of value should never come from the teacher, nor should group influences be so strong as to dictate a particular kind or type of product. We have seen that growth affects the products and also affects the aesthetic awareness of children, and any standards outside the child become false.

As we have gained a greater understanding of this peer group age, we can readily see how the teaching of particular techniques in art may stand in the way of children exploring and experimenting for themselves. As adults we help a great deal in the physical development of children by providing them with the proper nutrients and the place and encouragement for the development of the necessary physical skills; in the same way we as adults should provide the essential ingredients for children's artistic development, but we can not do this developing for them.

RELATED ACTIVITIES

1. Collect the drawings of a fourth grade class and tabulate how many children depend upon base line concept. How many use more than one base line? Have any children begun to use the space below the base line as a

plane? Compare these figures with drawings from the fifth grade, the sixth grade.

2. Save the drawings of a third grade child over a period of several months. Trace the development of symbols from a representation using geometric lines to a representation more closely related to nature.

3. Observe several group activities within a school setting at several grade levels. Which activities were the most productive? Which were most satisfactory from the child's point of view? Analyze the reasons why some activities were more successful than others.

4. Make a list of materials used in a fourth grade art program. Revise this list according to the meaningfulness of these art materials for expression at these age levels. Compare this list with what is appropriate at the kindergarten level.

5. Make a list of examples of the growing awareness of children for design and textural pattern in their drawings. Pay particular attention to clothing and objects important to the artist. Are there any sex differences? How does the extent of awareness compare with academic ability?

6. In working with clay, how many children model analytically (by pulling out from the whole) and how many synthetically (putting parts together)?

7. Keep a record of which children begin to make the sky come down to the base line. What is the first realization of overlapping beyond this initial step? Are these the same children who are also more socially developed?

## Notes

1. Agatha H. Bowley, *Guiding the Normal Child* (New York: Philosophical Library, 1943).

2. Viktor Lowenfeld, *The Nature of Creative Activity*, rev. ed. (New York: Harcourt, Brace & World, Inc., 1952).

# 8

# The Pseudo-Naturalistic Stage: The Stage of Reasoning, Eleven to Thirteen Years

THE pseudo-naturalistic stage of development is one of the most exciting and yet one of the most trying in the field of art. Since children of this age span the years from the usual elementary school into the junior high school level, and since for many of these children this will be the last formal public school art they receive, the importance of this level cannot be minimized. This age is also referred to as the period of pubescence or preadolescence. This is a time when girls start to develop mature sexual characteristics but boys do not. It is a time for seeking greater independence from adults and a time for following the demands of the "crowd." The child, although maybe the term *child* no longer applies, strives to be as much like his peers as possible, even to the extent of following fads and refusing to wear appropriate clothes and insisting on having his hair just so. It is also a period of great individual differences;

214

although this is most noticeable in physical differences, it is also true in the mental, emotional, and social areas as well.

Shortly the adolescent will be faced with the problem of finding himself as a person in relation to the adult world. Before he arrives at that stage, however, we get the awakenings of a critical awareness and the beginnings of a half-understood and not entirely welcome change in status. This is an age when emotion and strong feelings begin to be expressed, when the adult word is no longer accepted as gospel, when he begins to find that he is not a child, but is also very sure he is not an adult. The role of art in this stage of development should be both strong and clear: to give support to his individuality, to provide a socially accepted release for his emotions and tensions, and to ease the transition from the expression of a child to the type of expression expected of an adult.

The significance of this stage can better be understood when we consider it a preparatory stage to the approaching crisis of adolescence. After the child has properly gone through the gang age, he enters a stage in which he has developed intellectually to the point where he can tackle almost any problem; yet in his reactions he still is a child. The difference between children and adults can best be seen in the diversity of their imaginative activity. This can be observed in the different types of playing. The child may play hide-and-seek with abandon; with the same unawareness he may move a pencil up and down while imitating the noises of an airplane. Such unawareness is characteristic of children. Quite obviously, their imagination transforms a pencil into an airplane. All children use their imagination in such an uninhibited way; if an adult were to do the same he would be considered insane. For an adult a pencil is a pencil and the pencil is for writing. The child's imaginative activity is unconscious. The adult's imaginative activity in its effect is controlled. This change in the imaginative activity from the unconscious to critical awareness, signaled by physical changes in the body, is one of the most important characteristics of the crisis of adolescence.

One parent recalls this stage of development with his own child in the following words:

"When Tommy, my son, was in this stage, of course he was a member of a gang, he had his fun, he had his group of children. He was always tall and a little bit out of proportion to the other children, but he didn't even recognize that, he didn't see it. He associated with younger children who were not as tall. He had his wooden gun, or his wooden stick—and enjoyed playing. But there came a time when I came home from my office—when I saw that when I approached the house he sort of tried to hide the gun, and I said, 'Why don't you play with the children?' and he said, 'Oh, I think—isn't it silly?' I said, 'No, not silly at all, why don't you play with them? It is fun, isn't it?' And when I went into the house, of course he went on engaging in his pretend-to-be games. He felt again as though he were no longer being watched, and since the smaller children accepted him in the group—in the gang—well, he continued the game. But these interruptions became more frequent as he grew older, and I could see him with his wooden gun, sitting there and watching them playing pretend-to-be games, now and then participating or giving orders, but already standing outside. Until one day he put the wooden gun he had so carefully whittled into the basement, but still he could not part with it. Sometimes he went downstairs trying to improve it, but he no longer associated with the group, just watched them."

The important question will be, How can we prepare the child most properly for this change so that he can continue his creative production in spite of his critical awareness? Or, in other words, How can we prepare the child to create in such a way that he looks with pride on his work instead of being ashamed of it? During this stage, for the first time, the attention has to be shifted from the importance of the working process to an increased emphasis on the final product. Thus, the final art product becomes more and more significant with increasing age. This recognition of the growing significance of the final product is a clear demand on the part of youth, and it must be accepted by educators.

A healthy body can overcome the aftereffects of an operation much easier than a weakened body; therefore, it is important to strengthen the body before undergoing a contemplated operation. We take this procedure for granted when dealing with a physical crisis, but it is all too often neglected in cases of emotional disturbances. Neither art educators nor psychologists give the necessary attention to preparing the child for the crises of adolescence. Yet this stage of reasoning is the appropriate period for such physical and psychological conditioning.

Since art education affects the whole individual, his thinking, feeling, and perceiving, the teacher has an excellent opportunity to influence changes. Thus he may be able to help youth to overcome an important part of this crisis. Most commonly this change is seen in the fact that children are highly spontaneous, whereas adults, because of their critical awareness toward their imaginative activity, generally lose their spontaneous creative ability.

Another psychologically important factor deserves consideration. The closer we study adolescence, the more we see a distinction in the sensory reactions of the children toward their artistic experiences. We see clearly a preference by some children for *visual stimuli;* some others may be more concerned with the interpretation of *subjective experiences.* Visual experiences are defined as those that refer to our optical senses. They are concerned with the differences of color, light, and shadows, introduced through atmospheric conditions as well as with the perspective interpretation of space. Subjective interpretations are those that emphasize the emotional relationship to the external world in reference to the body self. Visually minded individuals refer in their pictures to environment, whereas nonvisually minded individuals are the expressionists. Children who have a preference for visual experiences feel as spectators, looking at their work from outside, and are more impressionists. Subjectively minded people feel involved in their work. As we approach the crisis of adolescence, during which preferences toward these different experiences crystallize, we have to pay increasing attention in our motivation to both of these important experiences. We would discourage a visually minded person by motivating him in referring to subjective experiences, emotional qualities, or body experiences; in the corresponding way we would inhibit a subjectively minded person if we were to motivate him by mere visual experiences. Since traditional art education is mainly built upon visual stimuli, a great part of our young people must feel not only neglected but frustrated. Many art educators use visual stimulations throughout the secondary level, not realizing that modern expressionist art is a clear indication of the importance of nonvisual stimuli in our present-day life. *Indeed, most of the children react in both ways, with a preference for one or the other kind of experience.* The knowledge of this fact together with the increasing shift of emphasis from the working process to the final product is of vital importance for art educators and educators in general who deal with this age level. A more detailed analysis will follow in the section "Art Motivation."

## The Representation of the Human Figure

We would naturally expect that changes in the representation of the human figure would follow the increased awareness and concern with changes that are beginning to take place in the bodies of the preadolescent

**Figure 63.** Notebooks and scraps of paper often reveal a child's interest and concern with himself and things around him. This form of spontaneous art expression should not be repressed.

period. Since girls tend to develop earlier than boys, we usually find the greatest interest in drawing the human figure among the girls. As biological changes occur, we find greater interest in drawing spontaneously in notebooks, on scraps of paper, or on book covers (see Figure 63). Usually the sexual characteristics of these drawings are greatly over-exaggerated, reflecting the concern of these children over their physical development. Often these drawings are concealed from adults, and in some cases a sense of guilt or shame accompanies these drawings. We will discuss later how the interest in the body can be used to an advantage in the art program.

At this point it might be well to mention the interest in drawing animals. It is especially true of girls that a great deal of interest can sometimes be focused upon drawing horses (see Figure 64). It is not necessary at this time to delve into the underlying reasons for this, except to say that by now children have generally lost their anxiety about animals and often project their own feelings into some animal form, and this identification with the dashing, romantic horse can also be used as a strong motivating force in art education. The emotional and psychological concerns of children of this age need to have constructive outlets, and at any age the feelings and concerns of an individual are the basis of true art expression.

Children who tend to be visually minded will strive for greater naturalism in their drawing of the human figure. That is, they will become more aware of the changing optical effects experienced in different light, space, and atmospheric conditions. From this viewpoint the drawing of clothes will become naturalistic as soon as the changing effects that take place when we sit down are *observed*: the clothes fold or wrinkle at the bent parts, lights and shadows are determined by the changes of the sitting body, and so forth. Until he reaches this stage, the child usually employs clothes only for characterizations, to show that "This is a girl" and "This a man." Henceforth we shall see that the visual child gradually develops the urge to add optical changes.

The child begins to observe visually; thus visual observation starts where mere characterization ends. There is generally a confusion between visual experiences on the one hand and mere recognition or characterization on the other. Stating that the dress is red does not imply a visual analysis any more than the bare statement "The boy wears pants." Both statements are mere characterizations. They will become visual experiences as soon as the changes of red according to light, shadow, and distance are observed or when the changing appearance of the "pants" while the boy is running or otherwise in motion are recognized.

**Figure 64.** Girls frequently like to draw horses; these are by an eleven-year-old girl.

Thus, observation is not the mere ability to see or recognize. It is the ability to analyze the visual image in its changing effects in space. One of the first signs of the discovery of these changing effects is the drawing of joints. Usually, at this time, children desire to include joints in their drawings of the human figure. If this is noticed by the teacher, he should include motions in which the use of the joints is important in his motivations.

In later stages this age level notices more detail. The child may even observe that clothes change with different motions. The visually minded child will start to concentrate more upon appearance. He will be eager to include "correct" proportions and motions. He will use exaggeration less frequently as a means of expression.

*Whereas the visually minded child concentrates more on the whole* and its changing effect, *the nonvisually minded child concentrates more on the details* in which he is emotionally interested. In his interpretation of expressions he still uses the method of exaggerating important parts. The visually minded child sees the human figure as a whole, while the nonvisually minded is particularly concerned with the details which are emotionally significant to him. Thus he refers more to the self and his body feeling than to the exterior qualities. His creative work belongs to the art of expressionism.

Since the best motivation is the one that is the most meaningful to the child, it is important to stimulate the child in the direction of *his* thinking and feeling. Thus, it not only would be fruitless to divert a child from his own feeling and perceiving but would be frustrating to him, for it would confront him with experiences he could not comprehend. Mere visual stimuli would just as much frustrate one group as stimuli that refer to the body self and its emotions would inhibit another group, although most children react in both ways. In a good motivation, visual effects are just as important as the emphasis on body experiences, expressions, and emotions.

## The Development of Two Different Space Concepts

We also find differences in approaches to the representation of space, depending upon whether a child has a preference for visual experiences or nonvisual experiences. A great number of children will tend toward both characteristics in their creative expressions, depending upon numerous factors, one of which is the degree to which a child is stimulated by the subject matter. However, we commonly find a preference for one type of experience or the other. Only for the purpose of clarifying these differences in experience are the two concepts discussed separately.

### THE DISCOVERY OF DEPTH BY THE VISUALLY MINDED

One of the important discoveries for the visually minded is the apparent diminution of distant objects. Closely related is the meaning of the horizon. With the recognition of distance, space in its three-dimensional qualities moves intuitively into the focal point of interest of the visually minded child. The child merely follows his growing innate demand and power of observation. With it, light and shadows in their changing effects begin to come into the mental picture of the child. All this is done without awareness. Therefore, the teacher should know that stimulation of optical changes in space is not to be given on the conscious level of perspective and "constructing" three-dimensional effects, unless the child asks for it.

The seeing of depth must be discovered by the *child*. To take this discovery from him by "explaining" perspective would deprive him of an important experience. The teacher must capitalize on the child's own findings and start on the child's own level. "What makes the tree more distant in your drawing?" Let the child become aware of his own discoveries: that he has drawn the tree smaller, because distant objects appear to be smaller to us; that he has included less detail, because we do not see as many details in distant objects; that he has given it a less intense color, because the air in between makes the color appear less bright. All this the child should find out for himself. It should be used as a frame of reference for later experiences that may be less simple. "I want the road going to the house in the background, but it looks funny" may be a remark a teacher hears. "Let's see whether the road is doing the same as the tree" would be a good starting point, using a previous experience for new discoveries. The child will soon find for himself that the road as it goes into the distance should grow smaller (that is, narrower) in his drawing as the tree does. It may also be less intensive in color. Such discoveries should always be supported by real experiences in nature. The teacher has no right to deprive the child of his own discoveries. On the contrary, he must pave the way in providing the child with the right stimulus whenever the need for it arises.

Much of the precious creative unawareness of the child has been spoiled by teachers who are too eager to see a child's taste adjusted to an adult's taste. However, it is necessary to prepare the child for the stages of critical awareness before this awareness has set in. The change from the unconscious creative approach to the stage of critical awareness has to occur gradually. The more gradually the child can move from one stage into the other, the less is the shock the child suffers from the results of the changes in his imaginative thinking. Thus, if we can *motivate the child in such a way that he comes in his unaware stages close to the concept he will finally attain,* we have succeeded in bridging the gap between the unconscious approaches of preadolescence and the approaches of critical awareness that start during adolescence. It is, therefore, a question of preserving the child's spontaneous creative power beyond the critical stages of adolescence. *If we can do this, we have not only saved one of the greatest gifts of mankind, the ability to create freely, but we have also kept one of the most important attributes necessary for proper adjustment —flexibility.*

## THE SPACE CONCEPT OF THE NONVISUALLY MINDED

It has been observed in many cases that children who have advanced beyond the base-line concept at some point return to the very same kind of space concept. This retrogression to a former concept can only be understood if we study higher art forms of nonvisual art. There we would see that the base-line concept is no longer an unconscious "childish concept." In Egyptian, Assyrian, or medieval art expression, the base line becomes the vehicle of space representations. In this light, base-line expressions represent a higher form of nonvisual consciousness, not a retrogression. Indeed, the new base-line representations are the forerunners of a more conscious nonvisual art expression. The retrogression, therefore, is only apparent. It is in reality the very same step into the nonvisual sphere as the three-dimensional tendency of space representation is in the realm of visual perception.

In general we see that the nonvisually minded children concentrate in their representations more on the expression of the self and the emotions resulting from it. For them space has significance only if it is necessary for their expression. We will be able to distinguish visually minded children from the nonvisually minded merely by the choice of representation. The visually minded child prefers environment, feels like a spectator. The nonvisually minded child concentrates more on the self and draws environment only when it has emotional significance for him.

Figures 65 and 66 show dramatic illustrations from the Bible. Moses strikes the rock that water might gush forth. Such stories should be told in such a way that environment and dramatic action are emphasized equally. Strong sentiments and feelings in the characters must be developed in the same way as mood, terrain, and atmosphere. Here also the two different reactions toward experiences can clearly be seen. In Figure 65, the painting by a nonvisually minded child, the experiences are centered in Moses alone and how in his anger he struck the rock so that water should emerge. Figure 66, on the other hand, the painting of a visually minded child, shows us a "spectacle." How grand it is to see that water flows out of the rock! In Figure 65 nothing but experience of the self is embodied. The experience of form is intensely personal and finds its strongest expression in the lineaments of Moses. In Figure 66 we feel that we are taking part in this great moment as spectators. In the former everything has been concentrated on expression and gesture; in the latter it is the arrangement of the figures, the rich colors, the motions of the

**Figure 65.** "Moses Strikes the Rock," as represented by a nonvisually minded thirteen-year-old boy. The boy feels as if he were striking the rock.

**Figure 66.** "Moses Strikes the Rock," as represented by a visually minded thirteen-year-old boy. This boy feels as if he were a spectator at the scene.

people, the water, the sky, and the environment—all that is visually perceivable—that has become the main problem of representation. We see the enormous effect the miracle had on the crowd. Some people have jars with which to fetch water, others are drinking it directly from the earth. Nowhere in this picture, however, do we perceive those intense personal sensations that hold our attention in Figure 65, in which even the water, the only object except the person of Moses, has been drawn in a compact mass as though it could be grasped rather than seen. The fact that in this picture the arm has been added later, also shows clearly the synthetic mode of procedure characteristic of nonvisual expression. This will be discussed in greater detail in the next chapter.

It should be emphasized that many children will be affected by both visual and nonvisual experiences. Although the child who is more purely visually minded will relate figure spacing to the proportion of landscape, the nonvisually minded child will establish space relations mainly through his body feelings and emotions on which the picture is centered. Many children will of course include both types of stimulation within their painting.

## The Importance of Color

The child does not develop in particular directions only but develops as a whole. However, in the interest of clarity, we discuss various trends separately. Space, color, and the self are fused in the creative development of the child and form a unity, a part of the total growth of the child. We see changing effects in color in relation to space and the representation of the human figure. Only the visually minded children show the tendency to see color in its changing effects. "This is green, red, or blue" means only that we can distinguish colors from one another. To have a percept of color means that we notice the *changes* color undergoes under different external conditions. The same color appears different in light and shadow. The surrounding colors reflect upon the focal color and make it seem different. Red in blue light looks different from red in orange light. Red in the distance looks different from red in the foreground. Red on dull days appears quite changed on bright days. Countless other factors impinge upon color to make it relative to prevailing conditions. To notice these changing effects is one of the attributes of visually minded individuals. *During this important period that precedes adolescence the visually minded child will begin to adjust colors to his visual impressions, whereas the nonvisually minded child depends greatly on his emotional reactions toward color.* Yet we must be aware that most of the children are between the extremes, and may show both characteristics.

Much has been written about the psychology of color and its emotional effects on individuals. Such emotional reactions to color are to a large extent determined associatively, through the effect of past experiences. Thus, to one individual, horror can mean red (he might associate it with blood), whereas to another it might be green (he might associate it with mold or decay). Psychology has made it evident that all rigid theories that refer emotional reactions to color are to a great extent outmoded. At least generalizations should not be applied to teaching that deny the child's right to creative approaches to color. Emotional reactions to color are highly individualized. The nonvisually minded child uses color often in contradiction to nature according to his individual emotional reaction. Color, therefore, becomes highly subjective in its meaning.[1]

Also with color, the main problem during this age period is to find means to gradually lead the child to the stages of critical awareness. If we now can motivate the child effectively to see or feel color, we will prevent him from being disappointed at his "inability" to express his mental picture. How this can effectively be done will be discussed in the section on motivation.

## The Importance of Design

With an increased awareness of form and pattern within the environment a conscious approach toward design becomes increasingly important. Whereas the visually minded child will more and more be concerned with the aesthetic function of design, expressed by the feeling for color schemes, rhythm, and balance, the nonvisually minded child will more and more show a tendency to either work directly with materials and use them functionally or concentrate more on emotional abstractions. Both groups should be given the type of motivation needed for developing properly. Burdening them with theories at this time would be out of place; the only effect would be an inhibited reaction at a time when children still proceed freely in their creative work. We shall see in the section "Art Motivation" how design and color may be closely interwoven.

The visually minded child might start to relate forms of nature to design. Many shapes, patterns, and forms in shells, wood, moss, or other objects in nature can provide the stimulation for design experiences. Since the laws of symmetry are more related to dogmatic periods of history, including periods of symbolism, it seems to be more and more out of place when individualism, emotions, and social changes dominate in our lives. Consequently, free forms or nature forms created by the child should be used for design purposes.

During this period the child should be made aware of industrial products as examples of good functional use of different materials. From the kitchen utensil and furniture to the streamlined car or machine, the child should learn how design is adapted to material. The child should be given an opportunity to use all types of scraps creatively, even if it is only for the pleasure of working out forms or shapes in different materials without relating them to a definite purpose.

If a potter's wheel is obtainable, the child will enjoy operating it. However, the child should be allowed to experiment with the wheel without being hampered by too many technical procedures. Skill and body coordinations definitely will greatly improve the child's confidence in his abilities, which is of vital importance. The creation of forms that can stand the critical evaluation of the adolescent will further help to bridge the gap between childhood and adolescence.

## Modeling—Two Different Approaches

The meaning of modeling during this preparatory stage is of special significance. Here, better than in any other field, we can build a bridge between the unconscious approach to three-dimensional expression (which we called *modeling*) and the conscious approach (which we shall call *sculpturing*). This can be done easier in clay than in painting, since the difference between modeling and sculpturing is not as great as the difference in the approaches to painting, in which, especially for the visually minded, the whole transfiguration from the plane into three-dimensional space takes place. No change of such importance can be seen in clay work. Therefore, it is much easier to prepare the child in this field to face his work with critical awareness, with confidence, and without the shock that endangers his further creative production.

Since environment is excluded or, at least, minimized in sculpturing, visually minded and nonvisually minded children face the same subject

**Figure 67.** "Cow and Calf," modeled by a thirteen-year-old girl.

matter. This also contributes greatly to make modeling a particularly effective means of stimulation (see Figure 67). The child should be lead from modeling to sculpturing in such a way that he does not become aware of this transition. This can best be done by modeling from real or imaginative poses. In real poses a person is posing throughout the session. An imaginative pose is one in which the person or the student subjectively poses only in the beginning of the art period as a means of motivation, but the actual modeling is done without the pose. The pose serves only as stimulus and control. The latter procedure, if well handled, is by far the better one. In both cases, however it is necessary to give the pose a definite meaning: "A Man Carrying a Heavy Load," "A Scrubwoman," "Tired," and so forth. The procedure of motivation will be discussed in the following section. If we did not give the pose a meaning, we would frustrate those children who have a preference for emotional interpretation.

The difference between the visually minded and subjectively minded approaches can be seen both in the working process and in the choice of subject matter. The visually minded group will concentrate on the changing shapes and forms caused by the differences of the motions of the posing figure. The nonvisually minded will use the posing figure merely as a stimulus and will model their subjective experiences of "A Man Carrying a Heavy Load," "A Scrubwoman," and so forth. In observing the working method, we see that the visually minded uses more and more the analytic method of pulling out the details from the whole. When we think of a tree, we first think of the tree in its entirety and then of the details—the structure of the bark, the branches, the kind of twigs, and the foliage. The synthetic method, that of putting parts together, will be used primarily by the nonvisually minded child. His thinking relates to the details that are of emotional significance.[2] He builds up his final impression out of a synthesis of partial impressions. It is therefore of vital significance not to divert to the analytic process a child who uses the synthetic method. We would only disturb or frustrate the child's thinking.

In the same way that we encourage the visually minded child in his modeling by directing his attention to the visual changes of form, we encourage the nonvisually minded individual by stimulating subjective experiences. This way we gradually move from the unconscious form of modeling to the conscious approach of sculpturing. Scenes such as Indian villages containing Indians do not satisfy the needs of approaching critical awareness. Modeling should shift gradually to sculpturing by eliminating all illustrative tendencies and by concentrating on the motion and expressiveness of the human figure.

## Art Motivation

Since this stage is of special significance for the development of the child, especially during the crisis of adolescence, the following generalizations will indicate the issues involved. As is the case throughout this developmental level, the most important contribution art education can make toward the adjustment of personality is to help bridge the gap between childhood and adulthood. The more gradually this can be done, the less this period will be characterized by disappointments, frustrations, or even shocks. As we have previously said, one of the characteristics of adolescence is the change of the imaginative activity from uncontrolled to controlled. He "can't draw anything" because his sudden critical awareness realizes the "inefficient" childish approach. The drawing expression seems childish and ridiculous because of the sudden awakening of an adult attitude.

*The problem is how to make this change gradual.* If we can develop the child's unaware production to such an extent that it reaches a "creative maturity," which will be able to stand the critical awareness that will set in, we have kept the child from making a sudden change and from disappointments in his changing imaginative activity. In general this can be done by making the child aware of his own achievements at a time when he is not yet aware of them. The graph indicates more clearly the effect of proper art motivation.

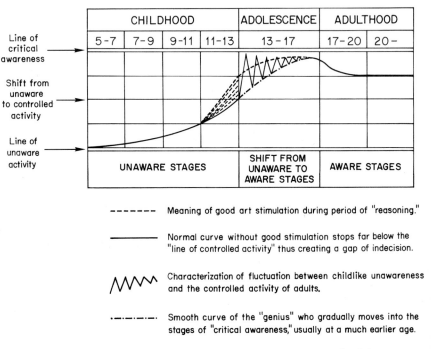

------- Meaning of good art stimulation during period of "reasoning."

———— Normal curve without good stimulation stops far below the "line of controlled activity" thus creating a gap of indecision.

∿∿∿ Characterization of fluctuation between childlike unawareness and the controlled activity of adults.

·—·—·—· Smooth curve of the "genius" who gradually moves into the stages of "critical awareness," usually at a much earlier age.

If we did not prepare the child for the oncoming crisis of adolescence, he would fluctuate greatly between unaware and controlled reactions as is indicated by the zigzag line in the graph. Such unstable behavior is typical for a crisis. The child feels torn between his childish reactions and his intellectual control. On the one hand he is ashamed to participate in childish play activities although emotionally he would love to participate in them, and on the other he cannot participate in adult activities because he is not accepted as an adult. How often do we see those "lonely" boys who whittle all by themselves or those girls who play with their dolls "secretly," because they would not officially participate in childish play activities and at the same time have not found social acceptance as adults.

The more we can raise the child's awareness during the stage of reasoning without doing undue harm to his creativity, the more do we condition the child to facing the crisis of adolescence properly. In the graph this raising of awareness is indicated by the dotted lines, which show the different degrees of rise. In the motivation this is as simple as this: "Johnny, tell me, *how* did you get this purple color?" or "Mary, tell me, what did you do to make your house look that distant?" or "Joe, how did you get this tense feeling in your figure?" It simply means making the child aware of his *own* achievements.

It is understood that such motivations must never occur during the creative process. There they would greatly interfere with the intuitive character of art. They must always occur afterward.

According to available evidence no such fluctuation occurs in the genius during adolescence. As indicated in the graph he moves smoothly from a stage of lesser maturity and perfection to one of greater. For example, the preadolescent Dürer and Mozart had the characteristics of the more mature artist. More research would be necessary to determine whether this characteristic can be used for purposes of guidance and prediction.

If in the following discussion on motivation a distinction is made between visually and nonvisually minded children, it should be borne in mind that these two groups are by no means distinctly divided. On the contrary, as has been pointed out before, and documented by research, these groups are on a continuum, frequently intermixed with a preference toward the one or other experience. It would be artificial to exaggerate a dichotomy. They are discussed separately only for clarification.

## MOTIVATION OF THE HUMAN FIGURE

For the visually minded the critical awareness during adolescence demands the drawing of correct proportions and motions with their changing effects. The nonvisually minded require greater concentration on gesture and expression. How can we stimulate these factors without doing harm to the unaware, creative approach of the child? Three approaches are particularly valuable during this period. *Proportions must never be measured.* Such a procedure would only inhibit further creative work, since rigid methods are the death of any creative work. Therefore, means of motivation should be found that make the child *experience* the correct kind of proportion. This can best be done by the choice of topics. *Topics that compare the sizes of the self to environment are best suited for such purposes.* Although it will not be useful to lead the child's attention consciously to the fact of comparing sizes, it will be important to include this factor in the discussion. As an example, we give this special emphasis to the topic "Fighting the Fire in a Burning House." After asking, "Who has seen a house burning?" we will receive many descriptions of burning houses. These many descriptions should have a proper balance of visual and nonvisual experiences. Some children will be attracted by the beauty of the flames and their glowing colors, others will "feel" with the people who were living in the house and will become emotionally involved in the fate of those who lost their belongings. Still other children will be more concerned with the technical procedures of fighting the flames. Especially the boys may become interested in this element. But at all times we have opportunities to direct attention to comparative proportions with questions. "How high did we have to climb to fight the fire?" "Did people jump out of the window?" "From what height did they jump?" "How long was the firemen's hose?" "How far up could the hoses reach without climbing the ladder?" Such questions will inspire both groups: the visually minded because they become visually aware of the comparative proportions, and the nonvisually because they refer in their drawings to the body actions and its emotional qualities. Many other topics like "Sitting Under a Tree," "Reaching for an Apple on a Tree," "Sitting in a Rowboat," "Looking Out the Window" and so forth, will stimulate the child to compare sizes. However, any "correction" of proportions by the teacher would only frustrate the child. If the child does not react to the mentioned stimuli, it is only a sign that the child is not affected by them. An imposition would not help him in his experience. However, his awareness may develop slowly.

The second approach suitable to prepare the child for the coming critical awareness of sizes and proportions is the use of posing models as a means of motivation. Here, too, we must give both groups a possibility for self-expression. That is why the posing model should be given a meaning, as has been said before. As an example, we cite a particular pose, "Feeling Tired from Work." "Have you ever worked very hard? Have you ever watched people who do heavy physical work? When? Have you yourself ever really been physically exhausted? What had you been doing? How did you feel?" (Let the boy or girl pose, assuming a tired-out attitude.) "I notice you are not standing straight and tall! Why? How do your hands, back, and feet feel? Why do you have your head and shoulders bent?"

All these questions will bring the pose into a higher consciousness. For both groups it will be of benefit if the posing model does not keep the pose. The visually minded will have to concentrate much more on their visual experience to retain the image, and the nonvisually minded will use the posing model only as a stimulus, concentrating entirely on expression, that is, on the mental picture he has formed, which is a result of his body feelings and emotional experiences.

The third approach for getting the representation of the human figure more closely related to that of the adolescent stages deals with a method of modeling. It is most stimulating to first characterize the personality of the clay figure and then let it go through the motion as if it were a motion picture. For example: "A visitor (your grandpa) comes to see you. He sits down and tells you a story." First grandpa would be modeled as he arrives and would finally be put into the actual position of telling a story. "How does your grandpa sit when he tells you a story? Does he hold a book in his hand? Does he support his head? Does he stretch out his legs or does he cross them?" The plasticity of clay permits the expression of this kinesthetic experience. While going through the motions, the child will grow more consciously aware of them, and in turn will bring himself closer to a more critical level of creative production.

## MOTIVATION OF SPACE

The motivation of spatial experiences again will have to be channeled in two directions: first, to prepare the visually minded child for a space concept that is more closely related to the adolescent concept of realizing the visual space; second, to prepare the nonvisually minded child for the importance of the emotional tie-up of space and the self. We know too well the frightening effect that the teaching of perspective has on some of our children. This effect is especially frightening for children who have no desire for such a space concept. This group, which is the nonvisually minded, has no comprehension of this way of perceiving space. Therefore, *there is no need for including perspective in our art program as long as there is no demand for it from the children.*

For the visually minded, means of introducing a visual space concept should be found that exclude the dry teaching of technical data of perspective. To do that, it is inspiring to refer to nonvisual means, to become aware of the different intensities of emotional experiences that are both far away and close to us. "What would happen if one among us were suddenly to die?" All children would immediately understand the tremendous intensity of this experience when it is closely related to us. At the same time the deaths of thousands of people on battlefields, in factories, and other places do not affect us much. The intensity of this experience grows and diminishes with the distance. Visual space, too, increases and diminishes in size and intensity, depending on the distance. However, in visual space this intensity depends only on the visual interest we take in objects close to us, whereas in emotional experiences we can focus our greatest interest even on things not close to us. Thus, the intensity of nonvisual space is governed by the emotions we associate with the experience.

Most important, however, is that a good teacher must always start on the level of the individual and extend his frame of reference from there on. If for a child the expression of distant space (that is, perspective) has become important (see Figure 68), the teacher must support the child's desire by using the child's present understanding. It would, however, be entirely wrong to impose such knowledge on a child who has no desire for it.

### MOTIVATION OF COLOR

Naturalistic color—the color of the visually minded—can only be stimulated by actual experiences with nature. The different intensities—brightness and dullness and the character of colors in distance, shadows, and lights—can be brought into the consciousness only by observing them. Few children, and by no means all adults, can do that. We ourselves realize how little we see in comparison with some artists' concept of color. And some of us know that we are unable to see the "blue shadow" we are supposed to see according to the old method of teaching. Not all of us can see the changing effects of colors, and there is no need for all of us to see them. What is a stimulation for one can be a frustration for another. There exist too many instances of frustrated children and unhappy adults, compelled to enroll in art classes in which they received visual stimuli only and in which they were forced to "see color."

*Personification of color* is a method that can be used for both groups, though it will appeal more to the nonvisually minded children. By *personification of color* is meant the seeing and dealing with color as if it were a living being. For example, the telling of some such story as the following would be effective.

"Imagine you feel very happy and want to go on a hike. Everything around you is marvelous, just wonderful. Environment is beautiful, bright,

**Figure 68.** "Thinking," drawn by a thirteen-year-old boy. A need for visual perspective is beginning to be felt by this boy, who here achieves a representation of depth.

and the atmosphere is happy. As you walk you see in the distance your friend, your most beloved friend. You thought how marvelous it would be to have him with you. And there he comes. Now you are talking about personal things, and you become so friendly that you feel very close to him. As you continue on your way, the atmosphere suddenly changes for the worse. It gets dark, dreary, and mysterious. As you go on, someone stops you on the way and tells you that you are not permitted to continue; this road is not for you.

"Now imagine that you are 'red' in this story. How does red feel in a marvelous environment, happy and bright? What color would you choose as an environment for red to make it happy? What color is the best friend of red, whom red expected to meet? When red and his friend were talking so intimately, to which color would they unite? As they went on and the atmosphere darkened and the environment became mysterious, how would red change? How would its friend change? How would environment change? What color would come in their way and prohibit them from continuing?"

Of course there are hundreds of such stories. Almost any story can be translated into "color." This personification introduces color as a living symbol. Verbal theory cannot give as good an introduction into the living qualities of color as such personifications. Such an introduction will also lead into an understanding of the nature of emotional abstract design. It is better than music as a means of stimulation, since we refer to real living qualities. Such an interpretation of color will be highly individualized.

Through such methods the child will gain more confidence in his use of color and will approach it more consciously, which is vitally necessary for the proper adjustment to the coming stage, the crisis of adolescence.

## MOTIVATION FOR SELF-EXPRESSION

Between the ages of eleven and thirteen we find many new problems arising for youngsters, and many changes are occuring both in themselves and in their relationships to their peers and adults. For example, by the time a girl is thirteen, she may actually be taller than her mother. Both boys and girls are beginning to break numerous childhood ties to the family and begin to question adults' authority. There is, of course, great concern about personal appearance, and the gradual awakening to the simple fact that they too will soon be adults. There is a great deal of idealism, and romantic feeling about the freedom of becoming an adult member of society, but also some fear and insecurity about the beginning stages of leaving childhood. They may even invent their own society in which they reign supreme, free from adult domination. The imaginary country "Connia," seen in Figure 69, was obviously drawn by a girl named Connie who wore glasses. All these reasons call for a strong art program that will give ample opportunity for self-expression.

**Figure 69.** "Connia," drawn by a twelve-year-old girl. The picture shows a strong desire for belonging. The artist projected her own image onto the total group.

Girls are no longer making wars on boys but seem to be too much concerned with their development to be bothered. A handsome film star may be a safe idol for a girl of this age; however, she often is more interested in admiring the female stars. Boys are somewhat aware of the fact that girls are not always trash but are far from being ready to admit this. Instead boys collect baseball statistics, try to develop their muscular powers, and seek out boys who have comparable interests in such things as motorcycles, BB guns, radios, or even chess.

In the preceding sections on motivation of the human figure, of space, and of color, the youngster would certainly express feelings about himself, especially if he could identify with the model or could project his own feelings into a color. The stronger the motivation, the more involved a child will become. It is not diplomatic to say, "Put your innermost feelings down on paper about some adult whom you feel has treated you unjustly." Since many children have been taught that it is not nice to have unpleasant thoughts about people, and since in some cases these feelings may very well be directed at parents, it is usually best to let

**Figure 70.** "The Hairy One," drawn by a twelve-year-old girl. By giving vent to her imagination, she had the opportunity to release feelings of aggression.

feelings of aggression, and in some cases love, be expressed unconsciously. A subject such as "The Ugliest Person in the World" would provide the opportunity for release of such feelings. "What would the ugliest person in the world look like? Would he have smooth or rough skin? Would he have a long or short nose? How about his ears? Would his teeth stick out? And his hair? What color would go well with him? Could the ugliest person be a woman?" (See Figure 70.)

Both boys and girls at this age can develop an interest in particular individualistic subject matter. Boys may like to spend a considerable length of time drawing guns or airplanes, whereas girls may spend a comparable time drawing horses or fanciful figures. Whatever the particular interest of these youngsters, this interest can be capitalized upon in the art program by expanding the frame of reference. A project—making many different types of airplanes, jets, transport planes, helicopters, and fitting all of these into a larger background of airstrips, tankers, and people—can provide an excellent art experience. Other individual interests can be utilized in comparable fashion.

Any art motivation should stress the individual's own contribution. At this stage of development it is important to reinforce individualistic thinking. An art program that is primarily concerned with productions may miss entirely one of the basic reasons for the existence of art in a school program, that is, the personal involvement of an individual and the opportunity for a depth of self-expression (see Figure 71).

## Subject Matter

Any particular group of eleven to thirteen year olds will find some exciting subject matter material from within their own environment and experience. Care should be taken, however, to insure that any topic gives support to the child's individual expression, provides for a release of tensions, and helps bridge the gap between the childhood unaware approach to art and the adolescent critical awareness. Occasionally topics are pushed upon the person responsible for an art program, topics that may actually be detrimental to the fostering of a meaningful art education program. Such topics as a poster for some local organization, the mass production of table decorations for the annual teachers' meeting, or the making of a monogram for the gym team may all be worthwhile activities, and if the teacher feels that he has time to do these himself, we will not complain. However, the art program has a much greater role than to fill its time with busy-work.

The following list of topics should serve only as examples for the different kinds of motivations and should be used flexibly.

## ACTION FROM IMAGINATION

"Farmer Rushing Home Before the Storm"

"Rowing a Boat on the Lake"

"Fishing in the Stream Near Home"

"Hunting in the Woods in the Fall"

"Working on the Gymnastic Equipment"

"Highway-Department Men Working on the Street"

"Telephone Men Digging a New Post Hole"

## ACTION FROM POSING MODEL

"Poor Woman Scrubbing a Floor"

"Feeling Tired from Work"

"Lifting a Heavy Load"

"Waiting at the Corner for the Bus"

"Worrying About My Homework at My Desk"

"Being Lost in the City"

## PROPORTIONS

"A Ladder Being Put Against a Burning House"

"Having My Hair Cut"

"Reaching for an Apple on a Tree"

"Looking Out the Window"

"Practicing on My Musical Instrument"

"Washing the Family Car"

## COLOR

"The Storm Gathers Above the Field"

"Cold and Snow in Winter"

"It's Dark and Windy Outside"

"A Happy Feeling Inside Me"

"Personification of Color"

Figure 71. Depth of personal experience is of prime importance in art activity. The meaningfulness of an art program can only be measured in terms of the individual.

MURALS

"Lunch in the School Cafeteria" (from preparing food to eating)

"Our Newspapers" (from reporting to printing)

"Landing on the Moon" (from blast-off to landing)

**Figure 72.** A twig transformed by a covering of frost dramatically illustrates the pleasing forms and textures that surround us in nature.

DESIGN

Finding pleasing forms (in puddles, clouds, leaves, stones, shadows, twigs, wood grain, moss). (See Figure 72.)

Collages (range of textures and colors for both abstract design and symbolic design)

Abstract designs made from different materials to learn their function (wire, sheet metal, glass, wood, cardboard)

Knowledge of industrial designs (utensils, furniture, flatware)

Printing and repeat designs from natural forms on material

CLAY MODELING

From posing model (topics as discussed)

Actions from imagination

Kinetic motions: "Picking up My Room," "Mother Holding the Baby," "Getting Tired," "Sitting Down, Reading a Book"

SELF-EXPRESSION

"The Ugliest Person in the World"

"A Fierce Villain"

"All Alone on a Dark, Cold Night"

"A Good-Looking Movie Star"

"What I Want Most to Do"

## Art Materials

Technique is closely related to the need for expression. The material that does not help the child to express his particular desires is not a good one. During this period the visually minded child becomes more aware of the visual characteristics of his environment. The most suitable material will be one that easily permits the portrayal of effects in nature. Since atmosphere and sky in nature are not opaque but have a transparent character, a medium having such transparent qualities would be most suitable. This medium is water color. At this stage we can even encourage the child to make visual use of the happy accidents that occur when the colors in a sky run together and form clouds of different shapes. At first the whole paper may be moistened with brush or hands before the child starts to paint. Since some children now approach paintings visually, such accidents as the formation of clouds or the mixing of colors will stimulate the child for his next work. Running of colors, which could have been most discouraging at a time when linear representation dominated the preschematic or schematic stage, is now most stimulating.

Referring to the quotation of Leonardo da Vinci to the effect that an art work should look complete in every stage will help in stimulating the visually minded child in building up a visual concept. The sequence in which a picture is painted can be of decided influence. For example, we are thinking of a painting in which farmers rush home before the rising storm. If we were to ask the child to stop painting after he has finished the stormy sky (which covers the *whole* sheet, of course), the sky as such could exist and could be called complete. If the child then added the field and we interrupted him, the picture again would look complete. The child might then add a barn or a tree and finally would paint the farmers in the foreground as they hurriedly leave the field. The picture has grown organically and looked complete at every stage. Besides that, we have the feeling that the sky is really behind the tree or the house without appearing to cut out the part of the sky covered by it. This *organic* growth of the picture is an important part of a method of approach that will help to bridge the gap to which we have referred during this period so frequently. In order to paint on the sky, the child must wait until it is dry; otherwise, the foreground would blur with the background. It is also of advantage to use opaque colors, such as tempera paint, for the foreground. This creates a still stronger feeling for the transparency of the atmosphere and the opaque quality of objects (see Plate 8).

For mural painting it is suggested that either egg tempera or ordinary poster paint be used. If possible, murals should be painted directly on the wall surface, but if this is not possible, good craft paper tacked on the wall or stretched on stretchers while it is moist (when it dries, it tightens) will serve very well. For painting directly on the wall, one or two coats of flat paint will serve as sizing. Bristle brushes for large spaces and hair brushes for details are advisable. Preferably, murals should not be carefully planned at this age level because careful planning destroys much of the intuitive quality and reduces interest. A small sketch, which tells approximately what will be on the mural, will be sufficient. Children should have all possible freedom in painting and organizing murals. Often it is good practice to permit a group of children to work on one mural. It must be remembered that *a mural is a decoration of a wall and that it should tell a story or have a message.* Sizes can differ according to importance. No further explanations need be given about the nature of a mural, but the teacher should have in mind that a purely naturalistic execution is contrary to the essence of decoration.

The use of clay gradually shifts from modeling to sculpturing and pottery. Also here, especially with pottery, no preplanning should be done. Starting with a preconceived notion of the finished product when working on a potter's wheel is nearly impossible for the beginning student, for much depends upon the consistency of the clay, the speed of the wheel, and the positioning of the hands and body.

Many of the art materials that have been discussed in earlier stages are also appropriate at this level. However, it is important to make sure that any materials used are also used by professional artists. That is, the child should be able to identify his work with those people who consider art a vocation rather than think of art in terms of children only. Exploring the qualities of charcoal and India ink with brush can stimulate an interest in the potential use of these materials. Exploring other possibilities, such as making papier-mâché moon-men, paper bag puppets (see Figure 73), or plaster and wire space sculptures can get the most reluctant youngster readily involved in art materials. When the child "is encouraged to invent or imagine unusual forms, such as strange machines, environments, and animals" his imagination can definitely be boosted.[4] Such projects as making color wheels or doing lettering exercises had best be left for a time when these exercises become more meaningful. However, the occasional use of finger paint or chalk on a blackboard can sometimes rekindle a fresh spontaneous approach to art.

We have found that at this level materials begin to play a more important part in the art program, but it should be emphasized that their main function is to provide for an increased knowledge, understanding, and expression in the arts and not to be an end in themselves.

## A Discussion of the Meaning of the Pseudo-Naturalistic Stage

We have seen that the child has gradually become more aware of his creative product. The young child creates in a straightforward fashion, projecting his personality into his work without inhibitions. The adult usually wants to conform to certain standards of beauty or perfection. These standards do not exist for the young child. The more this child

becomes aware of external standards, the less his work will directly reveal his personality.

This stage of development is one of very rapid changes. Girls discover the feminine role, trying desperately hard to be pretty and alluring. Boys' voices begin to change and most of them try hard to become very masculine. At the time that he is trying to make an impression upon his fellow students, the preadolescent not only wants to be liked by his peers, but also wants and needs the respect and attention of adults.

The development of a critical attitude has made him aware of the world that surrounds him. This growing naturalism is reflected in the drawings of objects and figures by children of this age. Usually the schema that we have seen in earlier stages has now disappeared. The continued use of a schema at this age would tend to indicate that the child has not become intellectually aware of the variety of details and individual differences within his environment. If there is a discrepancy between what might be expected for this age level and what is actually produced, the teacher will have to take positive steps to find a more forceful means of motivation. This primarily means involving the child more directly in the activities that are part of the art program. Retarded children may need a great deal more stimulation than normal children. However, certain past experiences in the art area may even have a negative influence upon the child's attitude toward art, and this may be, in part, responsible for a lack of sensitive awareness.

At this age children have not yet developed full control over their emotions, and often we find that a seemingly minor incident will be of extreme importance to a youngster. This intensity of emotion can often be utilized within the art program. The emotional relationships a child may develop with various segments of his environment can often be expressed either directly or symbolically. Topics centering around religious themes, individual justice, or the expression of love or hate can often involve a youngster quite completely. In such cases exaggeration or overemphasis of particular parts within a composition can be noted. Color in such cases can also be used symbolically, as in painting a face green. Such distortion should be looked upon as acceptable, and support should be given to the free use of exaggeration and distortion for emotional effect.

As we have already emphasized, this stage is characterized by, among other things, a tendency toward two different types of creation. These tendencies show themselves best in the preference for certain perceptual experiences. The extreme visual and nonvisual are relatively rare and most

gure 73. These hand puppets are made from paper bags and scrap aterials. Puppets may be used for acting out dramatic situations.

often both tendencies are expressed. The observation of wrinkles and folds when clothes are in motion is usually an indication of visual awareness. The mere characterization of a figure by means of its clothing usually does not include wrinkles and folds. The representation of light and shadow is an advanced awareness of the visual environment. Differences in color value in light and shade also can be occasionally noted. When a child has become aware of his visual environment, it can usually be seen first in the indication that distant objects diminish in size. In younger children the representation of space goes through very definite stages. Here, when we consider only the visually minded child, the representation of space begins to include not only an awareness of changes in size but also a feeling for the three-dimensional quality of objects. For some children who may have been taught the rules of mechanical perspective before they were psychologically ready for such teaching the drawing of space may be extremely rigid, and the expression of the child may be hampered because of the adherence to certain rules that are not thoroughly understood. We would find this to be especially true of the child who has nonvisual leanings. In any case painting is no longer looked upon as the reproduction of three-dimensional distance, and such instruction at this age should be limited to those students who voice a need for a further understanding of perspective.

An awareness and expression of texture and tactile sensations can often be observed in drawings and paintings. The expression of textural differences is often because of an increased awareness of such differences, developed by a first-hand working with such materials in collages or by working with three-dimensional materials. Needless to say, such sensitivity to textures cannot be achieved through "correcting" the product itself, but only through meaningful experiences in which the tactile sensations are stressed. The student who is inclined toward visual expression will be more concerned with form and color than with the expression of tactile sensations. We find the nonvisually minded is more inclined to use color in a flat pattern than to be concerned with changes in value. In the painting "My Barber" in Plate 9 we can see color used in this way.

It is usually during this stage of development that joints appear in the drawing of a human figure. We also find an increased awareness and exaggeration of sexual characteristics, especially in the drawings of the human figure by girls, for these sexual changes can no longer be experienced in a passive way. There is no reason to look upon these exaggerations as anything but normal. In fact, the very opposite may be true; that is, a child who is beginning to develop sexually and who does not include these changes within drawings may be showing a fear of expressing these changes. Drawings should not be censored; throughout history, art has been one area where intense concern and feelings could be portrayed. In this connection we find that greater detail is attached to the representation of clothing for both sexes.

The area of aesthetic growth has gradually become much more important. In earlier stages of development the child was not aware of the beauty of his products; now children are developing a greater sensitivity toward the aesthetic qualities. Making a meaningful whole out of a chaos of parts is one of the most important criteria of a work of art. Both the design and the content play a part in the meaningful distribution of the single parts comprising the creative work. If we turn a picture 180° and forget its content by looking at it as if it were an abstraction, we receive an impression of the abstract design qualities within it. It should be emphasized that this is not the time to teach the formal elements of design, but rather children can be made aware of the beauty in what they do. Obviously a drawing of loneliness will be quite different in design quality from a drawing portraying excitement.

The quality of the material used for expression should be closely related to the subject matter. It would be difficult to express the feeling of a rainy day, or for that matter even joy or excitement, with clay. The subject matter expressed and the materials used to portray this expression should have unity. This becomes a great deal more apparent if we look at the function and design of an object as simple as a spoon. Such questions as "Why isn't a spoon made out of cloth, or paper, or glass?" can begin to stimulate thinking about the relationship between material and expression. "Would the addition of holes in the handle of the spoon, or bumpy roses embossed upon the spoon bowl, help or hinder its function?" The development of aesthetic growth should not be minimized, and an increased awareness of tangible examples of both good and bad design should be explored. This is not the time for listing or memorizing rules to follow; rather it should be an opportunity for developing sensitivity to honesty and truth in art.

We have constantly emphasized that creative growth is one of the vital components of any art program. This is especially true between the ages of eleven and thirteen. Here the child is becoming much more critical of his own work, and the pressure to conform to the adult standards of behavior or to the standards of the "crowd" work to stifle the creative urge. An emotionally free and flexible child should have an experimental attitude. His approach toward his own mode of expression should never become rigid. The teacher should be sure that individuality in expression, exploration in untried directions, and the opportunity to delve deeply into one area of interest are supported and actively encouraged. It is important to stress that every product in which a child becomes truly involved should be accepted without any outside evaluation. That is, the child who produces pleasing looking products and the child who is not doing the type of work that suits the teacher's aesthetic taste should be treated with equal respect. However, in no way does this mean that a laissez-faire attitude should prevail. The very opposite is true! The halfhearted attempt, the stereotype, the presence of copying, should all be clear indications to the teacher that the program is not a meaningful one. To stimulate a child's thinking, to have him come to grips with a problem that is meaningful, to encourage a depth of expression, are all much more important than making "pretty" end products. We have discussed earlier the need for an environment that fosters divergent thinking. At this point the teacher should consider the development of creativity as one of the most vital areas of the art program.

In summarizing this section on growth characteristics of preadolescents as seen in their art, we have discussed several aspects of growth that are exhibited in the art of these preadolescents, and also we have found that the art program has a very real part to play in the total developmental process. *We can see quite clearly that art is not merely a subject matter area but is the expression of the total being.* As children grow into adults, an art program should constantly change to meet their needs.

This particular stage of development assumes greater importance when we realize that many youngsters have no further art experiences in the public schools after this time. It seems very strange indeed that at the onset of adolescence a program designed to provide an opportunity for the expression of feelings, emotions, and sensitivities should unfortunately be dropped for the majority of our secondary school population. To a great extent, then, the responsibility for a continued interest in the arts and the opportunity for active participation in art experiences rests with the attitude that children of this age develop from their art program in school. It is of vital importance that teachers of this age group show a high degree of involvement and enthusiasm in these art experiences themselves.

RELATED ACTIVITIES

1. Compare a twelve-year-old girl's representation of females over several months. Are there any changes in drawings, reflecting maturation? Compare these drawings with representations by girls a year younger.
2. Collect the drawings of a sixth grade. What proportion of the class are observing visually by drawing distant objects smaller? What proportion apparently are showing a nonvisual type of space representation?
3. Observe the working process while children are using clay. Which children give a subjective interpretation of the topic rather than a visual? Are these the same ones who model synthetically?
4. Record examples of behavior that show the change from an unconscious approach to that of a critical awareness of the child's own actions. Are there any indications of the child's becoming critically aware of his own drawings?
5. Have children of this age become aware of joints in the drawing of figures? Are differences in size and age characterized? Collect examples of such drawings. Are there differences in the ages when these changes occur?
6. Observe a class for several sessions. Can you pick out some children who seem to be less involved in art activities? Does their work show this lack of involvement? How? Analyze some of the possible reasons for the hesitancy or fear of expression. Plan definite steps to take to improve the meaningfulness of the art experience.

NOTES

1. Ambrose Corcoran, "The Variability of Children's Responses to Color Stimuli" (Unpublished doctoral dissertation, The Pennsylvania State University, 1953).
2. Alexander Zawacki, "An Experimental Study of Analytic Versus Synthetic Modelings and Drawings of Children" (Unpublished doctoral dissertation, The Pennsylvania State University, 1956).
3. Viktor Lowenfeld, "Tests for Visual and Haptical Aptitude," *American Journal of Psychology*, **LVIII**, No. 1 (1945), pp. 100–111.
4. Clarence Kincaid, "The Determination and Description of Various Creative Attributes of Children," *Studies in Art Education*, **II**, No. 2 (Spring 1961), p. 52.

# 9

# The Period of Decision:
## The Crisis of Adolescence
## Seen in Creative Activity

CRISIS means passing from one stage to another under great difficulty. This is true physically, emotionally, or mentally. When undergoing an operation, the time the body needs to adapt itself to the new status created by the operation is a crisis. Since adolescence is considered a stage in the development of human beings, this crisis is connected with the difficulties of passing from one developmental stage to another, from the period of childhood to that of maturity.[1]

Because the crisis of adolescence is connected with bodily, as well as with emotional changes, we deal here with a complex crisis in which body, emotions, and mind have to adjust to a new situation. Indeed, we can say that this is an *important period of decision* in human development. That it is a period of decisive changes can be seen in the different behavior reactions and attitudes of people before and after adolescence. How often we witness sudden changes from happy, open-minded children to shy and serious-looking youths. Much of this change is due to the degree of difficulty under which the individual has passed the crisis of adolescence. The less the child is affected by the changes of body and mind, the easier he can adjust to the new situation. The greater the difficulties were, the less the child was prepared to face the crisis properly. The question is: How can art education help to ease the crisis of adolescence? This can best be studied if we investigate the psychological changes that directly relate to the changes of the creative concept.

## The Psychological Change in the Imaginative Concept

For the purpose of investigating this change in imaginative concepts in the preadolescent and adolescent, the topic "Playing Tag on the School Ground" was given to a number of (1) elementary school children of the first three grades, (2) boys and girls of the upper elementary school, and (3) secondary school students, with approximately three hundred in each group. Children and students were under no compulsion to draw the topic, but did so only if they wished. Individuals without prior special training in art were selected for this study. Of interest are the different ways of expressing the experience of catching and being caught, on the one hand, and the spatial representation of the school ground on the other. But it is also important to note that 95 per cent of the younger elementary school children made some attempt to represent this experience, whereas only 35 per cent of the secondary school students tried to depict this well-known game. Both facts—the different kinds of interpretation and the small percentage of the secondary school students who attempted to draw the given topic gives us insight into the nature of this part of the crisis of adolescence.

In looking at the *children's* drawings, two striking features are apparent: (1) we see no attempt at naturalistic representations, either in the representations of the human figures or in the representations of the school ground; (2) the lower the age of the group, the less the attempt is made to indicate environment.

Let us select one drawing from the children's group and describe it in greater detail, stressing some of the attributes more or less characteristic of all the representations of this age group. The child, a boy six years and six months of age, introduced a representative symbol for boy, an oval

**Figure 74.** "Playing Tag on the School Ground," painted by a six-and-a-half-year-old boy. Notice the exaggeration of the arm that is doing the catching and the omitted arms of the captive. Environment is expressed only by a base line.

for body, and a circle for head. Arms and legs are expressed differently in the representation of the catching boy and the captive. Whereas the arms of the captive are omitted entirely, those of the captor are very much overemphasized, indicating the importance of the subjective experience of reaching out to catch. This finds its strongest expression in the exaggerated symbol of the grasping hands (see Figure 74). We also see a difference in the length of the legs in both figures. Looking at the other drawings of this age group, we frequently see the same difference in the representation of this part of the body—shorter legs for the captive and longer legs for the captor. We can conclude that shorter legs indicate slower running, whereas longer legs mean faster running. This confirms what we have discussed in the chapter dealing with preschematic and schematic stages. The school ground is indicated by a base line only, which shows that the subjective feeling of being a part of environment is the only spatial experience the child has.

The child's creative expression is mainly connected with such subjective experiences as bodily feelings, muscle sensations, and touch impressions. It is obvious that the child's way of perceiving space is determined by his subjective relationship to it, since the child's perception is derived from bodily, not from visual, experiences. The proportions in the child's representations are proportions of value, not the result of aesthetic evaluations. That is why it can be assumed that *the child's world of imagination is mainly bound up with the self,* with subjective feelings, and subjective relationships toward surroundings.

Let us look at another drawing that will lead us a step farther toward the period of adolescence. It is the drawing by a nine-year-old girl and is another characteristic example chosen from the three hundred of its kind. This drawing (see Figure 75) compared with the other, most obviously shows a greater relationship to nature. The girls wear dresses. There even is an attempt to portray the flying hair of the running girls. Although unimportant details can be seen, there still is a clear overemphasis

**Figure 75.** "Playing Tag on the School Ground," painted by a nine-year-old girl. Here we see slight exaggeration of important parts. Environment is expressed by two base lines on which the children and school are placed.

of the arm of the catching girl, thereby expressing the importance of this part. There is distinctly a greater emphasis on environmental objects. The school ground is indicated by trees and by a fence which surrounds the field, placed on the base line of the upper section. The lower section with the girls, as the focus of the experience, is placed on a base line close to the bottom of the page. Considering the motion of the figures, we see a great stiffness, even a lack of correlation between them. This is typical for the representations of this age group (see Chapter 7, on the Gang Age). On the other hand, a greater emphasis on single details, such as the flying hair, shows the interest in things of importance. The nicely designed dresses of the girls are both in front view. If the somewhat exaggerated arm were not drawn, the topic would scarcely be recognizable.

From this representation we can assume that a definite *tendency exists to replace mere symbols* (oval for body) *by a representation that is more related to nature.* But as we have seen in our general discussion of this stage, this approach toward a naturalistic representation is due to a greater consciousness of the self deriving from the thought "I am wearing a dress" and is not a result of a visual image. The proportion of value seen in the size of the girls who, compared with the trees, are drawn according to the degree of importance, still shows a strong subjective attitude toward the representation. Another fact seems important: the percentage of children who did not want to depict the topic has slightly increased, which shows decreasing confidence in self-expression. The lack of spatial correlation is a result of an egocentric attitude, which, as we have seen, is typical for this age level.

When we turn our attention to the drawings of the secondary school students, we see first of all that only a very limited number of students voluntarily depicted this topic (35 per cent). Those who did, tried to represent it as naturalistically as possible: some by the real movement of running with "well-proportioned" figures, including a part of the campus; others with the emphasis on the figures only, stressing the muscles and the function of the body (see Figure 76).

From this experiment it becomes clear that the closer the child approaches adolescence, the more he loses the strong subjective relationship to the world of symbols. The growing consciousness of his own body introduces a more critical awareness of the self. In some cases the higher consciousness of the self leads to a more detailed and determined expression of the body, whereas in other cases this growing critical attitude stimulates very strongly visual observation. *A conscious critical awareness*

**Figure 76.** "Playing Tag on the School Ground," drawn by an adolescent. This picture is an attempt at naturalistic representation. Space is portrayed through the use of visual perspective.

*now dominates all the creative production of the adolescent individual.*

There is, however, an intermediate stage, in which the individual has already lost the connection with his childish way of symbolic representation and has not yet found confidence in his own conscious approach. Through the strong desire of establishing a conscious approach, the child temporarily loses the subjective attitude toward his own creations. Consequently, the drawings show this feeling of insecurity. This period in which the youth has neither an unconscious childish nor a conscious approach of self-expression is marked by a very profound crisis, which sometimes shakes the whole self-confidence. This is the reason why so many individuals stop their creative work at this period. In the study of adolescence this particular phase of the crisis hardly has been recognized.

One of the most important tasks of art education during this vital period is to introduce means and methods of stimulations that will prevent the child from losing self-confidence. How this can be done is the main thesis of this chapter.

# The Development of Two Creative Types

We can now clearly distinguish two types of art expression both by the end product and by the attitude toward experience. When we investigate the artistic products of these two types in their pure forms we find that the visual type starts from his environment, that he feels as spectator, and that his intermediaries for experience are mainly the eyes. The other, which we shall call the haptic type, is primarily concerned with his own body sensations and the subjective experiences in which he feels emotionally involved.[2] The existence of these two distinct creative types, based upon two different reactions toward the world of experiences, is reported in *The Nature of Creative Activity*. In the course of this study it was found that imaginative activity, including the ability to give objective reference to creations of the imagination, by no means depends upon the capacity for perceptive observation. Furthermore, it was shown that the inability inspectively to notice visual objects is not always an inhibitory factor in creative activities. On the contrary, the very fact of not paying attention to visual impressions may become the basis of a specific creativeness of the haptic type. This is of greatest importance for art educators, especially for those who still are concerned with visual stimulations only.

A visually minded individual would be disturbed and inhibited if he were to be stimulated only by means of haptic impressions, that is, if he were asked not to use sight but to orient himself only by means of touch, bodily feelings, muscular sensations, and kinesthetic fusions. This much is clear, but what is not as obvious is that "seeing" may also become an inhibitory factor when forced upon an individual who does not use his visual experiences for creative work. Both facts are established by numerous experiments reported in the work referred to above.

An extreme haptic type of individual is normal-sighted and uses his eyes only when compelled to do so; otherwise he reacts as would a blind person who is entirely dependent upon touch and kinesthesis. An extreme visually minded person, on the other hand, is entirely lost in the dark and depends completely on his visual experiences of the outside world. This distinction is true for creative types as well as for individuals in general, as has been reported elsewhere.[3] W. Grey Walter in an encephalographical study (dealing with alpha rhythms, or recorded electrical waves from the brain) reveals that "individuals with persistent alpha rhythms which are hard to block with mental effort, tend to auditory, kinesthetic or tactile perceptions rather than visual imagery. In this group of persons the alpha rhythms continue even when the eyes are open and the mind is active and alert." He administered a test to 600 individuals, which enabled him to distinguish between a visualizer (the M type) with few if any alpha rhythms, a non-visualist (the P type) with persistent alpha activity, and a mixed type (the R type) with a responsive alpha rhythm. He raises the question "Why are the alpha rhythms so persistent when they appear in childhood?" He warns, however, that "we must be cautious about jumping to any such conclusion as that children only learn later to think in visual terms, although this is suggested by the extreme rarity of M type children." He continues, ". . . evidence already available, both statistical and experimental, strongly suggests that the alpha rhythm characters are inborn and probably hereditary."[4]

The result of another investigation in which 1,128 subjects were tested by means of specifically designed tests for visual or haptic aptitude was as follows: 47 per cent were clearly visual, 23 per cent were haptic, and 30 per cent either received a score below the line where a clear identification was possible or were otherwise not identifiable.[5] In other words, approximately half of the individuals tested reacted visually, whereas not quite a fourth reacted haptically. These figures are in close agreement with those in the study by W. Grey Walter.

*Most people tend to fall between these two extreme types.* Investigations have shown, however, that only a few individuals have equal amounts of visual and haptic predisposition. Seventy-five per cent have an appreciable tendency toward one or the other. Since the tendency toward these two antipodes of experience is important not only for the proper stimulation in creative activity but also to life in general (especially in the proper choice of occupation), we shall discuss this aspect of the problem in a separate section.

*Thus, apparently one among four individuals depends more upon his subjective reactions, such as touch and kinesthesis, than upon vision.* In a study by Drewes, using a variety of testing devices, Rorschach responses for what he called visualizers tended to be whole and three-dimensional forms, while the nonvisualizers in his population reproduced more kinesthetic movements and shading responses. Although these two extreme groups responded in significantly different ways on parts of an intelligence test, no differences were found in total intelligence scores.[6] Aside from its far-reaching significance in other fields, for art teaching this fact means that one fourth of the population cannot benefit from visual stimuli. They either are not reached or may become frustrated by this type of stimulation.

Each type should therefore be stimulated in the direction of his experiences and thinking. To do this, we should become acquainted with the nature of these two creative types, particularly because during the crisis of adolescence the individual is most unsure of himself. The kind of stimulation that is able to inspire him will not only contribute to his creative development but may also contribute to his self-confidence. In spite of the fact that most people fall between the two extremes, with merely a preference for the one or the other, an analysis of each type in its pure form seems imperative for the proper understanding of their "mixed" forms.

### VISUAL TYPE

The main intermediaries for visual impressions are the eyes. The ability to observe visually does not depend entirely upon the physical condition of the eyes. Inferior visual awareness is not necessarily determined by a physical defect of the eyes. On the contrary, as experiments have proved, the psychological factor of having the *aptitude* to observe is of deciding significance. This is of special importance because it implies that being forced to observe might possibly create inhibitions. Before one can remove inhibitions, it is necessary to recognize them as such. For example, it would be completely wrong to attempt to set free the creative powers of a nonvisual type of individual by trying to remove his "visual inhibition" and anxiously attempting to familiarize him with visual impressions. One would, in fact, achieve the exact opposite, just as one would inhibit creative ability by forcing a visualizer to pay special attention to tactile impressions. *Not being able to see, or rather not noticing visual impressions, is not always an inhibitory factor.* This haptic expression can be readily found not only in the field of art but also in literature and other areas.[7] Before the way is cleared for the development of artistic ability, it is essential to ascertain which creative type is involved. From this it follows that naturalistic modes of expression should not be used as the only criterion, for this may actually inhibit free creative expression. To ascertain the type being dealt with, the specific attributes of each have to be determined.

The *visual* type, the observer, usually approaches things from their appearance. He feels as a *spectator*. One important factor in visual observation is the ability to see first the whole without an awareness of details, then to analyze this total impression into detailed or partial impressions, and finally to synthesize these parts into a new whole. Apparently, the visual type first sees the general shape of a tree, then the single leaves, the twigs, the branches, the trunk, and finally everything incorporated in the synthesis of the whole tree. Starting with the general outline, partial impressions thus are integrated into a whole, simultaneous image. This is true not only psychologically but also for the act of creating. Thus, we will notice that visual types usually begin with the outlines of objects and enrich the form with details as the visual analysis is able to penetrate deeper into the nature of the object.

This visual penetration deals mainly with two factors: first, with the analysis of the characteristics of shape and structure of the object itself; and second, with the changing effects of these shapes and structures determined by light, shadow, color, atmosphere, and distance. Observing details is not always a sign of visual-mindedness; it can be an indication of good memory as well as of subjective · interest in these details. For visual-mindedness it is necessary to see the changes these details undergo under the various external conditions mentioned above.

Visually minded persons have a tendency to transform kinesthetic and tactile experiences into visual experiences. If, for instance, a visual-minded person acquaints himself with an object in complete darkness, he tries to visualize all tactile or kinesthetic experiences. "How it looks" is the first reaction to any object met in darkness. In other words, he tries to imagine in visual terms what he has perceived through other senses. A visually minded person who encounters an object in darkness thus tries immediately to visualize the object he has met. The visual approach toward the outside world is an analytic approach of a spectator who observes the complex and ever changing appearances of shapes and forms.

## HAPTIC TYPE

The main intermediary for the haptic type of individual is the *body self*—muscular sensations, kinesthetic experiences, touch impressions, and all experiences that place the self in value relationship to the outside world. In haptic art the self is projected as the true actor of the picture whose formal characteristics are the result of a synthesis of bodily, emotional, and intellectual comprehension of shape and form. Sizes and spaces are determined by their emotional value in size and importance. The haptic type is primarily a *subjective type*. Haptically minded persons do not transform kinesthetic and tactile experiences into visual ones but are completely content with the tactile or kinesthetic modality itself. If a haptically minded person acquaints himself with an object in complete darkness, he remains satisfied with his tactile or kinesthetic experiences of the surface structure of the obstacle or with partial impressions of those parts that he has touched. Since tactile impressions are, to a great extent, partial (this is true for all impressions of objects that cannot be embraced with the hands, where the hands have to move), the haptic individual will arrive at a synthesis of these partial impressions only when he becomes emotionally interested in the object itself. Normally, he will not build up such a synthesis and will remain satisfied with his haptic experience. Since the haptic type uses the self as the true projector of his experiences, his pictorial representations are highly subjective; his proportions are proportions of value.

In art education it is necessary to consider these attitudes toward the world of experiences as important as the visual approaches toward art. Thus, a motivation will be effective only if it includes haptic sensations as well as visual experiences.

## The Different Creative Concepts of the Two Types

To be able to separate pure optical perception from other sense impressions, we need an object of contemplation that cannot be influenced or disturbed by other senses. But associatively almost everything in our surroundings somehow influences all our sensations and experiences. We can therefore hardly ever speak of pure optical perception of things. Even color, considered in isolation from any object, awakes in us dark, bright, cheerful, or warm feelings, and a tree waving in the wind awakes in us some knowledge of the elasticity of the wood, the nature of the leaves, and so forth. Thus Van Gogh writes in a letter to his brother, "Yesterday evening I concerned myself with the gently rising terrain of the wood, which is completely covered with dry, dead beech leaves. . . . The problem is—and I find this extremely difficult—to bring out the depth of the color and the enormous strength and firmness of the soil. . . . Out of this soil grow the trunks of the beeches, which are a shining green on the side on which they are brightly illuminated, while on the shadow side the trunks show a warm, strong black-green. . . . I am affected and intrigued to see how strongly the trunks are rooted in the ground. I began to paint them with the brush, and was unable to bring out the characteristics of the soil, which had already been painted in thick colors.

The new brush strokes simply disappeared. Therefore I pressed roots and trunks out of the tube and modelled them a little with my brush. There, now they stand in it, grow out of it, and have firmly taken root."[8]

We see here how the optical impression has been influenced and formed by other sense impressions, how intellectual apprehension of shape and form fused with optical and emotional experiences. Can optical perception, therefore, be adequately perceived by means of seeing with the eye alone? We shall have to conclude that optical perception in its purest form is only an extreme case of visual perception in general. We must therefore use the term *visual perception,* when impressions coming from other senses are subordinate to those coming from the eye, when visual impressions are the *dominant* feature in a percept.

The artistic representation of visual impressions always starts from optical perception. It is concerned with the subjective experience of the self only as far as any creative activity is an individual mental act. *Being bound to the self* in this sense is not what we shall understand by the term later, because it does not seek its experience in bodily sensations, but *outside the body*. The self merely evaluates the experience.

"The further optical experience recedes into the background, the less important does the eye become as the intermediary of the concept."[9] Visual and haptic concepts are fundamentally different in their basic experiential content. As we are able to recognize them, we will be able to encourage the individual in the *direction* of his thinking and thereby provide the guidance he sorely needs.

### HUMAN FIGURE

For the visual type the human figure is a part of the environment. As such, the human figure is exposed to the same phenomena as environment. The main experiences related to the representation of the human figure are the qualities that can be discovered with our eyes. Correct proportions and measurements are, therefore, of prime significance for the visual type (see Figure 77). The changing effects of light and shadows in the different motions are necessarily a part of the visual image. In art stiumulation, therefore, the posing model is of different significance for the two creative types because the visually minded individual is mainly concerned with the visual analysis of his optical impressions.

The haptic type, however, uses the human figure as the interpreter of his emotions and feelings (see Figure 78). Since different parts of our body have various functions and importance, the proportions given these

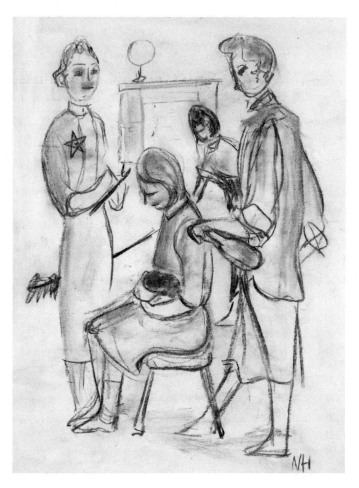

**Figure 77.** "A Scene at the Police Station," drawn by a visually minded adolescent. Correct proportions, lights and shadows, and three-dimensional quality are important to the artist.

parts will assume the emotional significance assigned to them. The wounds on the hands of Christ are of such significance in a Byzantine mural that the hands dominate in size and in importance. Another experience related especially to haptic types is the intense body feeling expressed in the desire to get one's body transferred to another place (that is, when late; related to the wish of catching up with time and space) or the desire to catch something that is already out of reach by throwing one's arm after it. These typically haptic experiences are in strong contradiction to visual observations. They spring from body experiences and kinesthetic sensations. Since these experiences are highly subjective in their interpretations, the haptic representation of the human figure and its meaning is a highly subjective one.

In *The Nature of Creative Activity* are numerous examples of the works of the blind, among whom haptic expression is much more common. Here is discussed the meaning of autoplastic sensations, the sensations of drawing all experiences from the body, and the significance they assume. The figure "Youth Imploring" modeled by a girl who has been blind since birth will illustrate these viewpoints. Its most striking characteristic is overemphasis on the imploring hands. We feel the strength of the elemental forces embodied in this figure when we observe the gradual increase in its proportions. It starts from the slender basis of the delicate legs and rising like a hymn to heaven finds in the great hands its mighty closing chord. The base has, as it were, been dematerialized: it is no longer earth-bound, and we have before us only the feeling "I implore!" (see Figure 79). In almost all sculptures by the blind, those parts of the body that have emotional significance are greatly exaggerated. We find, however, the same principles of representation in all epochs and cultures in which expressive qualities are of greater importance than visual ones.

**Figure 78.** "A Scene at the Police Station," drawn by a haptically minded adolescent. The elements of this composition are determined subjectively; proportions, lights and darks, and space are of emotional importance.

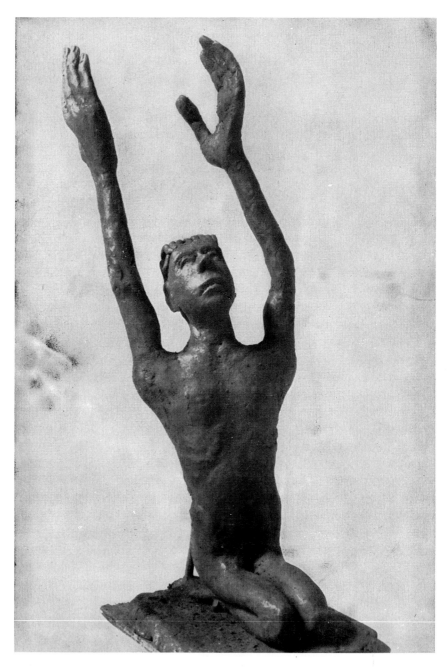

**Figure 79.** "Youth Imploring," sculpture by a seventeen-year-old girl who has been blind since birth.

In Egyptian murals the kings and other prominent persons are made larger in exactly the same way as in Byzantine paintings. In these cases large and small cannot be considered visual qualities: they are expressive evaluations; visual experiences have to make way for impulses lying outside the visual sphere. This is especially true for modern art in which the emphasis again is on the side of expressive qualities. This may help us in understanding some of the complex creations of Picasso in which space and time fuse, in which profile and front views are expressed simultaneously, in which the arm of a horrified mother becomes separated from the body as an expression of the intense feeling of reaching for her bombed child.[10] The nature of this art expression is at least as deeply rooted, historically and psychologically, as the visual interpretation of the world that surrounds us.

## SPACE

Space cannot be conceived in its totality. Its infinity is irrational, and it becomes accessible to our senses only when we circumscribe it. At the center of space, with nothing whatever to surround us, space itself would be infinite and therefore nonexistent. The self would cease to be a measure of value in space. It would vanish to nothing in infinity. Our senses and our psychological attitudes set limits to space, and each in its own way enables us to grasp space. *Visual space,* for which the eyes are the intermediaries, we perceive as the widest space. *Haptic space,* for which our organs of touch and our bodily sensations are the intermediaries, is the most restricted. Both spaces achieve a magical significance whenever the self is included in them through value judgments. We shall discuss the difference in the ways in which these two sensory spaces are pictorially represented. Both points of view are necessary for understanding the kind of stimulation the art educator has to use during this deciding stage so that he will neither neglect nor frustrate either of these types.

In relation to its environment the self grows or diminishes in size and in importance. Next to children we seem large, next to a skycraper, small; unimportant in the world at large, important in our own circle; most important, perhaps, when we are quite alone. These attitudes vary according to our psychological state. The narrower, the more restricted, three-dimensional space or the space of our psychological experiences is, the more importance is assigned to the self. Haptic space is of necessity restricted. In it, therefore, the significance and the importance of the self are very much emphasized.

The eye produces as a visual image an apparent diminution of distant objects. In drawing, this apparent diminution of distant objects is achieved by using laws of perspective. The outer limits of visual space are represented by the boundary of the horizon line. Distant objects in haptic space do not produce differences in size to the sense of touch or to emotional reactions. Thus, the visual image receives a decisive correction. When space is being explored tactually, distances can only have different values attached to them or seem of greater or less emotional significance. In haptic space, therefore, we find a predominance of subjective value judgments. The longing for freedom, however, grows with its remoteness. An individual without restrictions is unaware of boundaries. His eyes can easily rest on the horizon. The horizon of the sharecropper is his cotton field, the horizon of a laundry woman her tub. *The perspective of haptic space is a perspective of values.*

None of the creative interpretations of these spaces is true in a naturalistic sense. Both spaces are "distorted" by individual interpretations. Although philosophy has generally considered visual space as the more realistic, nevertheless it has less validity than the space of touch. Distant objects do not actually change in size, and the sense of touch records this truth. Bushmen who were shown photographs or reproductions of paintings of three-dimensional qualities were unable to orient themselves in the jungle of visual foreshortenings.[11] For them sizes do not differ with distances. Their spatial interpretations, however, are not "true interpretations" either, since they evaluate objects in space according to significance. We are completely one-sided in our judgments relating to the validity of our own visual space interpretations. Our civilization has become so accustomed to the photographic interpretation of space that we have to change our concept completely if we shift to the "unconventional" interpretations of haptic space, although these have been the conventional interpretations among historical cultures in which *expression* dominated the realm of art.

## The Two Creative Types Are Psychological— Their Significance for Personality Development

When we sit in a train, watching the swiftly passing landscape, we may or may not realize that the impression of the landscape as a whole exists only in our minds. Actually we do not see the whole thing, but only many little strips of landscape about the size of the window, each one quickly replaced by another. Some of us are quite satisfied with these many partial impressions and would even feel dizzy if compelled to integrate the fleeting glimpses into a whole. Others, however, do not need to be stimulated to put this picture puzzle together. While moving, they fuse all these strips together and see in their minds a whole landscape; more than that, they orient themselves quite well in it.

Members of the first group not only lose contact with the parts of the landscape that are left behind but often become irritated by the ever changing picture. Many of us have experienced how this irritation contributes to the discomfort of train travel. It is not only the fresh air that makes riding in an open car a pleasure, the smoothness of high-altitude flying that makes it more pleasant than the take-off; it is also the enlarged visual circle, which permits better orientation and a fuller sense of physical security. The body likes to know what is being done to it. The driver of a car does not feel the sudden stop as much as the passengers do.

The traveler who sits either comfortably or painfully in his compartment seldom realizes that this ability or failure to produce a single, unified picture out of the many successive impressions of the landscape may classify him according to a definite psychological type, which differs from other types on this and many other points, as we shall see.

An air-pilot training candidate who failed in his examinations explained his failure as follows: "In high altitudes I feel secure. However, the closer I come to the ground, especially in landing maneuvers, the more I become confused. Since I cannot take in the whole airfield, I lose orientation." This is exactly the problem of a blind sculptor, who, moving his hands over a face, receives only partial impressions. The inability of the pilot to integrate his partial impressions of the landing field into a whole, confused his sense of orientation. Having lost contact with the part of the airfield left behind, the pilot could no longer orient himself.

In primitive, haptic, and expressive art the same attitude toward the experience of senses can be observed with one striking additional factor. As a man sitting in a train loses contact with the area he leaves behind him, so does the haptic artist. But the train passenger, like the artist, may suddenly become bound up with something that quickly passes his eyes and strikes his personality, such as an old shack or a hawk circling in the air. From this time on the hawk will circle with him and grow in his mind as one outstanding, isolated impression of the many he has perceived in succession.

A blind person who made himself acquainted with a room became very much interested in a desk lamp. He could feel the bulb growing warmer when he turned on the light, and when he was asked afterward to model the room in clay, the lamp was the most conspicuous part, even overshadowing the desk. This impression became outstanding and most of the other parts disappeared. The lamp may have been for him a symbol of the unattainable or, perhaps, the unperceivable, which can easily change for the primitive man into any magic symbol. The creative result, however, shows the same expression for it—proportion of value.

The world of expressionist art is one of expression, feelings, subjective processes—*of haptic experiences*. Bodily feelings, kinesthetic experiences, muscular sensations are clearest examples of subjective processes. The bodily feelings of these uplifted hands in Figure 79 have become incorporated into the magic content of the expression of the whole sculpture. The same kind of expression can be seen in the works of some modern masters, as well as in the exaggerated hands of primitive African sculptures. It can be seen in every art that originates in haptic rather than in visual experiences.

Thus, the two creative types are psychologically independent of physiological factors. It has been demonstrated that there are completely and congenitally blind individuals who react visually or haptically in the same ways as normal-sighted people react both ways. A blind person reacts visually if he is able to receive from his touch impressions (which are partial impressions) a simultaneous image of the whole, like the visually minded, normal-sighted person who sits in the train and fuses all partial impressions into a simultaneous image. *Both final products are distinguished by the same visual attributes of emphasizing the external appearance.* Blind and normal-sighted haptic types, however, create entirely from within. Their inward feelings are expressed rather than any realistic external qualities. Actual differences in method of working with clay can be seen in the products of two sixteen-year-old youths (see Figures 80 and 81).

*The ability to give objective form to the creations of the imagination does not depend on the capacity to see and observe things.* This is of vital importance for art educators because it will affect the methods of motivation.

### THE CHANGE OF THE IMAGINATIVE CONCEPT

Proper art motivation is always determined by the factors that influence the growth and development of the individual during a particular age

**Plate 9.** "My Barber," painted by a fourteen-year-old boy. The haptically minded child frequently uses flat areas of color. He does not feel as a spectator but is bound up with his subject.

**Plate 10.** An interest in texture and an organization of spaces and colors demonstrates a growing aesthetic awareness. Nonobjective painting may be visually inspired or it may represent a nonvisual experience.

period. During the crisis of adolescence the individual has to battle for many far-reaching decisions. He stands on the threshold of adulthood, reached under circumstances that often affect his life very definitely. Adjustment from childhood to adulthood usually occurs under difficulties, physiologically and psychologically. Neither one can be separated from the other because the body is closely related to the mind and affects it greatly. We shall be concerned only with creative activity as a natural outlet and means of expression for the individual. Art education during this important period should by no means be offered to only a selected group but should be a natural means of expression for everyone. This conclusion is not in accord with common practice in the American high school, where art is taught to a small group of artistically "gifted" students. *Gifted* usually refers to skill in conventional interpretations of objects of nature. If we can eliminate this attitude toward "art expression" and at the same time develop self-confidence in the individual to accept *art as self-expression according to individual needs*, we have succeeded in our chief aim of making art a common expression of mankind.

Much of the confusion of adolescent critical awareness in our society is due to traditional concepts that establish a "naturalistic" relationship to environment, a relationship which develops a "true" (photographic) picture of the external world. The concept of truth should be established from as many angles as possible, especially with the help of works of art of different epochs and cultures. Truth is relative and the word should be replaced by *sincerity*. An African sculpture is as "true" to its creator as was the "David" to Michelangelo. The experience, however, that the African sculptor had with his work is vitally different from the experience Michelangelo had when he created the "David." Thus it is the difference in the experience that determines art expression, whether it be painting, music, architecture, or any other art form. Demonstrating this relationship between experience and art work in great variety will aid students in an unhampered interpretation of their own experiences.[12]

A work of art is not a product of nature; it is a product of human spirit, thinking, and emotions and can only be understood when the driving forces are of essential significance and everything else is only a by-product. If these driving forces are lacking, not even the most developed skills can ever replace them. That is why the works of the primitives can be great works of art while most skillfully executed works are not necessarily works of art if they lack the driving forces, the inner spirit that determines the greatness of an art work. They are like beautiful wrappers around nothing. The most diverse works of art of different epochs and cultures

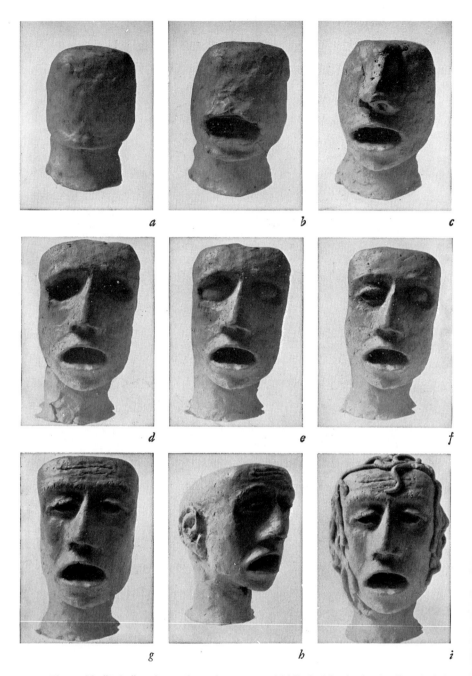

**Figure 80.** "Pain," sculpture by a sixteen-year-old blind girl who is visually minded. **a.** The general outline is made. **b.** The cavity of the mouth is formed. **c.** The nose is added. **d.** Eye sockets are hollowed out. **e.** Eyeballs are put in. **f.** Lids are pulled over. **g.** Wrinkles are formed. **h.** Ears are added. **i.** Hair is added. **Right (j):** In the finished product, all features are incorporated into a unified surface.

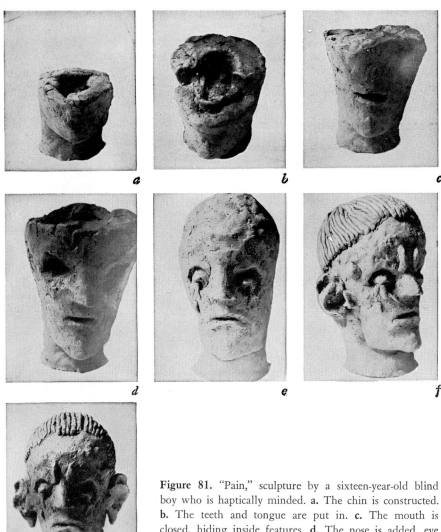

Figure 81. "Pain," sculpture by a sixteen-year-old blind boy who is haptically minded. **a.** The chin is constructed. **b.** The teeth and tongue are put in. **c.** The mouth is closed, hiding inside features. **d.** The nose is added, eye sockets made. **e.** Eye sockets are put in from inside, head is closed. **f.** Ears, muscles, and hair are added. **g.** The head is finished. **Right (h):** All features remain isolated as partial impressions on final product.

show the different qualities of these driving forces. It is important to demonstrate how in Greek sculpture the highest admiration of the beauty of the body has been expressed. This can be understood only if we realize that even a mother subordinated her feelings to the concept of beauty by disposing of a baby for the mere reason that its body was not perfect, as was the custom among the Spartans.

The driving forces that determined the expression of the "ideal" form and shape must be different from those that determined religious expression (as during the medieval periods). Ideal forms disappear when expression dominates. When we cry, we do not care whether we cry beautifully. The driving force represents the need to incorporate all expressive experiences into the single work of art making it a symbol of that expression. That is why in times when a general idea of expression was universal, like the general idea of religious expression during medieval times, the tendency toward symbolism or the general validity of expression is great. If the driving force, however, is individualistic—if expression derives from personal experiences—art expression will be highly individualized.

To illustrate, we have only to compare Picasso with Rouault to see the strong differences in their individual expression based on the difference in kind of experience (see Chapter 11). Whereas many of the experiences of Picasso can easily be traced to body sensations and kinetic experiences (as the desire to paint dynamically, front view and profile in one interpretation of a head), Rouault concerns himself greatly with associations of past experiences in which medieval art is often brought into a new light. Its greatest and most powerful expression is found in the dark outlines as seen in the medieval stained windows. How different is the origin of the driving forces in an impressionistic picture in which the external appearance—the changes of light and shadows, the illuminating qualities of surfaces, the complex idea of the breaking of colors—reaches its climax. How much in contrast to such external structures and appearances are the driving forces that make an African sculptor carve his idols or an Indian his totems. An analysis of these forces leads the student directly away from the mere imitative urge of reproducing nature.

Youths during the period of adolescence are eager to give their thinking an intellectual backing. They will readily absorb those differences in the nature of the driving forces that determine the art experience. The personal experience in our everyday life must be included in the discussion. When we see a burning house, the driving forces that determine our experiences related to it will be quite different for different individuals. The one might be affected by the beauty of the blazing flames flaring skyward, their reflections, and the dancing shadows cast by them. The other individual is deeply touched by the fate of the people who are now without a roof over their heads, suddenly deprived of everything they could enjoy a few moments before. This individual sees the weeping mother holding the only thing she had been able to save, the baby in her arms. Still a third individual might leave the scene thinking only of what he would have done in the same circumstances. Whereas the one would merely approach the accident as a spectator (emphasizing visual experiences), the other might become involved in the struggle for existence, setting the ego in a value relationship to the experience (emphasizing haptic experiences). The third might be affected by both experiences.

For the proper approach toward art experiences it is of vital importance to distinguish between what is essential and what is unessential. *Everything is essential that directly relates to the expression of the experience.* Unessential are those factors that have no direct relationship to the creation of the work. The essentials are the basis for a proper art motivation.

For example, our experience may be derived from a body motion: we were intrigued by a worker who carried a heavy load on his shoulder. Carrying a heavy load is now the most essential experience that we would like to express. Everything else becomes unessential. Thus, we do not care whether Mr. Smith or Mr. Jones carries the heavy load. Their faces might only detract from the essential expression in the same way as the face of the "Man with the Helmet" by Rembrandt would have contradicted his experience if it had overpowered the helmet. Rembrandt illuminated the helmet as the essential part, and put the face in deep shadows as if he wanted to say, "Under the helmet all faces look alike." It is not the portrait of Mr. Jones, it is the "Man with the Helmet." If we compare this great painting with one of Rembrandt's portraits in which the face has to stand out and the headdress is almost a silhouette, we will more definitely experience the meaning of these essentials.

Thus, while concentrating on the act of carrying a heavy load, we shall omit everything that does not contribute to carrying a heavy load, and concentrate more and more on the experience itself. Although we are quite aware of the meaning of carrying, especially when going through the experience ourselves, we will soon discover that it is the lack of active knowledge that prevents the student from portraying his experience.

"What are we doing when we are carrying? Are we bent or upright? Do we have our legs together, or apart from each other, to gain better support? How do we hold our load? Do we need to bend our arms or do we have them straight? Do we look at the ground or forward?" Such questions will activate the passive knowledge of the individual and at the same time stress the essentials necessary for the expression of carrying a heavy load (see Figure 82). It will help those who have no definite concept and will not disturb or restrict those who find it easy to express themselves. It is much more stimulating and easier not to start to draw from nature but to use the experiences derived from the self.

The complexity of nature, its details and lights and shadows, deflect the attention from the essentials and may in the beginning be too complex

**Figure 82.** This sketch from a posing figure interprets the topic "Carrying a Heavy Load."

and confusing. This way, we also will avoid imposing visual stimulations upon the whole group. Visual and haptic types will apply their individual application to this stimulation, which starts from the self. The visually minded individual will include environment in his visual concept and will project the experience of the self into his environment, whereas the haptically minded student will become absorbed solely in the qualities deriving from his own subjective experiences.

At some point, however, it might become essential to include more than one motion in a representation—for instance, if the repetition of a motion is essential for the atmosphere of the working situation. Digging potatoes and putting them into bags is a continuous activity requiring repetition. We would not do justice to the essentials to exclude this act of repetition. Sometimes monotony is one of the essentials; then we would not vary the motions but would place them parallel. Another time it is essential to show the type of motions workers go through while performing a job. Then it would be necessary to show the characteristic rhythm of the various phases of the working process, in one representation, "The Rhythm of Workers on a Construction Project."

The essentials might even become more complex if we include social atmospheres or emotional reactions. With gaining confidence the urge for expression grows, and the guidance of the teacher may diminish. The quality and sincerity of art expression are in close relationship to the urge for expression. Attention to details must grow out of the desire for expression, otherwise we are not dealing with creative activity. *The study of a detail must never be an aim in itself,* and in this respect art education often fails. The academic method, which uses rules for creative production, starts with details. A mouth separated from its environment loses its meaning and becomes an anatomical part unrelated to art. A mouth is a dynamic part of the face and ceases to exist as such when separated from the whole.

Form and expression are a unit and can never be separated from each other without doing harm to either part. If a student who paints a picture of a man pulling a boat gets "stuck" because he cannot express the essential quality of a pulling hand, the study of a pulling hand grows out of the desire to incorporate this hand into the whole experience of a pulling man. He will then proceed with his study, not as a separated, isolated detail but as a part of the whole, which becomes fulfillment only when it unites with the rest. Studying details in the academic meaning becomes quite superfluous within a curriculum of modern art education. *The urge for studying details develops from the individual need for expression.* This need, however, is very diverse, individual, and highly subjective.

From the foregoing discussion it becomes apparent that proper art motivation relates as much to personality development as to creative expression itself. This double function of art teaching signifies the importance of aesthetic experiences within this decisive period of development, and shows clearly why art should not be confined to a selected group but should become a means of expression for everyone.

RELATED ACTIVITIES

1. Compare the drawings of an eighth grade with those done by a fifth grade class. Point out the changes that show the development of a critical awareness toward creative expression.

2. Make a list of the characteristics of the child who tends to be haptic. What would be his preference for subject matter, his manner of representation, his use of color, his use of proportion? Plan a lesson that would emphasize nonvisual responses.

3. Make a list of the characteristics of a child who has a preference for visual stimuli and plan a lesson, as above, emphasizing the visual elements.

4. Discuss the changing relationship between the child and his environment as seen in the representations of space. Point out how the use of space changes and how these changes reflect changes in development as the child grows.

5. Make a collection of reproductions of recognized artists' work that show the differences between haptic and visual approaches to painting on the adult level. Collect some reproductions that show both influences.

6. Realizing that differences in training, education, and interests affect vocational choice, list some occupations that emphasize visual characteristics. List those that emphasize haptic characteristics. Defend your choices.

NOTES

1. Thomas Munro, "Adolescence and Art Education," *Methods of Teaching the Fine Arts,* ed. William Rusk (Chapel Hill: University of North Carolina Press, 1935), pp. 25–58.

2. *Haptic* derives from the Greek word *haptikos* and means "able to lay hold of."

3. Viktor Lowenfeld, "Tests for Visual and Haptical Aptitude," *American Journal of Psychology,* **LVIII,** No. 1, (1945), pp. 100–111.

4. W. Grey Walter, *The Living Brain* (New York: W. W. Norton & Company, Inc., 1953), pp. 214–218.

5. Viktor Lowenfeld, *The Nature of Creative Activity,* rev. ed. (New York: Harcourt, Brace & World, Inc., 1952).

6. Henry W. Drewes, "An Experimental Study of the Relationship Between Electroencephalographic Imagery Variables and Perceptual-Cognitive Processes" (Unpublished doctoral dissertation, Cornell University, 1958).

7. Paul B. Flick, "An Intercorrelative Study of Two Creative Types: The Visual Type and the Haptic Type" (Unpublished doctoral dissertation, The Pennsylvania State University, 1960).

8. Vincent Van Gogh, *Letters* (Berlin: Bruno Cassirer, 1928), pp. 14, 16, and 17.

9. *The Nature of Creative Activity*, p. 82.

10. Mural "Guernica," by Pablo Picasso.

11. Leo Frobenius, *Kulturgeschichte Afrikas* (Zürich: Phaidon-Verlag, 1933).

12. Thomas Munro, "Creative Ability in Art and Its Educational Fostering," *The Fortieth Yearbook of the National Society for the Study of Education* (Bloomington, Ill.: Public School Publishing Co., 1941), pp. 289–322.

# 10

## Adolescent Art

ALTHOUGH this chapter is primarily concerned with the art of the adolescent, it would be difficult to define this stage in artistic development. While our knowledge and understanding of child art have greatly expanded, the understanding of the art of the adolescent has been generally neglected.

*Child art* is a term that is meaningful to every teacher, parent, and psychologist. We know the attributes of child art, the forces that underlie it, its developmental stages, and its meaning for growth. It has been demonstrated that child art has its distinct attributes and, like childhood, represents a very important phase in our development. When we consider art of the adolescent, however, we find confusion. We are far from having arrived at a definite concept of adolescent art, and this is reflected in the art programs in the junior and senior high schools of our nation.

282

There is a crying need to determine the underlying principles of adolescent art and to develop and support a program that is concerned primarily with the needs of this age group. We know that adolescence is probably as distinct a period in the development of individuals within our society as is the period called childhood. The need is quite clear, and there is no real reason why we should not be able to arrive at an art program that is not only distinct in its nature but that can also provide the necessary basis for helping to satisfy the needs of this age and to unfold possibilities for continued growth.

Generally there have been three approaches in our secondary schools to adolescent art. One approach is mainly concerned with saving the precious attributes of child art. Teachers adhering to this method are anxious not to lose the fresh, spontaneous approach of the child. A highly intuitive teacher can strongly motivate children in such a way as to make them forget themselves and paint in a very fresh fashion, as though they were again young children. However, it is quite obvious that prolonging the spontaneity and unconscious approach of childhood can produce an insecurity within youth. Instead of giving him confidence in his own art expression, such motivation pulls him back into a prolonged childhood. Although the products of such strong motivations may at times be quite pleasing, they do not serve the individual in his own critical period of growth, and they can undermine confidence in his own natural form of expression.

A second and more common approach, found in junior and senior high schools, is that of emphasizing perfection. Here teachers try to approach "professional" standards. In many instances, to the pride of the teacher, one can hardly distinguish between a high school art exhibit and one from a professional art school. This striving to adhere to adult standards deprives the adolescent youth of his own expression, and in a sense harks back to days when children were trained how to draw, since their own expression lacked "artistic" qualities. It is fairly obvious that emphasizing perfection in the public schools completely counteracts the democratic meaning of education, for it is only the selected few who are able to conform to high standards of adult professionalism. This is especially alarming when we realize that if these same few students continue on to professional art schools, they often have to unlearn the techniques they have so laboriously perfected.[1]

A third approach to art is centered around what might be termed *school-type projects*. These are the type of art projects with no apparent relationship either to child art or to adult professionalism. They have the unhappy distinction of being important only because they are included in the curriculum. Much time and effort can be spent by the students and by the teacher in what is sincerely considered a good art program. Such projects may include embossing metal plaques, designing stained glass windows, making safety posters, designing monogrammed napkins, carving book ends, copying various lettering styles, or carving a football player out of soap. The list of such school-type projects is unlimited. These tend to parallel the May baskets and sewing cards on the elementary level. This approach to art education tends to make a sham and a frill of what should be a vital and dynamic part of the school curriculum.

In addition to the three approaches to art in our secondary schools mentioned above, there are some programs making an honest attempt at providing a meaningful art experience. It is in this direction that we will focus our attention. A meaningful creative program in art for the adolescent should be based upon an understanding of the nature and meaning of adolescence within our culture. It is only with a thorough understanding of the characteristics of this stage that we can deal intelligently with the problem of constructing a meaningful course of study.

## The Adolescent

When one is no longer a child, and yet somehow not quite an adult, that is adolescence. Just when one becomes an adult is questionable; it can be considered the age when one can legally leave public school or when one is of voting age. When one leaves childhood is easier to define, at least from a physical point of view. Puberty is generally recognized as being the end of childhood. Girls usually begin a period of rapid growth at about eleven years, and by menarche at about thirteen they will have developed the usual feminine bodily characteristics. Although girls do not reach their full mature height until about seventeen, growth becomes much slower. Boys start to shoot up about two years later than girls; they don't start slowing down until fifteen or sixteen, and they reach adult height at about nineteen. Their voices may begin to change, the Adam's apple grows, and a trace of fuzz appears on their faces at about fifteen years. With both sexes, there are skin changes, and it is not unusual for body parts to grow at different rates. All these changes are of concern to these youngsters and obviously have an effect upon how they view themselves in relation to the rest of society.

Adults—parents and teachers—usually look upon this age as a stage of awkwardness and turmoil. Small children can be looked upon as cute, but the comment "I don't know what this new generation is coming to" is aimed directly at the adolescent. What may be of even greater importance is that these teen-agers feel that adults have a uniformly low opinion of them; and at the same time parents believe that teen-agers have high opinions of themselves.[2] To a great extent the usual secondary school program tends to emphasize these feelings. Teachers are concerned with class control and discipline, whereas the adolescents tend to look upon school as an evil necessity. For some youngsters the legal age for leaving school can hardly come soon enough, and often secondary art courses are selected by these students to fill their waiting time in preference to taking other even more frustrating courses.

Sex has suddenly begun to play an important role. There is no doubt that the awakening of sexual urges gives rise to some of the greatest concerns of this age. Girls are bombarded with advertisements about how to make themselves more femininely alluring by the use of hair rinses, deodorants, cosmetics, by squeezing or padding the body, or by various dress styles. Romance and love are somehow just over the hill, and many hours can be spent in daydreaming. For boys greater attention is often focused upon muscle building and attaining masculinity. This is a real problem for the youngster who develops later than his classmates. Added to all of this, of course, is the general feeling that somehow sex is taboo. It has been shown that in other cultures this uncomfortable period between puberty and marriage may be considerably shorter. Although some girls leave high school for marriage, especially in the lower socio-economic levels, marriage can sometimes be delayed for others well beyond college.

To an adult removed from this age the teen-age society may look like an organized union with its own language, dress, and rules. However, there are in-groups and out-groups, which can seem very important to belong to or to shun. Conformity can be a powerful force extending not only to dress but to behavior as well. Being popular with one's peers is often more important than the longer term educational goals.

The young adolescent may also be very idealistic. He may be anxious to rebel against the confused muddle that adults have made of the world and is eager to work and strive for remaking his environment. Or he may become disgruntled and disillusioned and assume a so-what attitude. Rapid emotional changes can come about through a phone call from some special person or by being told by mother that he has to be home at ten thirty. Many romantic ideas of becoming an explorer or a famous movie star go out the window, with the realization that a living must be made in a few short years or months. Certainly the adolescent idealism can and should have some practical means of expression.

There should be no thought that teen-agers are all alike. Although all young people face changes within the self and are also confronted with resulting changes in their environment, every adolescent is a distinct individual.

## The Need for Adolescent Art

It is quite clear that a junior and senior high school program, if it is to be effective, must be built upon the needs of the growing adolescent. Above all, it must provide the adolescent with opportunities for expression of his thinking, his emotions, and his reactions to his environment. As Dr. Cole has said, "Adolescents need outlets for their emotional interests and for self-expression. Their constantly shifting social adjustments inevitably put considerable strain upon them. They have a real need for such subjects as music, art, dramatics, writing. In these subjects, as in the sciences, a clear distinction must be made between the few for whom the subject is a speciality and the many for whom it is a means of self-expression. The object of the work in these fields should be to provide for such self-expression as can be indulged in by the 'untalented.' "[3]

The production and sale of paint-by-the-number kits and the popular fill-ins point to the fact that many adults have a need for some art expression. That these kits are being sold shows the startling failure of the present art program within the public schools to make a meaningful contribution to the needs of these children. Making a picture of a bottle, a book, and a dried-up orange or designing a border for an ash tray certainly does not contribute to the adolescent's understanding of himself or of his environment.

Ideally an art program in the secondary schools should contribute to the continued growth of individuals. One of the important questions facing the teen-agers is that of self-identity. "Who am I, where do I be-

**Figure 83.**

long, where am I going?" Subject matter at this stage of development should be aimed directly at the adolescent himself. Adult orientation toward art and the striving for perfection is just as foreign as the unconscious approach of childhood would be. This age is filled with drives, questions, problems, and emotional upheavals; these should be recognized as suitable material for an art program, for as in the past, they are the basis for all true expression.

Art materials for the adolescent should be the same materials as those

**Figure 84.** A typical art class in high school includes students who will become businessmen, laborers, or professional people. Occasionally one may become an artist.

constantly used outside school. One of the aims of learning is to provide us with the ability and tools to perform more efficiently at the immediate level and to provide the basis for continued learning. The art program, then, should provide a means of continuing expression of the self, whether for Sunday painters, for the evening furniture builder, or for the man with his own photographic darkroom. We will deal in a later chapter with some of the questions about the "gifted" child; however, the person who is serious about continuing his professional training in art will have ample

opportunity in art school or college to develop knowledge about specialized art techniques. Certainly there is no reason for engraving, etching, lithography, copper enameling, or bronze casting to be included in the usual high school program. There is no question but that the youngster with an energetic teacher can get enthusiastic about these subject matter areas and the perfecting of techniques, but to a great extent these skills will avail him nothing once he has left the high school, nor do they afford the opportunity for self-identity.

The art program should also provide the basis for a cultural directness and honesty. We discussed earlier the schizophrenic tendencies of our society. The negative implications and effects upon our thinking processes of accepting falsehoods and imitation within our own culture as being normal should certainly be emphasized. Attention should certainly be focused in our art program on such discrepancy in our living. Pointing out dishonesty and sham when it occurs in architectural planning, in the purchasing of accessories, or in our political life should make for a greater realization of the importance of integrated thinking.

Art courses in the secondary schools are usually thought of as being creative. To what extent this is true depends upon how the courses are conducted more than upon the subject matter itself. We have stressed the necessity for encouraging and developing creative thinking throughout this book. In looking back through history we find that many people considered creative began producing early in life. The adolescent age is filled with emotional energy; with proper guidance in the art program this energy could be channeled into a vigorous creative drive. The fourteen-year-old may be so concerned with conformity and peer-group pressure that real support needs to be given to original and individualistic thinking. By the time a student is a junior or senior in high school, however, he has begun to focus his attention upon the adult world of work. Here is no child, but a person who has developed the ability to think abstractly, who has become aware of social problems, and who is full of drive to make a better world. Here especially the adult can be responsible for guiding and sharing learning experiences and providing meaningful problems, which require divergent thinking and creative action. Without question, art at the secondary level should provide for the stimulation of creativity and foster its development whether the student will continue in adult life as an artist, scientist, housewife, or plumber (see Figure 84).

It should become apparent from the preceding discussion that there is a need for an art program keyed to this exciting age. Emphasis should be placed directly upon the student and the depth of his experiences. Fiddling around with art materials and procedures has no place in the secondary schools. However no art program can be designed without an understanding of the particular environment in which it will be placed. The general characteristics of the age group should be considered as should the individual characteristics of the particular student. Both play an important part in program planning.

# A Consideration of Subject Matter

Adolescent art has its own special characteristics—it is neither the unconscious childish mode of expression nor the art form of the professional artist and craftsman. It is, instead, the art expression of the adolescent youth, regardless of whether or not he will later engage professionally in art activities. That such art activity is highly personal and only in special cases is of highly skilled and aesthetic quality should be kept in mind.

Subject matter should be considered as the means of developing an interest in, and enthusiasm for, art experiences. Subject matter should never be considered as restricting the adolescent to a predetermined topic. Ideally, each youngster should be so motivated that the main task of the teacher is to guide the progress in such a way that a truly meaningful experience results. The adolescent has a wealth of ideals, drives, and dreams; his reactions to himself, his wishful thinking (see Figure 85), his reaction to his society (see Figure 86)—all make excellent source material. Teaching methods that restrict the individual instead of making him free are poor. Subject matter that has no relation to the individual needs of the student can restrict freedom of expression. Art should not be looked upon as a duty, nor should a student feel that the assignment needs to be completed because of the pressure of grades or as an obligation to adults. Rather the student should feel that the art experience is of his own choice and that the problems he faces and the failures and successes he achieves are truly his.

Subject matter at the secondary school level should be considered a means for involving the student in an individually rewarding experience. That is, the subject matter should open up areas of interest and not be considered merely as rigid problems to perform. Students will develop the need for acquiring certain skills, for these will be necessary to gain satisfaction and a sense of accomplishment. The teaching of skills and techniques, therefore, should be considered as a means to an end, and should be born from the need for expression.

The need for a more complex technique will follow the development of complexity in expression. This need can be satisfied by the individual with guidance from an alert and sensitive teacher. Skills and techniques that are copied either from the teacher or from how-to-do-it books are unsuitable for self-expression, for these are basically rules and formulas for achieving a certain type of product. As we have seen, the visually

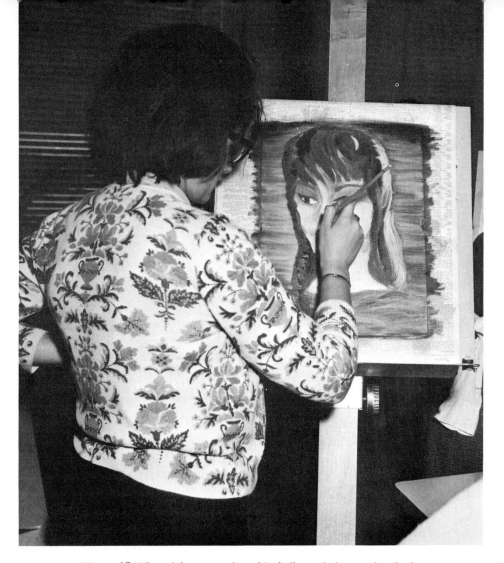

**Figure 85.** The adolescent projects his feelings, desires, and attitudes into his work. His personal expressions should be respected.

minded person may have a very different approach to art from the haptic person, who may be frustrated by exercises such as painting a picture in the pointillistic method. Particular techniques of art will be discussed in greater detail in a subsequent section; what needs emphasis here is that without the necessary desire for expression, teaching skills or techniques would be only an escape from the real problem. A method of art is good if it brings out the innate qualities of an individual by developing self-confidence and the desire to go ahead.

Essentially there are two basic needs to consider for an art education program. These are the individual psychological needs of the adolescent and the broader needs of society. Clearly the needs of today's society are not those of fifty years ago. The professional artists today need study and experience beyond the high school level regardless of their area of specialization. Certainly, gifted youngsters should be given the opportunity to explore possibilities in the arts and not be limited to making an end product to satisfy the teacher's preconceived list of art projects. The search for honesty and truth in the arts needs to be carried on by all members of our society whether they are planning to continue their education beyond the secondary school or not. Art education should be concerned

**Figure 86.** Subject matter should provide the opportunity for the adolescent to express his reactions to society, as shown in this social comment.

**Figure 87.** Understanding and sensitivity are basic
requirements for the art teacher.

with the needs of the individual, for the needs of individuals make up the
needs of society. *Subject matter cannot be selected at random but rather
must be an integral part of the life of the adolescent within his particular
environment.*

# Some Suggestions for Subject Matter in a
## Secondary School Art Program

An attempt has been made in the following course of study to relate the needs of the adolescent and the needs of society to a meaningful art program, which can feasibly be considered within the present structure of the secondary school. There are no arbitrary grade levels established, but rather the content is grouped under five main headings, each dealing with experiences of the teen-ager as the basis for the topic area. These are (1) Experiences of the Self, (2) Experiences in the Home, (3) Experiences in the Community, (4) Experiences in Nature, and (5) Experiences in Industry.

Needless to say, the success of this or of any other curriculum rests with the qualifications of the teacher (*see* Figure 87), with his broad understanding of the importance of art and with his sensitivity to the needs of his pupils. The *you* and *your* in the outline refer to the student.

## EXPERIENCES OF THE SELF

I. Experiences of the self in the home
   A. Understanding personal moods
      1. Sculpturing
         a. Modeling a clay mask referring to the self
           (1) Yawning
           (2) Laughing
           (3) Thinking hard
           (4) Whistling
           (5) Crying
           (6) Singing
           (7) Smiling
           (8) Being frightened
         b. Casting a mask in plaster, using a one-piece mold
         c. Modeling a full head in which the position of the head also contributes to the expression
         d. Carving
           (1) Tiredness
           (2) Singing
           (3) Excitedness
           (4) Looking out

  e. Cutting in soft stone
    (1) Listening
    (2) Being sad
    (3) Turning around, searching for something
    (4) Praying
  f. Casting a head in plaster
    (1) In a waste mold
    (2) In a piece mold
  g. Modeling a figure referring to the self
    (1) In action at home (studying, carrying, getting up)
    (2) A movement of emotional significance
2. Drawing with crayon, charcoal, conté crayon, pen, or brush
  a. Reaching for something at home
  b. Going upstairs
  c. Coming downstairs
  d. Reading a book
  e. Being tired
  f. Lying on the couch
3. Painting in tempera, water color, oil, or combination of these
  a. How you feel in the morning
  b. How you feel on a rainy day
  c. How you feel in the evening
  d. Feeling sleepy
  e. Feeling angry
  f. The ugliest person in the world
  g. A pretty, pretty girl
4. Designing emotional abstractions of moods (gay, laughing, excited, calm)
B. Home relations
  1. Modeling
    a. A group of two friends
    b. Mother and child
    c. You and your brother (sister)
  2. Carving
    a. Your pet
    b. A creature from outer space
  3. Drawing
    a. An evening at home

    b. Playing with friends

    c. Listening to music

    d. A date

4. Painting

    a. Home life (farm home, city home, country home, mountain home)

    b. Saying grace

    c. Life in a cabin where you would like to be

    d. An abstraction of musical rhythms (jazz, dance, march, waltz)

5. Design

    a. The type of home you would like to be in

    b. A relationship of textures of different materials (satin, silk, linen, cotton, wool, burlap; different kinds of wood, metal, glass)

    c. A drawing to scale of the living room of your family. Cut out the furniture to scale and move it on your drawing until it serves the function best and you also like it

6. Framing or matting one of your paintings or drawings

C. Social life

1. Painting

    a. In the playroom

    b. At the fireplace

    c. Dancing at a party

    d. Going out with a friend

    e. Watching television

    f. At dinner

    g. In the attic

    h. Helping to burn leaves

    i. Shoveling snow

    j. Mother cleaning the kitchen

    k. Holiday preparations

    l. A look out of the window

    m. Different social atmospheres in different homes

        (1) In different countries

        (2) In slums

        (3) In well-kept homes

    n. Back yard belonging to a family that likes

   (1) Gardening

   (2) To hang their laundry

   (3) To play

  2. Posing a model

   a. Raking the leaves

   b. Pushing the lawnmower

   c. Reading a book

   d. Climbing a ladder

   e. Carrying a log

  3. Design

   a. Decoration for your house

   b. A "No Trespassing" sign for your door

   c. Christmas-tree decorations out of scrap material

  4. Grooming

   a. For different occasions

   b. Trying out color effects for different types and complexions

   c. What colors look best on you

   d. How clothing affects you

II. Experiences of the self in nature

 A. Sensitivity to form

  1. Sculpturing

   a. Finding forms of nature and bringing out the innate qualities of rocks, shells, wood forms, and so on

   b. Making a collage of forms of nature

   c. Finding forms in nature suggestive of fantasy

  2. Painting

   a. Cloud formations

   b. Different forces in nature

   c. Flat desert

   d. Mountains

   e. Sea

   f. Rock formations

   g. Plant forms

  3. Design (graphics)

   a. Snowflakes

   b. Speed of wind

   c. Rhythm of movements in nature (waves in water, in fields)

   d. The force of fire

   e. Different textures brought together

     f. Forms in plant life
   4. Photography
     a. Forms in plants, in close-ups
     b. Rocks and animals
     c. Leaf structures, moss, barks, and so on
     d. Crystals, surfaces of weathered rocks, crevices, and so on
     e. Shells
     f. Skins, webs, beehives
     g. Ripples on waves
     h. Shadows on different textures
B. How nature affects you
   1. Sculpturing
     a. Abstract forms in nature expressing personal meaning
     b. Forms that affect you positively
     c. Forms that affect you negatively
     d. Walking against wind
     e. Relaxing in nature
     f. In a storm
   2. Painting
     a. A hot day
     b. A dull day
     c. Wide open on a plain
     d. Between narrow gorges
     e. In a drizzle
     f. Walking in snow
     g. Different moods in nature
     h. Sandstorms
     i. Floods
     j. Twilight
     k. Moonlight
     l. Seasons
     m. Afraid of lightning
   3. Design
     a. Mobiles with gentle motions and with speedy motions
     b. Collages of smooth textures and of rough textures
     c. Abstractions of "feelings" in nature
       (1) Glowing
       (2) Cool
       (3) Lonely

    (4) Gay

    (5) Forlorn

    (6) Spooky

    (7) Wet

  4. Costume

   a. Costumes for different seasons

   b. Costumes for different climates

  5. Architecture: how nature affects housing

 C. Social life in nature

  1. Drawing motions in outdoor sports

   a. Swimming

   b. Jumping

   c. Running

   d. Playing football

   e. Throwing

  2. Painting

   a. Hiking in nature

   b. Mountain climbing

   c. Skiing

   d. Skating

   e. Picnics

   f. Tenting

   g. Farming, plowing, haying

   h. Traveling (by car, by train, by horseback)

  3. Design

   a. A bench and tables for picnics

   b. An outdoor bungalow

   c. Garden furniture

  4. Costume

   a. Different uniforms for sports

   b. Costumes for hiking in mountains, in the tropics and so on

III. Experiences of the self in the community

 A. Relationship of self to the community

  1. Painting

   a. Visiting in stores

   b. The way to school

   c. Walking down the main street

   d. Helping in community drives

   e. Going to church

    f. Dancing

    g. Using recreation facilities

    h. Helping out with work in the neighborhood

    i. Looking for mail

    j. Going shopping at the supermarket

    k. At the barber shop

    l. Going through slum sections

    m. Going through residential areas

    n. At the fair

    o. Going to the movies

2. Sculpturing

    a. Praying in church

    b. Greeting the neighbors

    c. A fountain for the schoolyard

    d. A football player

    e. What you want to be

    f. Listening to a concert

    g. A beggar

3. Drawing

    a. At the shooting stand

    b. Sitting on a roller coaster

    c. Stepping into a bus

4. Design

    a. Why you like certain buildings

    b. Why you dislike certain buildings

    c. Light patterns at night—traffic, neon

    d. Abstraction of how you feel

        (1) On a roller coaster

        (2) When dancing

        (3) When listening to music

    e. Studying historical places and buildings of the community

5. Excursions

    a. Museums

    b. Factories

    c. Recreation areas

    d. Craftsmen

    e. Historical buildings

6. Costume design appropriate to the occasion and the individual

    a. Sports clothes

          (1) Romantic girl or boy

          (2) Athletic girl or boy

     b. Street wear

          (1) Stout person

          (2) Slender person

          (3) Tall person

          (4) Slim or average

     c. Evening clothes to fit personality, build, complexion, and coloring

     d. Costumes that will make a tall person look shorter

     e. Costumes that will be becoming to a short person

     f. A wardrobe for yourself (hat, bag, gloves, tie, socks, handkerchief)

  B. Relationships of self to other communities

    1. Painting

     a. Traveling by car

     b. Staying overnight

     c. Waking up elsewhere

     d. A mural of the important events of your visit

     e. How it feels being a stranger

     f. Visiting stores

    2. Cartooning

     a. Collecting various types of cartoons

     b. Analyzing for technique and effectiveness

     c. Drawing several cartoons based on school, local, or national issues

IV. Experiences of the self in industry

  A. Adventures in industry

    1. Painting

     a. Impressions from a visit to the dairy, steel mills, coal mine, brick plant, coke oven, tannery, lumber mill and so on

     b. How you feel while observing the operation of machines

     c. Identifying with workers in different industries

          (1) Being in a steel mill

          (2) Serving the furnace

          (3) Being on the assembly line

    2. Design

     a. Abstraction inspired by machine parts

**Plate 11.** The imagination may be given free rein when the student creates imaginative forms from papier mâché. Topics of this type appeal to a wide age range. Figures represent anything from moon creatures to unheard-of animals.

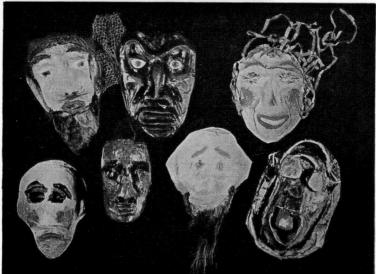

**Plate 12.** One aim of the art program is to develop the ability to think creatively. These papier mâché masks display great diversity in interpreting the problem. Each student's work reflects his degrees of originality and flexibility in the use of the material.

**Plate 13.** Adult art has a tremendous range. Artists work in every area of our life, changing the shape of things around us and seeking new forms of expression. The adolescent should be aware of the possibilities and scope of art. "Numbers in Color" by Jasper Johns is encaustic and collage on canvas. (Courtesy Albright-Knox Art Gallery, Buffalo, New York, Gift of Seymour H. Knox)

      b. Abstraction inspired by motion, rhythm, and accuracy of industry

  3. Drawing

      a. Movements of workers

      b. Carrying a heavy load on the shoulders

      c. A group of workers on the highway

      d. Swinging a pick

      e. Pulling a rope

      f. Pushing a cart

      g. Lifting a bag

      h. Climbing a ladder

      i. Two persons carrying a log

      j. Digging a hole

B. Appreciation for tools and processes in industry

  1. Pottery

      a. Visiting a commercial pottery

      b. Working on the potter's wheel

      c. Experimenting with firing methods

      d. Experimenting with glazing

  2. Textiles

      a. Visiting or seeing a film on the textile industry

      b. Discussing ways of textile printing (block, stencil, silk screen, batik, tie and dye)

      c. Trying one of above methods

  3. Weaving

      a. Using different looms

      b. Hooking

  4. Woodworking

      a. Designing and executing a wood panel

      b. Building a child's toy

      c. Making a simple, functional piece of furniture

  5. Metal working

      a. Use of wire and sheet metal

      b. Designing jewelry

C. Industrial products you buy and use

  1. Displaying objects from your personal belongings that you consider good industrial design and contrasting them with what you consider poor

2. Enumerating the differences
3. Purchasing from a local store an inexpensive article that you consider good industrial design and defending it
4. Selecting from advertisements good industrial products

## EXPERIENCES IN THE HOME

I. Evolution of the home
   A. Evolution of building materials: studying basic materials used in construction of homes during different periods and cultures
   B. Evolution of architectural features (relating to different types of materials: mud, clay, branches, wood, bricks, stone, steel, glass)
      1. Collecting pictures of homes built with different materials
      2. Comparing different kinds of covers (roofs) of houses that were used for protection in different periods and cultures
      3. Discussing what means man has invented to get from the ground level to other levels
      4. Discussing doorways in houses of different cultures
      5. Discussing how hardware developed
      6. Comparing doorknobs
         a. Egyptian
         b. Greek
         c. Roman
         d. Medieval
         e. Renaissance
         f. Colonial
         g. Modern
      7. Drawing conclusions from this comparison
   C. Evolution of furniture
      1. Showing the evolution of a chair, a chest, and so on
      2. Making a list of all movable furniture
         a. In a colonial home
         b. In a contemporary home
      3. Discussing how furniture can function toward better home life
      4. Comparing furniture styles with the change of home styles and home life
      5. Finding in several contemporary chairs what was important to the designer in determining his plan
         a. Material
         b. Function
         c. Design

D. Evolution of utensils
   1. Listing utensils for various rooms
      a. Discussing which were adopted from an older civilization
      b. Discussing which are of contemporary origin
      c. Discussing which are functional
   2. Listing materials used in the making of utensils today and comparing with previous periods
   3. Tracing the development of a spoon
      a. Primitive
      b. Egyptian
      c. African
      d. Greek
      e. Roman
      f. Medieval
      g. Renaissance
      h. American Indian
      i. Colonial
      j. Contemporary
   4. Doing the same with other utensils
      a. The key
      b. The knife
      c. The vase
      d. The lamp
E. Art activities
   1. Design
      a. Drawing to scale the living room of your family and comparing it with that of other periods
      b. Adapting a plan of a colonial living room to present-day use
      c. Discussing what changes were necessary and why you made them
      d. Redecorating your own room or any other room with which you are well acquainted
      e. Making an abstraction of different steps or ramps
      f. Making an abstraction of different building materials
      g. Finding a poorly designed piece of furniture and redesigning it
      h. Discussing what changes were necessary and why
   2. Drawing
      a. Doorways in your locality
      b. Different kinds of stairways in your locality

      c. Different kinds of roofs

      d. Someone sitting in chairs of different periods, to show how posture is determined by the design

        (1) Sling chair

        (2) Contour chair

   3. Painting

      a. How you would feel in different home situations

        (1) Living as a hunter in a paleolithic cave

        (2) Living on a Mississippi River houseboat

        (3) Living in a colonial mansion

        (4) Living in a contemporary home

      b. Abstractions using colors that refer to the different living conditions

      c. Murals

        (1) The evolution of homes

        (2) The evolution of stairways and ramps

        (3) The evolution of the chair

   4. Photography

      a. Gates of different periods in your locality

      b. Entrance doorways of different periods

      c. Houses of various ages

II. Planning the site

  A. Home surroundings

    1. Discussing how character of landscape influences and determines the essential features of house design

    2. Collecting photos of homes that are influenced by the character of the landscape in which they are built

      a. A house in a desert

      b. A house in the mountains

      c. A house on a shore

      d. A house on a hill

      e. Houses in warm climates

      f. Houses in regions with cold winters

    3. Collecting photos of driveways and garages adapted to different surroundings

  B. Location of home on lot

    1. Deciding how you can best locate the house on the lot

      a. Privacy

      b. Sufficient garden area

       c. Outdoor-living area

       d. Convenient garage

       e. Maximum benefits from air, light, and views

   2. Considering restrictions of street or property lines

   3. Suggesting effective means for creating privacy (screens, levels, plantings, trellises, and so on)

C. Building ordinances

   1. Studying your community ordinances prescribing such factors as the location of house on lot, frontages, minimum costs, building materials, and window space

   2. Going through your community to compare the houses according to the restrictions of building ordinances

D. Art activities

   1. Design

       a. Planning a home to conform to a particular area in your own community, keeping in a mind natural trees, lakes, ponds, streams, scenic beauty, and terrain

       b. Designing a house

          (1) On a shore

          (2) On a hill

          (3) In a desert

          (4) In warm climates

          (5) In a cold climate

          (6) On rocky terrain

       c. Collecting products of nature of your vicinity and combining them in an effective arrangement

       d. Designing an outdoor living area for your own home

       e. Designing an outdoor living area for a particular location (mountain, shore, and so on)

       f. Trying to redesign your own house to make it fit your own lot better

   2. Drawing

       a. Landscapes in your immediate vicinity and houses that fit the character of the landscapes

       b. Views from windows, trying by changing the size of the windows, to improve the view

       c. Various outdoor living areas with various activities going on

       d. Crowded areas and slums, showing how you would improve them

3. Photography
   a. Houses on different terrains
   b. Houses with various landscaping
   c. Effective entrances using environment as part of design
   d. Views through windows, keeping the window sill as part of the picture
   e. Views through doorways, of patios, of terraces
4. Sculpturing
   a. Designing outdoor sculpture for specific yards
   b. Designing a fountain sculpture for the yard

III. Interior design
   A. Designing rooms for specific families: zoning according to needs of the family
      1. Diagraming the inside area of your home according to activity zones and quiet zones
      2. Deciding what different zones your family needs
         a. Entertaining
         b. Living
         c. Sleeping
         d. Studying
         e. Eating
         f. Other
      3. Discussing the needs of a family of five
      4. Showing how exterior and interior of a house should harmonize
         a. Collecting pictures in which they do harmonize
         b. Collecting pictures in which exterior design contradicts the interior
      5. Deciding if your room reflects your needs and personality
      6. Deciding how you would change it if you had no limits
   B. Structural parts of rooms (doors, windows, built-in units)
      1. Finding out what kinds of doors you have in your home, collecting illustrations of doors, and deciding which doors (free-swinging, non-swinging, sliding, folding, all glass, flush wood, paneled wood, and so on) you would prefer and why
      2. Collecting illustrations of different kinds of windows
         a. Finding out the different ways by which they can be opened
         b. Going through your community or the outskirts of it and finding out which of the houses with picture windows adhere to the principles that picture windows should make the

landscape a part of your daily enjoyment without interfering with your privacy

3. Deciding what built-in units you know of
   a. Collecting pictures of various fireplaces, bookshelves that are part of the interior architecture, closets of various sizes serving different purposes, seating arrangements.
   b. Examining all these pictures for the relationship of function, design, and material used

C. Choosing colors
   1. Considering exposure, size, use, and personal taste
   2. Making a model room and experimenting by changing the colors of the walls with different color schemes
   3. Deciding what you would do to make the room appear wider, longer, narrower, higher, lower
   4. Planning color schemes for different rooms serving various functions (a quiet room, a music room, a dining room, a bathroom)
   5. Planning color schemes for light rooms, for dark rooms, for different exposures

D. Choosing lighting
   1. Deciding where fixed lighting is needed
   2. Comparing different kinds of lighting fixtures with the design of the home
   3. Comparing fluorescent and incandescent lighting, to decide where you would best use each
   4. Studying different types of lamps (desk lamps, table lamps, floor lamps, wall lamps, ceiling lamps)
   5. Deciding what kinds of lamps you would like to have in your room and why
   6. Studying the difference between the lighting in utility rooms (kitchen, bathroom) and living rooms

E. Furnishing rooms
   1. Studying contemporary designs of furniture for different purposes
   2. Relating function, design, and material to various pieces of furniture

F. Art activities
   1. Design
      a. A table lamp (The base may be made of any material—

plastic, wood, ceramics. The shade must belong to the base. In which surrounding will it be used?)

    b. An outdoor light for a porch, entrance for a driveway, a garage, or activity area

    c. A coffee table

2. Drawing

    a. A home plan, dividing it into activity zones

    b. Activities in different rooms

3. Painting

    a. When you look out the window from different rooms

        (1) Your room

        (2) Your corner

    b. A personal mood as related to your house or your room

4. Weaving place mats (combining different materials)

5. Making on a potter's wheel

    a. A vase

    b. A bowl

    c. A dish

6. Building

    a. A model of a one-story home with two bedrooms, kitchen, living room, bath, showing the division of the interior into rooms (Consider minimum hallways, traffic system, windows, storage, view, doors, built-in closets.)

    b. A table with a tile top from ceramic-tile scraps

    c. A candle holder from wood or metal

    d. Remaking or refinishing a chair, bookcase, and so on

IV. Home life

  A. Family life

    1. Sculpturing

      a. Modeling: Mother and child

      b. Cutting in soft stone: Your family

      c. Carving: Child and his pet

      d. Modeling

        (1) You and your younger brother

        (2) Praying

    2. Drawing

      a. Experimenting with crayon, charcoal, conté crayon, pen, or brush

      b. Going to church

    c. Going on a hike

    d. At the dinner table

    e. An argument

    f. Portraits of the family

  3. Painting families of different incomes, as if you were a member; how people live

  4. Mural painting: Family life from morning to evening

B. Things to do to improve the home

  1. Sketching

    a. Changes you would like to make in your home

    b. Changes in the landscaping of your home

  2. Designing

    a. Bird bath

    b. Fireplace utensils

    c. Mailbox

    d. Towel rack

  3. Hanging pictures so that they can be seen, considering the best light, interference by other items, the level of the viewer

  4. Flower arrangements

    a. Relation of flowers to container

      (1) Color

      (2) Size

    b. Combinations of flowers

    c. Branches

    d. Arrangements of products of nature on trays (moss, shells, rocks, foliage, flowers)

C. Gardening and landscaping

  1. Dividing your yard according to functions

    a. Living area

    b. Recreation area

    c. Play area

    d. Gardening area

      (1) Flower

      (2) Vegetable

  2. Making a plan of your yard

  3. Considering the lawn area in relationship to the planted area

  4. Considering the relationship among shrubs, trees, and flower area

  5. Sculpturing

    a. An out-of-doors figure

    b. A mobile

6. Painting

    a. Your impression of your garden

    b. Your feeling about flowers

    c. A close-up of the part of your garden that you like most

    d. What happens in your garden

7. Woodworking

    a. A bench for your garden

    b. Designing and making a special fence (louvre, slat, solid, woven)

    c. Designing and making a bird house or feeder

8. Design, using as an inspiration the textures, shapes, and colors you find in your garden

    a. A collage

    b. An abstract painting

## EXPERIENCES IN THE COMMUNITY

I. Community planning

  A. Present conditions

    1. Surveying present conditions in your town that need improvements

      a. Painting

        (1) Traffic jam

        (2) Slum areas

        (3) Narrow streets

        (4) Poor housing

        (5) Poor working conditions

        (6) Floods

        (7) Lack of playgrounds

        (8) Children playing on the street

        (9) How people live

        (10) Different social atmospheres

      b. Drawing

        (1) Life on the street

        (2) A building in progress

        (3) Children playing on a vacant lot

    2. Surveying present conditions that you accept

    a. Painting
        (1) Your recreation area
        (2) Your playground
        (3) Newly designed streets
        (4) The skating rink
        (5) A residential area
    b. Drawing
        (1) The new school
        (2) The airport
        (3) The bus station
        (4) The city hall
        (5) Fairs, parades, festivities
    c. Mural painting
        (1) For the school cafeteria
        (2) A cross section of town
            (a) Important activities
            (b) Important buildings
            (c) Important facilities
            (d) Important events
    d. Window display
        (1) A display that stresses uniqueness and quality
        (2) A display for a sale
        (3) One window of a store arranged for a special day
B. Future improvements of your town
    1. Painting
        a. The city of the future
        b. Future traffic
        c. The future city at night
        d. Living in the city of the future
    2. Design
        a. A future airport
        b. A future bus station
        c. A plan for redesigning a part of your town
        d. Shopping center or mall
        e. A bridge
    3. Photography
        a. New and old housing
        b. Narrow and wide streets

      c. Details of architectural designs

      d. Interesting shadows

      e. Textures (various pavements, various building surfaces)

      f. Contrasts (a lonely tree on a building lot, a church near a skyscraper, a bird in traffic)

C. Architectural and landscape design

   1. Art history

      a. The influences on the buildings in your town

      b. The oldest building in your town

      c. The first building that broke with traditional pattern

         (1) Kind of building

         (2) Relationship of the building to the town

         (3) Builder—one person, private group, public group

         (4) Affect on other buildings

      d. Historic buildings, arts, and crafts in your town

         (1) Paintings that refer to your town

         (2) Objects that relate to your town

         (3) Crafts that are peculiar to your town

         (4) People who have contributed to your town

   2. Design

      a. A plan of an ideal farm

      b. An effective, aesthetically pleasing parking lot

      c. A public park

         (1) Landscape areas

         (2) Recreation areas

         (3) Play areas

         (4) A pond

      d. A small city park in front of one of your public buildings

D. Transportation and communication

   1. Design: Inventing your own road signs (stop, slow, curve, crossroad)

   2. Mural painting: A mural for the airport, bus station, post office

   3. Making a soap box racer, a rowboat, or a dinghy

   4. Visiting and discussing the uses of art

      a. Newspaper plants

      b. Television studios

      c. Publishers

E. Interaction with other communities and countries (finding out where the population of your community came from; inviting people from different countries to talk to your group; finding out about their customs and cultures)

1. Painting a mural
   a. Where the people of your town came from
   b. A community festival
   c. The lives of people in various countries
2. Art history
   a. The relationship between art and life in the different periods of history in your town, and in different epochs and cultures, as shown by different houses and how life must have been in them
   b. Influences in your community of other periods and cultures (in buildings, in furniture, in art objects, in merchandise, in utensils)

II. Education and citizenship
   A. Health
      1. Sketching out-of-door activities:
         a. Tennis
         b. Golf
         c. Baseball
         d. Flying kites
      2. Painting
         a. Contrasting clean and dirty (houses, restaurants)
         b. Various functions of a hospital
         c. Emotions or experiences during illness
         d. Unhealthy conditions in housing
   B. School environment and education
      1. Improving the appearance of your classroom
         a. Reorganizing furniture for better function
         b. Adding a well-designed display area
      2. Illustrating your favorite story or book
      3. Visiting museums
         a. Works of local artists
         b. The permanent collection
         c. Types of displays
         d. How traveling exhibits are hung
      4. Exhibits
         a. Arranging products of nature (shells, rocks, moss, plants)
         b. Arranging an exhibit according to a specific topic

        (1) Technique
        (2) Theme
        (3) Material
        (4) Subject matter

5. Excursions
   a. Local artists, musicians, collectors
   b. Newspaper printing
   c. Local craftsman (carpenter, potter, jeweler)
   d. Factories and industries

6. Painting
   a. Listening to a concert at the theater
   b. A visit to the museum
   c. Fire
   d. Studying
   e. Reading in the library
   f. Helping accident victims
   g. In the school bus

III. Recreation
  A. Theater
    1. Formal aspects of stage design
      a. The effect of horizontal and vertical lines in relationship to mood
      b. The effect of different levels
      c. The effect of lighting
      d. The meaning of big spaces versus small spaces
      e. The meaning of foreground and background
      f. The center of interest
      g. The emotional content
      h. The social atmosphere
      i. Period and style
    2. Designing a stage set and lighting
      a. A dramatic scene
        (1) A graveyard
        (2) A wilderness
        (3) A prison
      b. A mass scene
        (1) A riot
        (2) A festival

      (3) A fair

    c. A small village square

    d. A scene in an industrial section or factory court

    e. A drawing-room comedy

  3. Costume: studying the characters of one play and designing the costumes and make up

  4. Masks

    a. Making masks for a specific play

      (1) Fantastic

      (2) Grotesque

    b. Studying masks of different periods and cultures

  5. Puppetry: designing stage set and characters for a puppet show

B. Music

  1. Design

    a. Listening to various musical moods and painting your impressions in abstract designs

    b. Painting abstractions interpreting sound

      (1) A trumpet

      (2) A drum

      (3) A violin

      (4) A flute

    c. Trying to catch rhythm and mood

      (1) A symphony orchestra

      (2) A band

      (3) A jazz orchestra

      (4) A chamber ensemble

    d. Designing a cover for a specific record

  2. Poster designing

    a. Announcing a music festival in your town

    b. Announcing a band concert

    c. Announcing a choir concert

    d. Announcing a chamber-music recital

  3. Sculpturing

    a. A three-dimensional form suggesting music

    b. Masks

      (1) Singing a sad song

      (2) Singing a blue song

      (3) Singing a happy melody

    4. Painting
      a. Listening to a concert
      b. Jazz
    5. Sketching motions of players during a rehearsal
    6. Drawing a layout for a specific program

C. Dance
    1. Costume designing
      a. Costumes for a creative dance (mourning, a clown, depression)
      b. Costumes for a folk dance
    2. Decorating for dance
    3. Designing abstractions of various dance rhythms
      a. Blues
      b. Tango
      c. Jazz
      d. Folk dances
      e. Ballet
      f. Creative dance
    4. Sketching dance motions, one movement in time sequences
    5. Art history: Representations of dance through different periods and cultures
    6. Painting your personal feeling for dance
    7. Sculpturing
      a. A dancer performing a specific dance or rhythm
      b. An abstract form suggesting dance

D. Motion picture, radio, television
    1. Studying a motion picture for its intrinsic qualities
      a. Use of close-ups to direct attention to specific forms or actions
      b. Use of various spaces and times
      c. Use of movement
      d. Mass movements
      e. Insertion of seemingly unrelated parts (such as clouds, storm) underscoring emotions
      f. Fading in
    2. Studying the various forms of films
      a. Entertaining
      b. Instructional
      c. Documentary
      d. Historic, dramatic

3. Studying the differences between stage production and movie making
4. Design
   a. Enclosures for a radio (table radio, portable radio, built-in hi-fi or stereo)
   b. Enclosures for a television set (table model, floor model, built-in unit)
5. Studying television as an art medium: quality of intimacy, spontaneity

E. Outdoor recreation
1. Recreation areas in your community
   a. Desirable locations
   b. Facilities
      (1) For children
      (2) For youth
      (3) For adults
2. Designing a functionally spaced recreation area on a specific locality in your town
   a. For various sports
   b. For playing and games
   c. For sitting and eating
3. Designing and building
   a. A table-bench combination
   b. An outdoor fireplace
   c. Outdoor cooking utensils
4. Sketching actions from nature (sport and play)
5. Painting
   a. Life at a recreation area
   b. The feeling of noise and motion
   c. Cooking outdoors
6. Designing a fountain or sculpture for a recreation area

## EXPERIENCES IN NATURE

I. Interpretation of nature's principles
A. Changes and growth
1. Painting
   a. How plant-life growth or death affects the landscape (desert, barren land, farm land)
   b. Seasonal changes (summer, fall, winter, spring)

       c. Sky and cloud changes, showing effects of time of day on nature and cloud formations

    2. Discussing and painting

       a. How increases in population affect our landscape

         (1) Urban

         (2) Rural

       b. Effects of industry on nature

         (1) Factories

         (2) Strip mining

         (3) Coal mining

       c. Effects of rise and fall of population on nature

B. Nature's varying moods: painting or abstract design

    1. How you feel on rainy days

    2. How you feel on cold days

    3. How you feel on hot days

    4. Varying winds, storms, tornadoes, and floods

    5. Sunshine after a heavy rain

    6. Shifting mists on the hills

C. Nature's motions

    1. Photography and mobiles

       a. Effects of wind on nature

         (1) Sand and snow

         (2) The moving clouds

         (3) The swaying trees

         (4) Fields of grain

       b. Effects of water on nature

         (1) Raindrops

         (2) Waterfalls

         (3) Swift rapids

         (4) Whirlpools

    2. Sketching

       a. Galloping horse

       b. Hopping frog

       c. Flying bird

D. Color and light

    1. Abstractions

       a. Seasons' colors

       b. Climatic effects on color and light

(1) How weather affects landscape (red hills, desert, mountains, snow coverage)

(2) Various lights (rainbow, moon, sun, stars)

   2. Outdoor water-color and oil painting

E. Texture and collage

   1. Photography of weather and wear

     a. Sand and water ripples

     b. Rock and pebble forms

     c. Tidal effects

     d. Snow drifts, an individual snowflake

   2. Design

     a. From sea structures (sea gardens, sea shells)

     b. Based on sea inhabitants and organisms

     c. Based on land structure (rock formation, landscapes)

     d. From dead or alive tree parts, stones, plants

     e. Based on texture qualities of soil through man's manipulation (cultivation, harvest time)

II. Getting the most from nature

A. Natural resources

   1. Abstract design

     a. Making a decorative piece from bark, rock, leaves, wood

     b. Making a collage of natural materials stressing variety of line, shape, form, texture, and color

     c. Making pottery and ceramic pieces from native clay

     d. Carving interesting shapes from local wood

   2. Studying the source of materials, providing experiences in making dyes, pigments, paper, tools for carving and modeling

B. Landscape design

   1. Design

     a. Arrangement of an informal garden for your own home

     b. Color sketches that show plans for a year-round pleasing effect in a garden

     c. Planning, designing, and building a model of a home that utilizes the landscape design as a purposeful part of the living arrangement

   2. Public landscape design

     a. Designing and sketching suitable landscape arrangements for a public building in your community

   b. Planning and making sketches for a spacious-appearing city park to include activities adaptable to many interests and age levels

   c. Planning a design to scale for a state forest-conservation park

III. Clothing

  A. Climate

   1. Seasons: considering your clothes according to weight of material, style, colors from nature

   2. Weather: studying weather-proof materials, weight of materials, style

   3. Latitude: studying weight of materials, style and colors according to highlands or lowlands

  B. Costume design

   1. Clothes for boys and girls for changes in weather and latitude.

   2. Outfits for various sports

IV. Geographic and climatic influences on culture

  A. Nature's way with materials

   1. Studying the effects of weather and time on various materials—such as iron, wood, brick, paint—to determine which age or weather "gracefully" and the implications of weathering for architecture

   2. Collage: weathered materials

   3. Photography: architecture with well-weathered materials

   4. Sketching shapes in nature influenced by weather in their growth or through wear of the elements

    a. A weathered rock

    b. A weathered pine

    c. A rock hollowed or shaped by a stream

    d. Stalagmites and stalactites

   5. Looking at weathered textures through a microscope

   6. Design: An abstract painting using the textures of nature

  B. Art history—comparative study of cultures influenced by nature

   1. Art activities: finding photographs of art work from different cultures (Egyptian, Greek, Chinese, Japanese), noting the use of native materials, and listing common qualities

   2 Mural painting: the relationship of natural setting, culture, and art work in your region, characterizing the variety of terrain, types of vegetation, climate, weather

**EXPERIENCES IN INDUSTRY**

I. Crafts
   A. Pottery
      1. Wedging the clay
      2. Working on the potter's wheel
      3. Firing methods
      4. Glazing
      5. Tracing the history of pottery from the early beginning to contemporary designs of dinnerware and showing its relationship to social changes
      6. Discussing relationships between material, design, and function
         a. A Greek vase
         b. Mexican pottery
         c. Italian majolica
         d. English Wedgwood
         e. Contemporary dinnerware
      7. Visiting a pottery shop in your town and noticing the different places where the pottery was produced
      8. Finding clay deposits in your environment
      9. Making a simple outdoor kiln
      10. From broken glazed pottery, making a mosaic—sticking the parts to a paper, framing it, pouring plaster or concrete over it, and then removing the paper
   B. Textile design
      1. Discussing and experimenting with textile printing
         a. Block printing
         b. Stencil printing
         c. Silk screen
         d. Batik
         e. Tie and dye
      2. Discussing and experimenting with weaving
         a. Hooking
         b. Needle point
         c. Gobelin
      3. Collecting and discussing textile prints in different cultures and countries
      4. Discussing the difference in a printed textile when flat and when hanging in folds

5. Following the history of the loom from the self-made loom of tribal primitives to that of our modern cloth factories

6. Relating the type of weaving, its pattern and design, to the culture in which it was produced—comparing a Mexican rug, for instance, with a Persian rug

7. Making a simple handloom and experimenting to find different patterns that grow out of the process of weaving

8. Visiting a rug store and finding out where the rugs were made

9. Tracing the history of Gobelin and relating the technique used to its period

C. Woodworking

1. Discussing how the tool determines the shape of the object and the object determines the tool

2. Showing differences of carving marks in soft and hard wood

3. Carving
   a. A free form
   b. A spoon
   c. A wood sculpture

4. Turning on a lathe
   a. A candle holder
   b. A lamp base
   c. A bowl

5. Carpentry design and execution
   a. A table
   b. A toy
   c. A bench

D. Paper working

1. Folding the paper and cutting it

2. Shaping paper forms and combining them

3. Forming with papier-mâché

4. Tracing the history of paper from the early Egyptian papyrus to the present day

5. Listing and experimenting with the different uses of paper (and related material such as cardboard and fiberboards)
   a. Making fold cuts, and folding the paper in different ways
   b. Making paper sculptures by combining the different processes of folding, shaping, and cutting
   c. Using different lighting effects on paper sculpture
   d. Using paper bags for masks and combining with other

processes, such as cutting, folding, or shaping

e. Using papier-mâché for making a free form, a mask, an animal, a strange creature

E. Metalworking
1. Shaping
   a. A copper bowl
   b. A wire sculpture consisting of round and flattened wire
   c. A ring with a setting for a stone
2. Forging
   a. A metal frame for a chair
   b. A fireplace set
   c. A hot-dog fork
3. Soldering
   a. Wire sculpturing with use of soft solder wire
   b. Jewelry making with use of hard solder
      (1) Pins on brooches
      (2) Settings on rings
4. Selecting works of arts and crafts and finding the various processes that were used
   a. A French gate
   b. A forged English sword
   c. An Italian Renaissance bowl
   d. Mexican jewelry
   e. Contemporary silverware
5. Visiting metal shops
6. Relating the process to design in various metal products of different periods and cultures

F. Synthetic materials
1. Experimenting with methods of handling (shaping, pressing, molding)
2. Exploring the use of different synthetic materials such as plastics, vinyl, rubber, Fiberglas
3. Making a simple platter, a bowl, a sculpture
4. Investigating the use of vinyl, rubber, asphalt, and linoleum tiles in building. Experimenting with floor patterns for kitchen or bathroom floors
5. Listing as many objects now made of synthetic materials as you can think of, then discussing what they were formerly made of
6. Making a mold as a form for plastics

   G. Relating different materials to each other
      1. Making collages of different materials
      2. Making a floor lamp using different materials
      3. Exploring various relationships of materials in furniture and architecture
         a. Textiles and wood
         b. Stone and metal
         c. Metal and wood
         d. Wood and stone
         e. Glass and metal
      4. Tracing the combination of different materials through various periods and cultures

II. Assembly-line and other industrial processes
   A. Effect on the self
      1. Discussing how the assembly line affects your standard of living
      2. Discussing how problems of production were solved in the era preceding the assembly-line procedure
      3. Naming advantages and disadvantages caused by assembly-line production
         a. Sameness of work
         b. Quality of work
         c. Effect on individual problem solving
         d. Mass participation in inventions
         e. Prefabrication
         f. Reduced prices
         g. Equalization of standards
         h. Individual expression
   B. Effect on the community
      1. Discussing how your community has been affected by industry
         a. City planning
            (1) Mass settlements
            (2) Apartment houses
            (3) Air and water pollution
            (4) Parking and traffic problems
         b. Planning of homes
            (1) Functional furniture
            (2) Kitchen and utensils
            (3) Bathrooms
            (4) Outdoor living

        c. Environmental changes caused by industrialization
          (1) Mining
          (2) Factories
          (3) Transportation facilities
          (4) Agriculture

III. Advertising
    1. Designing an appropriate container for a specific article (perfume, auto parts, ink, milk, foodstuffs, mechanical instruments)
    2. Making a model package, considering proportions, color, public appeal, material, novelty
    3. Designing an advertising layout for a product
        a. In a magazine
        b. For a billboard
        c. For a newspaper page
    4. Studying psychological appeal of advertisements

IV. Consumer education
    A. Self
        1. Selecting inexpensive household utensils of good design
        2. Discussing the relationship of function, purpose, design, and material
        3. Selecting from a furniture catalogue the table and chair you like best
          a. Comparing them with those you like least
          b. Naming at least four major differences between the "good" and "bad" table and chair
        4. Selecting from a book on houses the house you feel comes closest to your taste
          a. Why you like it, in detail
          b. Utilization of space
          c. Harmony of inside with outside
          d. Functional use of materials
          e. Use of textures
        5. Selecting and studying a painting with which you would like to live
          a. Reasons for appeal
          b. Agreement (or disagreement) with your environment
        6. Studying the appeal of various types of package design by showing several kinds of people different designs and recording their reactions

B. Home
1. Studying the proper choice of furnishings and household equipment (iron, washer, stove, table, chairs, lamps) in relationship to income (the best-designed washer or easy chair for low and high income groups, for instance)
2. Evaluating home furnishings according to price of product, design quality, material, and durability
3. From the houses of your community, selecting and discussing homes of good design for low and high income groups
4. Discussing poorly designed and well-designed prefabricated houses

C. Community
1. Redesigning a poorly developed housing section of your community
2. Discussing the effect of advertisement on the appearance of your community
   a. Billboards
   b. Neon lights
   c. Advertisements on houses
   d. Window displays
3. Selecting "good effects" on the appearance of your community
   a. Determining the characteristics of good effects
   b. Determining what you consider poor
4. Studying means by which you could make your community more "art conscious"
   a. Placing good paintings or reproductions in the town library
   b. Starting a display in your library of various crafts or other well-designed articles
   c. Starting an adult art program
   d. Asking stores to collaborate in the display of well-designed products

V. Transportation
A. Evolution of design
1. Discussing the evolution of car designs
2. Comparing the evolution of car designs with designs of other things
   a. Living areas
   b. Kitchen appliances
   c. Churches

     d. Schools

     e. Factories

B. Design topics

  1. Highway patterns resulting from intersections

  2. Effective highway signs for intersections, or other warnings

  3. Studying the design of various kinds of vehicles according to their functions

     a. Truck designs

       (1) For lumbering

       (2) For moving

       (3) For hauling dirt

       (4) For loading and unloading

     b. Airplane designs

       (1) For passengers

       (2) For hauling loads

       (3) For various war purposes

     c. Boat and ship designs

       (1) For passengers

       (2) For carrying airplanes

       (3) For carrying freight

       (4) For various war purposes

       (5) For pleasure

C. Painting your personal feeling when traveling

  1. In a train (the landscape swiftly passing by)

  2. In an airplane (cloud formations, patterns of various landscape textures)

  3. In a car (highways, endless or rolling terrain, curves)

  4. In a boat (water in its different moods, reflections)

  5. At a railway terminal

  6. At a bus stop

  7. At an airport

D. Sketching

  1. Trucking at night

  2. Impressions on the highway

  3. A marshaling yard (at night in the rain, during busy hours, when idle)

E. Landscaping

  1. Planning a roadside rest area

  2. Designing landscaping for a section dividing highways

# The Meaning of Skills and Techniques in the Secondary School

The development of skills is an important part of a program in art education for the secondary schools. It is through these skills that the adolescent gains confidence in his art expression. The characteristics of adolescent individuals must be seriously considered in motivations. Ambition, persistence, self-criticism, introspection, and also a desire for romance and adventure are traits that will best be served by an experimental attitude toward skills and toward the development of art techniques. It can be seen, then, that the crafts can assume an important role in the art program. It must, however, be kept in mind that a balanced program necessitates emphasizing the meaning of those forms of art where the adolescent individual can directly project his thinking, perceiving, and feeling.

As we have discussed in the preceding chapter, the adolescent suddenly becomes critically aware of the immaturity of his product. He can easily become discouraged by the "primitiveness" and "naïveté" of his drawings, and often seems afraid to project his thinking directly upon the paper. The adolescent is disturbed by the discrepancy between what he produces and what he feels is appropriate for an adult to draw or paint. A very direct approach to this problem would be to enlarge his concept of adult art. Certainly the fresh, and in some cases the blunt, painting of some contemporary artists may awaken the adolescent to new possibilities. Even older masters such as Chagall and Klee painted in a very unsophisticated manner. Another fruitful direction is to involve the student with materials and techniques in which the end product is not as readily comparable to adult products. The adolescent has now developed the ability to work with more intricate procedures, and in some cases these can be a real challenge (see Figure 88).

Before discussing specific techniques for the secondary school, it seems important to refer to the distinction between procedures and techniques. Procedures can be explained, but techniques are highly individual and therefore develop according to personal desires. The relationship of an individual to his technique is more an outcome of his experiences in the world that surrounds him than a result of learned skill. If a technique becomes separated from individual expression, it is then only a handicraft, which may even restrict the individual instead of encourage him. For example, a haptically minded student would become discouraged with oil

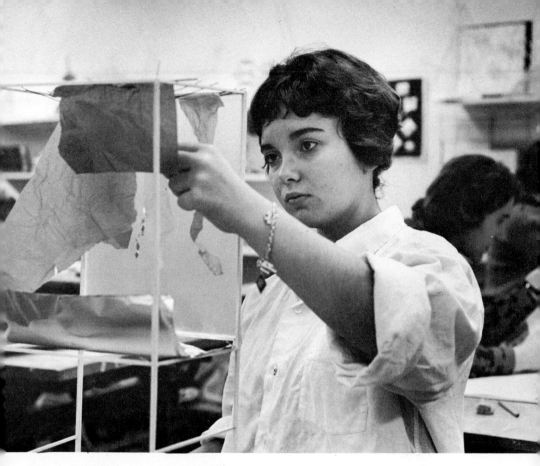

**Figure 88.** The student is challenged by the possibilities of a fresh approach to using materials, because in this way there are no set adult standards.

painting if he were shown an impressionistic method of painting nature. The complex colors that are the results of visual analysis would only confuse him, whereas his thinking and experiencing might be more related to an expression of line and subjective color relationships. Technique and individuality are closely interwoven; therefore, techniques should be developed and not taught. Procedures are those steps to prepare materials, to maintain their working consistency, and to clean and preserve the results.

There should be no inference here that the instructor is to hold back or refrain from discussing new or different methods of working with materials. Rather, these techniques should not be imposed upon students. The student who reaches an impasse, or who becomes dissatisfied with his means of expression, should be given encouragement, and many suggestions for possible solutions should be exchanged. Success in creative art does not come easily, as any practicing artist will testify. The working through a problem, the development of several possible solutions, the encouragement toward flexibility, and the final achievement of at least partial success will lead to a development of technique. The best technique is therefore developed by each individual and will permit him to express himself more easily and with greater depth.

Since art education in the secondary school does not prepare for a profession but rather serves to develop the mental, aesthetic, and creative growth of the individual, the teaching of skills must be focused upon the problem of finding adequate means of expression for the student. All skills, therefore, must be introduced with the purpose of fostering the individual's free expression.

### SKETCHING

The putting of marks from a pencil, charcoal, or other drawing material onto a page of paper is a very direct and fundamental art experience. At one time the mechanics of drawing or sketching were considered essential for students to learn before the student could actually draw or sketch. Much time was spent practicing various types of strokes and in drawing boxes at various angles. Once the student had mastered these mechanics of "how to draw," he was expected to be able to sketch from nature and develop coordination of the hand and eye. However, sketching can be a means of personal expression, since the line itself is an abstraction. The line can have kinesthetic origin, the feeling of motion, or it can be symbolic of form, an outline. Although there are many drawing instruments available, a wax crayon or marking crayon has good qualities for quick direct sketches. Since erasing is impossible, no attention should be paid to making a finished, polished product. In fact, in expressive art every line has significance, for even unintended lines have expressive quality, somewhat like the quality of *Fehlleistungen,* which plays a role in psychoanalysis.[4] Direct expressive sketching tends to be akin to handwriting in that it tells about a visual scene rather than reproduces it. Smooth paper is preferable to paper with a rough texture because the latter would divert from the smooth, gliding, one-dimensional character of a line. Brush and ink, brush and paint, lithographic pencil, conté crayon, or charcoal can also be used for sketching.

Charcoal, because of its adaptability to changes of shading, can be easily used for three-dimensional sketching. The visually inclined student who is concerned with changes in atmosphere, light, shadow, and distance will find that charcoal is flexible and changeable. Soft pencil, graphite sticks, or chalk can also be used with advantage for sketching three-dimensional subject matter. For these techniques coarse paper is preferable since it lends itself to texture and to the effect of depth and atmosphere.

## PAINTING

We are discussing here the contained, individual painting whether done on an easel or on the floor, whether small in size or as large as a wall, whether painted with oil paint, tempera, casein, or water color. This type of painting is usually not illustrative like a mural but rather is more the artist's direct approach to the world of his experiences. It is an intimate expression of emotions, ideas, or observations, both visual and nonvisual, of the artist's surroundings. The student's personality and the subject matter will determine the appropriate method of approach to achieve the desired expressive qualities. It is the responsibility of the teacher to recognize individual differences and guide students into the method that is most suitable for the attainment of their own goals (see Figure 89). As we discussed, some students will want models for visual inspiration; other students will be hampered by what they see, since they use means other than visual stimuli as starting points for their artistic experiences. Still other students will be more concerned with structure and the design quality of their paintings; some will be more imaginative in their thinking and treat a painting in a more fanciful manner.

There is no one "correct" technique of painting. Not only does each student need to develop his own approach to painting, but also his method should vary with the subject matter and not be considered a rigid formula. A medium such as water color lends itself to quick, spontaneous impressions, whereas tempera paint can be used much more deliberately. Indeed, tempera does not lend itself to studies of nature or to atmospheric effects; however, it can be used very effectively in a decorative manner or where atmospheric effects would be distracting. Many students look upon oil painting as the professional painter medium, and therefore it has much appeal for this age. The plastic quality of oil painting is better suited to some students than to others, and there is no reason to impose this material upon all students. Paper or cardboard can be used successfully with water color and tempera paint. The ground for oil paintings can be stretched canvas, hard-board panels, or plywood.

The preparation of the painting surface and the care of the painting medium should be a part of the total painting experience for the student.

**Figure 89.** Students must be encouraged to set their own goals and develop their own techniques.

For the teacher to prepare in advance materials for student use tends to make this experience less effective as a means for continued expression after the student leaves school. That is, the experience of painting should be looked upon as a continuing interest and the student should not be dependent upon the teacher for preparing these basic materials.

Painting from nature can be an exciting experience and historically includes the bulk of artists' endeavors. Often quick sketches can be made of nature and these can be combined into a painting. The direct painting from nature is usually done in one sitting, and water color lends itself to this nicely. Painting with water color on a paper that has been previously soaked can give quite a different effect from painting on a rough, dry surface. Different textures from smooth to very pebbly can also change the results. Different brushes, from small hair brushes to bristle brushes, may be tried by students. It should be pointed out that the teacher is primarily concerned with developing enthusiasm and fostering the students' own expression rather than trying to make everyone an "artist."

Tempera does not lend itself very well to painting in nature because its contours are sharp and its colors are not "atmospheric." However, experimentation in tempera can be tried, and its opaque color can sometimes be combined with water color for interesting effects. If tempera white is added to water colors, the technique is called gouache. Although tempera paint and water color are usually not mixed in one painting, there is no reason for not doing so, particularly if a student is impressed with the transparency of the air and the surface structure of a nearby object.

In oil paint there are many approaches to the painting of nature. The surface may be built up with a series of thin washes, or the paint may be thickly applied with a palette knife. Colors can be mixed directly on the canvas, can be applied in an impressionistic fashion, or can be mixed on the palette. A teacher should have a broad understanding of the technical possibilities and be able to adjust these to the individual desires of his students.

### MURAL PAINTING

Whereas an easel picture is an expression of emotions, ideas, or impressions, separated from its surroundings by a frame, a mural is a part of another whole—architecture. The size of the mural is predetermined by the architect. The painter has to adjust to whatever problems arise from the use of a wall as his painting surface (see Figure 90). The first problem in designing a mural, therefore, is to adjust the composition to the architecture for which it is planned. In some cases the shape available can be an interesting challenge to the student. In a good mural, architecture and mural should be closely interwoven so that one improves the other.

The second problem is that the mural must be part of the wall, and of the architecture as a whole. The painter should not paint a "hole" in a wall but rather should consider the mural as a decoration not in conflict with its architectural meaning. Therefore, a mural cannot stress a perspective of depth, but should distribute the composition over the whole wall space.

A third problem in mural painting relates to content. Since a mural is painted as part of the wall, it must be adapted to the purpose of the structure within which it appears. For example, the subject matter of a mural in a dance hall would be quite different from the subject matter of a mural in a church. A mural is therefore much more than a picture; it is also a means of communication, telling a story or transmitting an idea or concept.

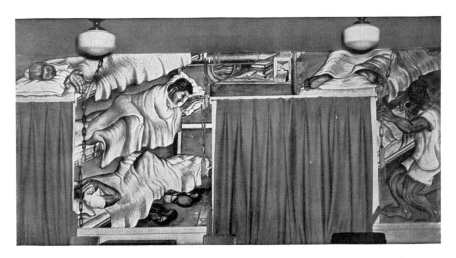

**Figure 90.** This is a section of a large mural painted by John T. Biggers. Here the architectural features provided a challenge to the artist to adjust his composition to take advantage of the space available to him. The result shows a unity of the mural with the architecture.

A mural can either be considered a permanent part of a building or be thought of as being a temporary decoration. If the mural is planned to be of lasting character, it must first be planned in detail. Historic, social, religious, or scientific themes can be used very successfully for mural paintings, and thereby provide an excellent opportunity to integrate learning in other fields with art. Schools usually have many walls that can be utilized for a mural. The cafeteria, auditorium, gymnasium, and of course the many halls—all provide potential surfaces for a mural. If proper care is taken to insure the adhesive quality of the paint, these murals may be painted over at some future time if necessary.

In contrast to the planned mural, the direct mural is applied directly to the surface with only rough sketches. These murals are used for special occasions rather than for lasting value. The surface may be the wall itself, a canvas secured to the wall, or large building boards. The subject for a direct mural is usually some special occasion, a dance, graduation, or some sporting event. It will be removed after the occasion is over and will be replaced by another. This type of mural is usually popular with the student body and is easily understood and appreciated. A latex-base paint can be used, and large brushes or rollers can cover areas quickly.

Groups of students can work satisfactorily on the direct mural. This has distinct social values, particularly if every participant subordinates his own contribution to the whole and the spirit or theme of the mural predominates. This is especially true if the mural is going to be used for a background for a play or other production where the student can feel a part of a larger accomplishment. Proper organization is important so that all students can participate in some function. In the planned mural some loss of artistic unity is to be expected if the mural is painted by a group. Where a long hall or very large wall is to be painted, individual panels can be integrated into a total with rather dramatic results.

## SCULPTURING

The three-dimensional expression of emotions, thoughts, or impressions of nature is the essence of sculpturing. Since the representation of environment is of necessity excluded, many students who have little desire and understanding for expressing themselves in painting will find much release and enjoyment in the realm of three-dimensional expression. The more visually inclined student will be more concerned with surface appearances and differences in sizes and proportions, whereas the student who is more haptically inclined will concentrate more on his subjective expression and kinesthetic experiences in the sculpture. We will continue to find some students who will build a total from many partial impressions in a synthetic technique and also some students who will achieve a form by cutting away unnecessary parts until the final form is reached through an analytic process. Most students, of course, will use both methods or whichever is most appropriate to the material at hand. Since the chief aim of teaching sculpturing in the secondary school classroom is to promote growth, and not to give special professional training, any method that is natural for the student can be used as a basis for developing understanding and knowledge about sculpturing for expression.

Clay is the most popular material for three-dimensional work. The simplest approach is to model from a solid lump of clay, with no parts standing out, so that an armature or wire frame is unnecessary. Clay can be kept in workable consistency by the use of wet rags and a plastic wrapping. Properly handled and prepared clay sculpturing can be fired if the facilities are available. However, this is often difficult to do with large pieces, and the danger of air bubbles and fragile parts adds to the firing difficulties. If it is necessary to make the clay sculpture into permanent form, it is often necessary to cast it into another material.

Casting should be looked upon not as merely transferring a clay sculpture into a more permanent form but rather as an extension of the artistic production. The rationale behind casting is quite simple; however, the procedure can get complicated. The material used is usually plaster, which is poured over the clay form and allowed to dry. This outside husk is then taken apart along a seam of metal shims, which were, hopefully, put into the clay before the plaster was poured. Once the clay is cleaned out of the parts of the mold, the inside is cleaned and given a coat of soap to seal the plaster. When put back together, the inside of the mold can be poured full of plaster or coated with molten metal. Once dry, the original mold can be chipped off. It is suggested that students try several castings to understand the process rather than be concerned with making a perfect reproduction of their original clay work. The final product should look as if it had been cast and not be an imitation of the original.

A more direct approach to permanency in sculpture is to use plaster directly over a wire frame or rough screening. This approach allows the student to mix the plaster in small containers (the inside of half an old rubber ball does nicely) and to build his sculpture with a feeling for the quality of the material itself (see Figure 91). Sand or sawdust can be added to the plaster for a variety of textural quality. A combination of building up areas by addition and chipping or filing down areas can be achieved in one sculpture. It should be emphasized that the creative concept must grow out of the material from which it is created. Many subjects are not suitable for sculpturing. Making a sculpture of a hazy autumn day would be quite ridiculous, and the student should be aware of this.

Carving in wood and cutting in stone are decisively different from working in clay or plaster. In a plastic material the student may choose

**Figure 91.** "Man Reading." This plaster sculpture takes advantage of the natural qualities of the material.

to build, up a sculpture out of partial impressions or to form it from the whole, whereas in carving or cutting the sculpture must be arrived at by the process of elimination. We can therefore expect that some students may have difficulty in visualizing the form within the block of stone or chunk of wood.

Carving in wood and cutting in stone must grow out of the material itself. Different woods have different grains, different cutting qualities, and these differences should be utilized in the working process. It seems logical, therefore, that the sculpture cannot be preplanned, but the planning process must go hand in hand with a developing knowledge of the material itself. Some woods lend themselves to cutting small details, whereas other types of wood are best for subjects utilizing rough texture.

Woods commonly used for carving are apple, pear, chestnut, walnut, mahogany, and some varieties of pine. In stone cutting almost any stone without faults or cracks or definite grain can be used. The harder varieties are much more difficult to use unless a pneumatic hammer is available. Softer stone can be readily worked by hand tools, however, and smaller size sculpture can often be done in the schoolyard. Artificial stone, building blocks, or blocks of insulation material can also be used; these materials should not be considered as substitutes for stone but should be approached as having sculptural qualities of their own.

**Figure 92.** This papier mâché mask of an ugly hag, complete with adhesive bandages, resulted from an adolescent's experimentation with the expressive possibilities of the material.

Mention should be made of masks and puppets, which can be a most inspiring and useful art form. These are sometimes carved from wood, made from clay, fashioned from fabric, or formed out of papier-mâché (see Figure 92). Satirical self-portraits, portrayals of particular moods or emotions, representations of particular personality types such as the school athlete, a crotchety old woman, the play-boy—all lend themselves as subject matter for puppet making. Psychologically these have value in developing a greater awareness for the adolescent of himself and of those feelings and emotions portrayed. This is especially true if these puppets and masks are actually used to put on spontaneous drama.

Masks and puppets are usually painted, because this adds to their expressive quality. They are not intended to be natural. Sculpture itself, however, is rarely painted since the material that has been carved or cut should have its own characteristics and beauty. Painting tends to hide or conceal these natural qualities. When three-dimensional works are used for a purpose beyond themselves, such as communicating a message or mood in the theater or in a medieval altar group, the sculpture loses its meaning as an expression itself and becomes a part of another symbolic form. In this case the beauty of the material itself becomes subordinated to the literary meaning of the work of art, and paint can be added to further this meaning.

## PRINTING

The printing or graphic techniques are removed from a direct approach to art because the student must alter a block, plate, or stencil, which in turn prints the final product. Because of this intermediate step in the art process, students who tend to be more spontaneous in their art approach may not get the satisfaction from this type of art experience. Because of the time involved in getting to understand particular printing processes and the questionable value of having many examples of a particular print available, printing tend to be less popular in the secondary schools. In some instances where courses are offered in one or more of these printing techniques, so much time is spent in learning the technical process and developing the necessary mastery over the materials that little time is left for true artistic creation. Except for producing Christmas cards few people beyond the secondary school ever develop or continue an interest in the graphic procedures. For those students who develop an interest in the area of prints much work in the technical process is required beyond what can be offered in the public schools. However, there are simple

possibilities such as printing with natural materials as in Figure 93 that can be used to broaden the student's viewpoint in the arts; in some cases printing can rekindle an interest in painting or sketching.

The linoleum print can be mastered quite easily. It is essential that the student be given ample opportunity to cut lines and shapes into a linoleum block so as to develop an understanding of this material rather than to merely transfer a drawing to the linoleum. The final print or design should be readily recognized as a linoleum block print and not attempt to be a naturalistic representation (see Figure 94). In principle, wood-

**Figure. 93.** Sensitivity to natural forms may be developed by printing with materials such as potatoes, onions, peppers, and carrots.

cutting is the same as linoleum, except for the effect of the grain upon the print and the greater difficulty in mastering the carving and gouging techniques.

A monoprint can sometimes be used to stimulate interest in the effect of a technique upon the product. Printer's ink is rolled upon a sheet of glass in some interesting pattern, and a sheet of absorbent paper is pressed or rolled over the ink. A variety of textures can be added to the ink, or the paper can be drawn upon while it is on the inked surface. This procedure is one that capitalizes upon the accidental and therefore cannot be

**Figure 94.** A linoleum cut by a thirteen-year-old child shows the nature of the cutting process determining the design.

thought of as a truly expressive material. It does have value, however, for those students who feel restricted in their approach to art.

The silk screen is used primarily as a two-dimensional, decorative printing device. As a modified form of the stencil its main function is to make easier the mass production of one design. Since the role of the public schools is not that of training employees for industry and since the textile designer needs specialized training, it is inappropriate to spend considerable time upon the printing methods.

### DESIGN

Too often design is thought of as being primarily a decorative addition to a surface, to an object, or to some structure. We have often seen a teapot with a "cute design" placed on one side. There are many trays, pieces of furniture, large appliances, or even whole houses available in "colonial style," "modern style," "provincial style," or "Victorian style." The secondary school is an excellent place to begin to re-educate toward a feeling for design as an integral part of the function and use of an object or of a material.

The word *functional,* therefore, refers to three equally important relationships: (1) the relationship between design and material, (2) the relationship of design to tools or machinery, and (3) the relationship between design and purpose. For example, a piece of pottery made on a potter's wheel should look as if it were indeed made on the potter's wheel. How often we see the beautiful form of the dynamic whirling effect, which is a natural and functional outcome of the process of turning, spoiled by having the surface smoothed and "perfected" until the relationship of the pottery to the potter's wheel is lost. The object will perform better with the principles of functional design when this relationship between the design and the material and its tools are maintained. The more we hide the effects of the working methods, the more we move away from the truth of functional designing. The purpose of a vase may be purely decorative, in which case it needs to be able to stand, or be hung, or be heavy enough so that it will not be easily knocked over. If the purpose of the pot is to hold flowers, however, its glaze must not compete with the flowers, nor should the pot be too wide or narrow for such a purpose.

The greater the variety of materials with which a student works, the wider will be his range of experiences. Whether he is working in clay, wood, metal, or cloth, he should be aware of the close interdependence of the material and the purpose for which it is intended. It is only when the nature of the material is thoroughly understood that plans can be made for this material. Therefore, many experiences are necessary to acquaint the student with the qualities inherent within these materials.

The interrelationship between textures, colors, and qualities of different materials can be very stimulating. Scraps of wood, metal, textiles, plastics, and paper can be arranged in such a way that they produce an excellent "symphony" of textures and shapes. Actually touching and enjoying the variety of textural qualities can be pleasurable in itself and can also stimulate the visual experience associated with the different types of textures, such as different grains of wood, weaves of textiles, and so forth. Such designs can be two- or three-dimensional, static or mobile (see Figure 95). Seeing how such experiments relate to interior designs can be exciting. The functional qualities of a material itself provide an important basis for design.

It is quite apparent that few people would purchase a toothbrush with a Victorian handle or one with an embossed design of flowers. The bristles

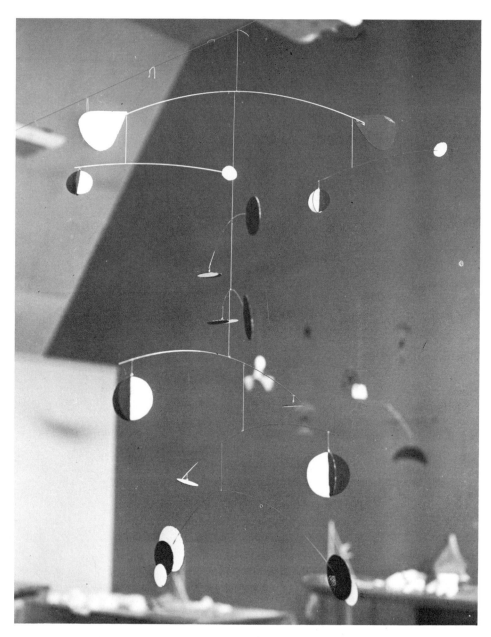

**Figure 95.** Materials may relate to one another in unusual ways, as in this mobile where forms are visually and physically interdependent.

of a toothbrush are not arranged in little scalloped designs, nor do they attempt to look like something other than bristles. However, we often find tableware with roses on the handle, lamps with scallops on the shade, and chairs with lion's paws for legs. The average American is rather up to date when it comes to the matter of finding a better kind of transportation—the newest car cannot be new enough—or a better kind of range or refrigerator. In his living room, however, he apparently wants to hide from today's world and is content with the furniture styled for his ancestors, electing flowers for his living room rug and a colonial weather vane for his garage. The question is more than that of just introducing the correct type of modern furniture or contemporary homes to the public. Our youth must be made aware of the discrepancy between the demand for truth and the quest for scientific knowledge on the one hand and our acceptance of imitation, eighteenth-century styles and cute designs of flowers on the other. To a great extent this must be a first-hand learning experience, for there is no formula of "right" answers.

The main characteristic of good design is a relationship between materials, tools, and purpose. This means that the student should have a concept of the interrelationship between these while working on a project. For example, a piece of furniture should have no meaningless ornaments, since they do not contribute to the purpose of the furniture. On the contrary, as dust-collectors they would only be detrimental to living comfort. The design itself grows out of the beauty of the different materials used. The natural qualities of the materials should be utilized and preserved as much as possible. Wood, glass, textile, metal, should each be used in its own right. Simplicity in line is an important principle of modern functional furniture, with variation introduced by the use of different materials. Fine workmanship is an integral part of the design itself, and joints and braces need not be hidden under a decorative cover.

Many people within our society walk around blind to much of the natural beauty within our environment. This area should not be ignored. Focusing attention upon producing art only will sadly neglect the tremendous impact and pleasure that can be derived from a sensitive awareness of the beauty in nature. In the next chapter we will focus upon aesthetics, but it is important to emphasize that materials and textures, a batch of grass seed (see Figure 96) or a large panorama, a fish net (see Figure 97) or the cast of shadow, can contain the essence of beauty for those who are sensitive to it.

Much of the art that is done by individuals after leaving the secondary

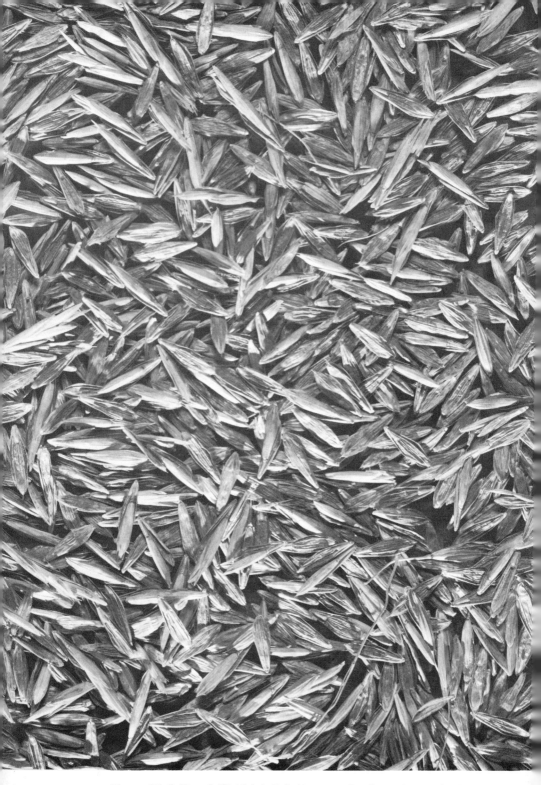

**Figures 96 (left) and 97 (right).** It is important for the student to develop a sensitivity to the beauty that occurs in his surroundings. Commonplace things such as grass seed and fish nets may be aesthetically satisfying.

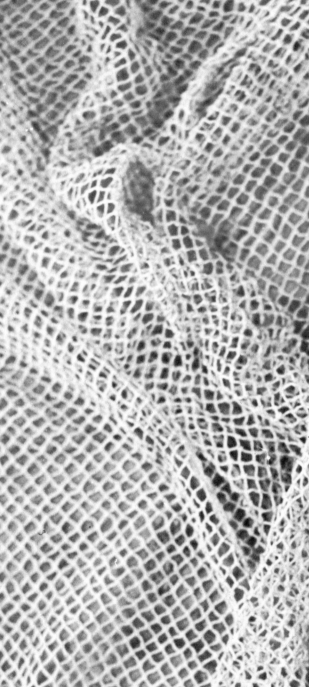

schools is of practical value, such as furniture making, rug weaving, pottery making, or even furniture repair and refinishing. Considerable time within the framework of the curriculum should be set aside to make this area meaningful for the potential home craftsman. It is obvious that much misdirected time and effort is presently channeled into nonworthwhile activities by the "easy-to-make, just-follow-the-pattern" type of project. People need to have control over, and identify with, a project of their own choosing. From the first conception of the idea, through the problem solving and technical mastery, to the final very personal result—this entire process must be grasped by the individual. Thus, any such creative activity should be an honest representation of its creator and of the material and be designed for its true purpose or function. Art education is ideally suited to maintain this self-identification with the whole span of production, usually unattainable to any one person in our modern technically oriented age.

RELATED ACTIVITIES

1. Survey the art classes in a local high school to determine who actually takes elective art courses. What major sequence of courses are these students following? How do their academic abilities relate to the total high school population? What are the vocational interests of these youngsters?

2. List the materials presently being used by students in a junior or senior high school. What type of use is made of these? Which of these art materials are used by adults who enjoy and actively engage in art, other than professional artists? On what basis can the use of the rest of the art materials be justified?

3. What are some of the characteristics of adolescent art? How do these differ from child art and from the art of professionals?

4. List a range of three-dimensional materials suitable for sculpturing. Which of these materials need to be chipped or filed away to make a sculpture? Which need to be built up to make a form? Which materials can be used in both ways?

5. Compile a list of occupations that could be considered under the heading "Artists." What are the specific differences between these occupations? What are some of the skills or training necessary for each of these occupations? What are some of the common backgrounds needed for all fields?

6. Observe an adolescent group outside school. Record the way in which these youngsters express themselves, both verbally and socially. Pay close attention to dress, hair styles, cars, verbal expressions. How much of this ex-

pression is controlled through pressure to conform to group standards? How do you see this expression relating to the school art program?

NOTES

1. For further discussion of this point see W. Lambert Brittain, "Creative Art," *Curriculum Planning for the Gifted,* ed. L. A. Fliegler (Englewood Cliffs, N.J.: Prentice-Hall, Inc., 1961), p. 294.

2. Robert Hess and Irene Goldblatt, "The Status of Adolescents in American Society: A Problem in Social Identity," *Readings in Child and Adolescent Psychology,* ed. L. D. and A. Crow (New York: Longmans, Green & Co., Inc., 1961), p. 178.

3. Luella Cole, *Psychology of Adolescence* (New York: Holt, Rinehart & Winston, Inc., 1950).

4. According to Sigmund Freud, *Fehlleistungen* are unintentional actions revealing the individual's subconscious reactions. Misspellings often belong to this category.

# 11

# The Meaning of
# Aesthetic Criteria

AESTHETIC criteria cannot be separated from creative development as a whole. They develop according to the specific need of the individual and *should not* be taught but must grow out of the individual work of the student. They are closely bound up with personality. If these criteria are taught academically—as a subject matter in itself, detached from the work —they become dead knowledge, which will inhibit rather than help an intuitive urge. Thus, the rigid teaching of composition may be more harmful than useful when freedom of expression is more important than learning rigid rules. If, however, composition grows out of individual needs, if it becomes a means of helping the student to express what is in his mind, it will be an important tool, more so for the *teacher* than for the *student*. It is not the student but the teacher who must learn the meaning of composition, and understand it, in order to guide the student. In this

352

way certain qualities or needs of expression or aesthetics can be achieved with the least effort and discouragement. We shall discuss those problems of aesthetic criteria a teacher should know for guiding his pupils. Although composition unifies all elements of expression into a whole, we shall not be able to understand and analyze this unification without knowing the meaning of the single elements. The meaning of line, space, color, and their different relationships to one another becomes important.

## The Elements of Expression in Picture Making

Growth is on an ever changing continuum and we find that this is also true in the area of aesthetics.[1] Aesthetic growth appears to be the component of growth responsible for the changes from a chaos on the lower end of the continuum to the most complete harmonious organization on the upper end. This striving for higher forms of organization does not necessarily refer to the elements of art; it may also refer to a more intense and greater integration of thinking, feeling, and perceiving and thus be responsible for our greater sensibilities in life. Indeed, one of the distinctions between the basic philosophies in art education and those in the fine arts may be a difference in emphasis on harmonious organizations. Art education primarily deals with the effect that art processes have on the individual, whereas the so-called fine arts are more concerned with the resulting products. It is then quite logical to say that art education is more interested in the *effect* of a greater and more integrated harmonious organization of the elements of art on the individual and his development, whereas aesthetic growth in the fine arts generally refers to the harmonious organization of the elements of art themselves.

Herbert Read calls aesthetic education "the education of those senses upon which consciousness and ultimately the intelligence and judgment of the human individual are based. It is only in so far as these senses are brought into harmonious and habitual relationship with the external world that an integrated personality is built up."[2] Thus, Read refers in his statement to the effect that aesthetic growth has on the individual rather than to the aesthetic product he produces. Although we are lacking basic research in this area, there seems to be a strong indication of an intimate relationship between the two. Thus, aesthetic growth appears to be essential for any well-organized thinking, feeling, and perceiving, and the expression of these. Depending on the medium used, we then deal with the different art forms as expressions of this organization, such as words, spaces, tones, lines, shapes, colors, movements, or any mixture of these. Aesthetic organization does not start at any arbitrary line. It may start at any level, conscious or subconscious, and anywhere, in life, in play, in art. That is why our whole personality is affected by aesthetic growth. Wherever organization is lacking, the mind disintegrates. Aesthetic growth, therefore, not only affects the single individual but also, under certain circumstances, a whole society. Aesthetic growth is organic with no external set of standards; it may differ in its expression as well as in its meaning from individual to individual and from culture to culture. "One must strictly refrain from forming a fixed code of laws to which one can submit artistic phenomena from the beginning on."[3] It is this that distinguishes it from any arbitrarily set organization. Also in art expression, aesthetic criteria are intrinsic to the individual work. It may therefore be said that a creative work is governed by its own intrinsic aesthetic principles. If we were to attempt to regiment harmonious relationship and organization, we would arrive at dogmatic laws. This has important implications for aesthetic growth in art education. It implies that all set rules rigidly applied to any creative expression are detrimental to aesthetic growth. Yet in most of our schools, on all levels, such matters as proportions, balance, and rhythm are still regarded as separate extrinsic entities with no relationships to the intrinsic qualities of the individual aesthetic product or to the intentions of the creator and his developed sensibilities. Proportions, when "corrected" on the basis of external, most often visual attributes, may be in complete disharmony with the aesthetic entity of a creative product and the innermost expression of the creator. Rhythm, according to generally applied "principles," may be in utter discord with the harmonious integration of an individual's desire for expression.

How then can aesthetic growth be fostered in today's art education, if there is no apparent set of rules that can readily be applied to any individual? The most decisive aesthetic education does not take place merely by the criticism or guidance an individual receives for his aesthetic product. It is much more a total task of education, in which the individual's sensitivity toward perceptual, intellectual, and emotional experiences is deepened and integrated into a harmoniously organized whole so that his "senses are brought into harmonious and habitual relationship with the external world." However, in this educational process art can play a major role, inasmuch as no art expression is possible without a heightened sensibility toward the external world and the ability to bring our inward senses in harmonious relationship to it.

## THE MEANING OF THE LINE AND ITS RELATION

If we drew a line, it would be a creation—very primitive, but a creation nevertheless—because this line would express something related to our feelings or ideas. The line might be bold, black, and direct, starting and stopping at definite points and thus showing decision of character. The line might be timid, dainty, wavering, indefinite, as a child just starting to take his first steps, not knowing where he will end. Or the line might be dreamy, as it seems to us when we are suddenly at a place without knowing how we reached it; or the line might be sketchy, consisting of many parts, whose synthesis finally might approach the mental image it followed step by step. It might be an intellectual line, well thought over and carefully controlled. It might be a calm line, in which everything is quietly and carefully but determinedly drawn, like the uniform waves of the calm sea; or it might be an excited line, in which no motions can be predicted, ever changing as our emotions change when we live through great excitements; or a *felt* line drawn unconsciously, intuitively following an emotional drive; or we might have drawn the line with a utilitarian purpose in mind, perhaps to separate two areas, as an architect who wants to indicate that this space has to be divided. Or did we have in our mind a symbolic sign like the "minus," thinking only of its function or meaning, which through repetition has received general validity? Or were we aware of its quality as it flowed from our pencil as we can see it in the signatures of vain persons, who play with the line like a lady who can never handle her powder puff elegantly enough when she feels conscious of being observed? Or is it an interrupted line, drawn in two or many continuations, showing thoughts that are not spoken out, as in letters in which we like to express continuations of thoughts by merely adding a few interrupted lines? Or is the thought so important that we have to underline it; or did we draw entirely mechanically, as we doodle while waiting at the telephone for an important call; or did we want to emphasize rhythm by placing one line parallel to another, weighing carefully the different widths of the lines, as we do when designing; or were we finally unsatisfied with the whole approach and did we cross it with two bold strokes indicating that it no longer exists?

These are only some of the distinctions of lines that will lead to a better understanding of the individual and his work; however, we would not

do justice to the meaning of the line within a composition without discussing the different relationships of lines to one another. Such a discussion of merely the meaning of the line itself without its relationship
to environment would be like a life story that is concerned only with the
facts dealing directly with the person and not with the interdependent
causal connections that determine the life of an individual: "Up to this
date Miss X was a student at this college. She could not continue her
studies." That really is like an interrupted line. But why is it interrupted?
Was she compelled to interrupt her studies, or did she do it voluntarily?
Will it be merely an interruption or won't she come back at all? What
tragedy sometime lies behind such simple words as "She could not continue
her studies." Lack of money, illness, death, or whatever the reason—we
never would be satisfied with a life story that only mentions the facts.
The circumstances under which she interrupted her studies will make the
facts interesting and dramatic to us. In the same way that we would like
to see the accompanying lines in her life, we also would like to see the
circumstances under which lines are interrupted, or in general, the relationships of lines to one another.

Two indefinite lines that finally meet at a definite point after long and
many interruptions are like two friends who, after long-interrupted contact, meet again. If, however, these two lines are definite, starting at a
definite point, steering consciously toward the meeting point from the
very beginning, their meaning is quite different. It is the same as if two
persons reach for something they already have in mind. The more this
something is removed from their reach, the more inaccessible it becomes.
It is the same with the two converging lines of a Gothic arch, whose
meaning has gone into the realm of inapproachable religious faith. People
and ideas can meet under diverse circumstances; so can lines. The line
becomes a living symbol, and as soon as we have reached this point, we
need no longer ponder over this symbol's meaning, because we can
draw our experiences and relationships directly from life.

We know from the very beginning of creative activity, from scribbling,
what *repetition* can mean. In scribbling, repetition meant a greater consciousness. But we know from life how different the meaning of repetition
can be, depending upon the circumstances under which something is repeated. If a bold line is repeated by a dainty sketchy line, it might mean
mere imitation, like one who tries to imitate the original but is not quite
sure of himself. However, repetition that is done over and over with the
same degree of certainty might have the same effect as the uniform

ticking of a clock, which creates a monotonous rhythm that is noticed only when the clock stops or when the rhythm changes. Thus it might mean equality or pure rhythm, depending upon the circumstances under which the lines repeat themselves.

If a person loses something valuable to him and asks someone to help him search for it, both would do the same thing—both would search for the lost article. The emotions, however, with which both are participating are of different intensity, since the lost object belongs to one. Thus, parallel lines would not do justice to such an expression. Both people search differently. How different it would be if the emotional factor were cut out, as with the workers in a field who harvest potatoes or beans all day long! Here, the parallel lines would get their real meaning: of an *everlasting* repetition. If we were to interrupt these parallel bent motions by upright figures, these interruptions would then introduce a pause, as in Millet's famous picture "The Gleaners." The more upright the line (or the figures), the more definite is the interruption.

If, however, we deal with parallel lines that are in perpendicular relationship to a base line, the meaning of the parallel lines changes again. The perpendicular line, the most absolute line, which is neither influenced from the left nor from the right, expresses the same stability that a flagpole expresses as the bearer of the symbol of the country. If those lines of stability are repeated at equal intervals, they will have the same meaning as soldiers, in whom equality and stability are unified. If, however, one line stands out from this uniformity, it immediately catches our attention like one civilian in the midst of a row of soldiers. The circumstances under which this line stands out determine its meaning. It might be an odd line with a little slant, as a felled tree in the midst of a forest of skyward-growing trees has lost its *stability;* or it might stand out in height, overlooking all other lines like the officer on horseback. We might, however, just as well raise the base line in a convex curve, as a hill overlooking the valley, or we might introduce a protecting line, a concave line like a protecting hole.

If the relationship of lines is well balanced, if one line takes care of the other, as in a building in which all stones hold together, we speak of *static lines.* If, however one stone is removed, all other stones start moving. We then speak of *dynamic lines,* lines that are no longer balanced but moving. Lines might be *open, receiving,* like our arms when we meet again after a long separation. But just as we might not be quite sure whether the person we are about to greet is indeed the long-unseen friend, since he has changed during his absence, so will the circumstances determine the meaning under which the open lines are drawn. Or lines might be *closed*. This could mean protection as well as prison, depending on the kinds of lines expressing the meaning of closing. If they are bold, rough, and determined like bars of a cell, we surely associate them with prison; if they are round, carefully surrounding the hole, they will be protecting. If, however, one line breaks through such a protecting line, like the arm of Michelangelo's Adam, which reaches out from the earth to communicate with God, the circumstances under which the line breaks through will determine its meaning.

In this connection the different height of the horizon in a picture might receive its real significance. A high horizon that because of its height will not be interrupted serves as a protection, whereas a low horizon makes the landscape stand out and, with the frequently interrupted horizontal line, introduces a more unquiet and restless atmosphere. A high horizon may include all people living in this space as a protecting line. A low horizon, however, exposes man to the elements.

Although this discussion on the meaning of the line and its relationships is by no means exhaustive, it has shown the close interdependence of line and experience and has thus demonstrated that the line, as a vital element, can be understood only as part of expression.[4]

### THE MEANING OF SPACE AND ITS RELATION

Space can generally have four meanings: (1) in its unlimited quality, (2) within a restricted boundary, (3) in relationship to other spaces, and (4) in subjective relationship to ourselves.

The unlimited space cannot be conceived in its totality. Its infinity, the universe, is incomprehensible. Space becomes accessible to our senses only when we circumscribe it or when we assign to it a definite meaning. As long as we think of the inaccessible space of the universe, space remains incomprehensible. As soon as we think in terms of sky, we relate the sky to a definite atmosphere or mood; we have assigned to space a definite meaning, and as such it becomes accessible to our senses, especially to our optical sense. If we think of restricted space, like the space in a room, it becomes accessible not only to our eyes but also to our kinesthesis or acoustic reactions. This space can be measured and therefore objectively determined in its sizes. The quality of this space, however, depends upon our subjective relationship to it. *Objective* space is space perceived optically. Its pictorial representation is governed by the laws of perspective. Its clearest depiction is produced by the photographic camera. *Subjective* space is the space in which we include the self. In it, therefore, we find a predominance of subjective interpretations or judgments of value. They can refer to sizes and their subjective values, or they can refer to the qualities of spaces as expressed through different emphases on light and shadow and color.[5]

A simple story will illustrate the meaning of these subjective relationships and their interpretation in art. You and your friend are standing in front of a door not knowing what or whom you will meet when the door is opened. Your present relationship to the space inside the door is therefore undetermined. The only thing you know is that you and your friend will soon enter a room. In art we would say that a *definite* space experience is contrasted to an *indefinite* one, thus creating the same tension and interest that you feel now as you are waiting in front of the door. The door opens. You enter a small, low room. This room is bare and empty. You look around and find nothing but two additional doors. Your friend goes through one, you through the other. You enter a very small room, almost the size of a closet; your friend, however, enters a spacious hall. Both of you are compelled to stay in your rooms. After some time you come back into the room from which you entered. Your impressions are different. You find this small room very large; your friend, accustomed to his spacious hall, finds it smaller than before. Your subjective relationship to the size of the room has changed. Through the inclusion of the self the relations to the sizes of the different spaces have become subjective.

In art these subjective interpretations of value relationships in space are of prime significance. Not only does the significance, which is assigned to the self, change in relation to environment, but the spaces also change in the emotional significance they have to us.

Before discussing this experience of spatial relationships with regard to sizes in its pictorial representations, let us continue the story about the rooms, adding to the subjective relationships of sizes the relationships of qualities.

Again you and your friend are standing in front of the first door. The difference in your impressions is that you both now have different but definite feelings of what will meet you when the door opens. Having lived in the closet for such a long time, you will have in your mind a comfortable-sized room, whereas your friend, having lived in the spacious hall, will remember this room as small. The door opens, and you are both surprised when you discover a comfortably furnished room. Again you don't stay here, but each of you enters your well-known room. Again you are greatly surprised to find your very small room as beautiful as you could imagine a room to be. It has changed to a perfectly decorated room, and at once you feel quite at home. Every glance reveals something new, gives more satisfaction of well-spaced and perfectly furnished environment. Your friend, in the meanwhile, has entered his room. The big hall has not changed except that it now appears barer and grayer than before. The walls have become dirtier, the atmosphere more gloomy. He feels quite lost in this big hall and anxiously awaits the time when he will be allowed to leave. How different are your impressions when you both return to the middle room. To you, coming from your most perfectly decorated room, the middle room, though larger than yours, will appear quite common, neither attractive nor distinctive in any respect. How different is the reaction of your friend. He will be delighted with everything in this room; everything will appear wonderful to him. Though he comes from his big hall, the middle room now seems to him better than anything he could imagine.

We conclude from these two stories that big space may mean much space and freedom as well as being lost and restricted (in one's comfort). Small space, however, may mean restriction of space and freedom as well as greatest satisfaction in being in a world of one's own. These problems could be further complicated by the addition of the problem of different personalities and their emotional reactions. The latter is the problem of Beethoven, who wrote, "I hate the world at large, with its grimaces; how well I feel in my four walls," as well as the problem of a little dancer who sits at home weeping because she cannot find the way to the world at large.

How are the subjective relationships expressed in art? To be more specific, these compositional elements will be analyzed by means of three pictures representing the same subject in different space relationships. The topic is the same, "A Wood Chopper," and we shall see how his spatial relationships determine not only the meaning of the pictures but also change his character and emotional relationships.

The problem is the same as with the rooms. Like the entrance room in the former story, here the wood cutter remains in fact unchanged. What does change is his relationship to the surrounding spaces. Figure 98*a* shows the relationship between sky and earth; in Figure 98*b* the immediate space in which he lives becomes characterized by a higher horizon;

*a*          *b*          *c*

**Figure 98.** "Wood Chopper."

and in figure 98*c* the space around him becomes restricted. If we investigate these changes, we shall find phenomena closely parallel to the problems developed in the story of the rooms. Vast space, as expressed in Figure 98*a*, means here unrestricted freedom. The space surrounding the woodcutter is almost unrestricted. In this space, in which he is uplifted by the convex line of the hill (see discussion on line), he stands out as a symbol of power, a master over nature, cutting wood, chopping trees at his own will. No one interferes with him. How different is the effect of Figure 98*b,* where he is no longer surrounded by free air in free space. Through the raised horizon he has become a part of the earth, of his earth, characterized by stumps of trees and lumber. It is his earthly life that surrounds him. In Figure 98*a* we were able to forget that woodcutting is a job with which to earn one's living, but in Figure 98*b* we definitely are not only reminded of that but become aware of what it means to cut wood all day long. The self is struggling with its environment. No one is victorious, and the only thing standing out above the horizon is the axe, a reminder that in it lies power and that with it the man earns his living. The subjective relationship of the wood chopper to the space that surrounds him has changed. It has narrowed his field of vision and has brought him down to his daily occupation. How this relationship has changed in Figure 98*c*! Now even the horizon has disappeared. The trees stand like the bars of a prison. The man has become the victim of his occupation, perhaps of society, a prisoner of the trees, which seem to take away from him air and freedom. How small he appears now, how beaten down by his environment, especially if compared with Figure 98*a*.

However, as we have learned from the story about the different rooms and their relationships, much space not only means freedom but may also mean the feeling of being lost, whereas restricted space may mean the greatest satisfaction of being in the world of one's own. These relative value judgments in art are of great significance. They help in understanding the works of art and provide the teacher with the proper perspective for understanding art products of children. How often we see a student struggle for a definite expression, without even being aware of the problems involved. Being aware of such psychological principles in the use of the elements of composition will help the teacher guide his students in their struggles. This different expression of much space with the feeling of being lost, or of restricted space with the feeling of happiness in one's own world, is demonstrated by means of the following three illustrations. Again the central figure remains unchanged. The topic is "Coming Home."

*a*        *b*        *c*

**Figure 99.** "Coming Home."

Figure 99*a*, which corresponds to Figure 98*a*, shows the person standing out from the horizon and exposed to storm in vastness of space. But here, unlike Figure 98*a*, where standing out meant power, the same spatial relationship means loneliness, the feeling of being lost in the vastness of almost unrestricted space. In Figure 99*b* the horizon is moved up as in Figure 98*b*, and characterizes more the immediate space of action. But unlike Figure 98*b*, where it meant more restriction, it now has the significance of greater protection. The man can no longer feel as lonely and lost as in Figure 99*a*, for he is surrounded by protecting elements. This feeling of security is increased in Figure 99*c*, "Coming home," where the space is completely restricted. It is not the restriction of a prison as it was in Figure 98*c*, it is now complete protection, which creates the feeling of happiness.

How can the same space relations create such diverse impressions? It is exactly as in the story of the rooms. Here also all depends on the circumstances under which these space relationships occur. If we compare Figure 99c with Figure 98c, we will immediately recognize that in Figure 98c restriction in space is expressed by lines that are determined—determined and bold because they start and stop at definite points, going over the whole length of the picture, as the trees do. They are dynamic and exciting lines because we cannot predict where they will start, where they have their base. This gives us the feeling that even trees might come closer and closer, thus expressing unlimited restriction. How different are the lines used in Figure 99c where restricted space obviously expresses the feeling of protection. Here we have the restricted space expressed by utilitarian static lines, symbolizing the boundaries of the room, by lines that are not in contrast to the central figure (as the trees are contrasted to the wood cutter) but that unite with him. They find in him their continuation, as it can be so well seen in the arms of the boy and the motion of the woman. All lines either unite or protect.

The very same difference in the use of lines holds true. Whereas in Figure 99b the lines are all curved around the central figure as if to frame him, almost like a protective umbrella, in Figure 98b the lines are all opposing the central figure, stinging against him, as it were, pointing swords toward him irregularly.

From this discussion it becomes clear that the means of expression determine the particular meaning of spatial relationships.

## THE MEANING OF LIGHT AND SHADOW

Throughout the history of art the meaning of light and shadow has gone through the most interesting and diverse phases. If one were to write a history of art, based only upon the changes in the meaning of light and shadow during the different epochs and cultures, he might produce one of the most dramatically written histories of art. The use of light and shadow in art in its different meanings and qualities not only indicates a different creative concept but allows us, as we shall see, to draw conclusions concerning different attitudes toward life and their psychological implications. A period that has not yet discovered the existence of light and shadow must be quite different from one in which light and shadow are accurately used according to our visual percept. How different must be a period that not only uses light and shadow but accentuates them by exaggerating light and deepening shadows. How different from such an epoch must be a period in which light and shadow are used as effects, as illuminations, dramatically, as on a stage. And again how different must be a time in which light is used only as a source of light, in utilitarian meaning, as it were, to turn on the light in a dark room only for the purpose of better visibility. And how different must be a period in which light and shadow are used independently from naturalistic laws, through their own forces, governed only by intuitive means, thus creating a mysterious atmosphere. Or we see an epoch, perhaps on the opposite end of the scale, that is not only satisfied with the visual recognition of light and shadow but analyzes the way the impressions of light and shadow reach our eyes. Again, how contrasted is the experience with lights and darks if we exclude external visual impressions and emphasize the expressive qualities of the warmth of light, or the frightening attributes of lightning or the emptiness and loneliness of darkness; and how different is a period that deals with light and dark only in their qualities as design, that is, the proper distribution of both values.

Of course, we have shown here only a few meanings of light and shadow; many more may be found, especially when we consider that rarely does one of these attributes appear independently. The more complex mixtures of different attitudes toward light and shadow give a deep insight into the struggle for the predominance of certain experiences. In order to get such a deeper insight into the nature of the meaning of light and shadow (or, better, lights and darks), we shall discuss the psychological origin of these different concepts. Such a discussion is important for the understanding and appreciation of the works of art of different cultures and epochs and also for the proper motivation and understanding of students who want to express something definite by means of light and shadow but, unaware of their real significance, use lights and darks in a conventional way. A teacher who knows these most diverse origins of the experiences with lights and darks will be able to direct the students' thinking into adequate channels and avoid discouragements, which always result from a discrepancy between the mental image and its actual representation.

If we perceive an object without using our eyes, the impression we receive from this object is not connected with lights and shadows. If we try to perceive a head by touch only and glide our hand along the profile, our impression consists of the contour, of a line along which we move our fingers. Indeed, we speak in psychology of the touch line, meaning the main line of touch impressions that characterize the object. This line has a kinesthetic origin, the meaning of moving along the outline. Only the line can have this meaning. Consequently, we should find in all nonvisual or haptic epochs of art an emphasis on the line as a means of representation. In other words, an artist who is more concerned with the subjective experiences, the haptic artist, will predominantly use the line as a means of expression and not the visual experience of light and shadow. Lights and shadows in their real meaning are expressions of the three-dimensional qualities of space. The line as a boundary can become a symbol of the thing itself. The three-dimensional qualities become meaningless in comparison to the essential meaning of the object (see Figure 100). These essential qualities are neither connected with the surface nor with the substance of the thing. Therefore, neither light nor shadow will be able to signify them. The line, itself of abstract quality (we do not see lines in nature), will be the best representative for these spiritual values.

**Figure 100.** A Byzantine mural emphasizes unnaturalistic meaning of the line.

Therefore, it can be easily understood that in those periods of art in which the spiritual forces diminish, the meaning of the substance and surface increases. It is possible, however, that the meaning of substance is so subordinate that light and shadow indicate only the three-dimensional quality of the thing and nothing else. Light and shadow merely characterize the representations. In such works of art light and shadow are confined to objects of expressive importance. The visual experience, which always needs a source of light, is subordinate. Therefore, all works of art in which either expression or the mere abstract characterization of form and substance predominate show light and shadow only as a means of emphasizing the meaningful parts.

If a visual experience is reported, light and shadow go beyond specific objects and include environment as well. These naturalistic representations (reports on nature) use light and shadow to characterize nature itself without accentuating the subjective relationship to it. The more the desire grows to give an exact report, the more light and shadow obey laws related to perspective. These tendencies are best seen in creative works of individuals who emphasize naturalistic or utilitarian relationship to the object. If the experience of light and shadow becomes a dominant experience, if the three-dimensional quality of form becomes the main discovery in a work of art, light and shadow appear exaggerated. This can often be seen in drawings of youths or in periods of art in which the discovery of light and shadow has the quality of a first experience. Such a discovery often leads to the need to find and indicate the source of light. In such works of art the relationship of light and shadow is shown, and also the source from which the light comes (see Figure 101). Paintings of interiors often deal with the discovery of a special meaning of light.

Epochs and cultures that are dynamic and not content with the mere visual experiences use light and shadow to give expression to this dramatic quality. In such cultures the work of art is more like a gigantic stage design. Neither life nor atmosphere is real. Both appear in the dramatic illuminations of baroque art in which the fight of earthly with spiritual qualities is deeply symbolized by the specific use of light. When light and shadow lose the quality of dramatic interpretations as well as of naturalistic representations, they no longer obey the laws of nature. The artist himself then freely determines lights and shadows. He creates his own laws, which are governed only by the relationship of his intuitive forces to the world outside. The atmosphere created by these forces is necessarily magically mystic. The best representative is Rembrandt in his latest works. His greatest strength, and his most precious gift to mankind, is his light vibrating in the darkness and his power of dealing with lights and darks in unlimited and absolute freedom (see Figure 102).

**Figure 101.** "Entombment of Christ," after a painting by Caravaggio, Vatican, Rome. Light and shadow are exaggerated. (Courtesy of Bettmann Archive).

**Figure 102.** In a painting by Rembrandt, lights have a mystical quality.

The antipode to this mysterious way of directing lights and shadows intuitively is an art that not only prefers the bright daylight in which nothing can be hidden but tries to analyze these daylight impressions as to
quality of light, shadows, and color (see Figure 103). Here visual ex-

periences are emphasized, and attention is focused upon the variety of surface appearances and upon atmospheric qualities. Impressionistic art is visual art in its extreme meaning. Light, shadow, and color are no longer means to an end but ends themselves. The evaluation of lights and darks obeys only the rules of visual perception.

Opposed to impressionistic art we shall find those creations that use lights and darks no longer in connection with visually perceivable appearances. This type of art in which light sometimes is an expression of happiness, another time has a mere symbolic meaning, is purely expressive. It places light and dark in value relationship to each other, using them emotionally, expressively, and symbolically. In this art lights and shadows are not governed by rules nor do they obey any external laws (see Figures 104 and 105).

How different is the significance of lights and darks when we finally look at the art in which they seemingly have the purest meaning. In design

**Figure 103.** "Haystack and Sheep," after a painting by C. Pissarro. Light and shadow express atmosphere, surface appearance, and distance. (Courtesy of Bettmann Archive)

**Figure 104.** In this painting by Picasso, lights and darks are used expressively, with an effect entirely different from that of a visual impression. (Collection, The Museum of Modern Art, New York. Gift of Mrs. Simon Guggenheim)

**Figure 105.** In a painting by Roualt, lights and darks are emotionally determined. (Collection, The Museum of Modern Art, New York)

light and dark are not connected with any subject matter, but rather their significance lies in their proper distribution.[6]

From this discussion it follows that lights and darks must be treated differently according to special meaning. It would be entirely wrong to motivate an individual who intends to express his inner feelings through the use of lights and darks by means of visual methods referring to the visual appearance of lights and shadows. It would be just as wrong to motivate an individual who is mainly interested in the impressionistic qualities of lights and shadows by referring to his emotional responses. It is important that we know the different meanings of light and shadow as elements of a composition, so as to understand their value as creative forces.

## COLOR, AN ELEMENT IN COMPOSITION

Color, as an element of composition, is a means of artistic expression. Only our subjective relationship to color, the meaning color has to the creator, will be discussed within this section. Thus, we exclude the science of color, which is just as remote from our discussion as the teaching of "correct proportions" as seen in the "golden mean" (a geometric progression of 8, 13, 21, 34, 55 . . . considered perfect proportion by the ancient Egyptians and Greeks[7]).

Color can have as many meanings as line, space, or lights and darks. The simplest is mere characterization. Color merely characterizes the object: the grass is green, the sky is blue, the bark of a tree is brown, the foliage is green, and so forth. An artist who uses color merely to characterize objects must put his creative emphasis elsewhere because he must be more concerned with other means of expression than with color. Color has for this artist a subordinate meaning. It has descriptive meaning, which finds its parallel in the early stages of speech development. The main aim of this descriptive meaning is the establishment of a relationship between color and object, or in speech, between word and meaning. The origin of this relationship in art can be visual or haptic: visual when the description is according to our visual percept, which uses the eyes as the intermediaries; haptic when the description is an outcome of emotional or body reactions. Both relationships can be general and bold or individual and sensitive, depending upon epoch and culture and artist personality. The more complex these relationships between object and color become, the greater becomes the problem of color. The most general and bold visual relationship is the assignment of one local color always related to the same object. (See the discussion of color in Chapter 6, on the schematic stage.) The visual percept can thus be satisfied merely by distinguishing objects roughly by their colors. The most general and bold haptic relationship between object and color is the repetition of one color for the same emotional experience. A rigid relationship between emotion and color represents the most primitive haptic color experience. Through repetition the color becomes a symbol. Color symbols are thus the most primitive haptic means of color expressions.

The more complex visual color experiences become, the more we see the need to refrain from using local color. With the increased desire to see and observe color, the quality of color assigned to the objects and the relationships of the colors to one another become more differentiated. Visual relationships of color deal with the optically perceivable influences of one color upon another. Red will appear different in a blue or yellow environment. The reflections of colors on one another may, however, assume such importance that local colors cease to exist. In this art the relationship between object and color has shifted its center of gravity from the importance of the object to the meaning of color. In impressionistic art the visual percept has attained its highest significance.

The more complex haptic color experiences become, the more we abstain from color symbols of general validity. Color expression becomes highly subjective. Associations with past experiences become fused with emotional reactions to present experiences. With the increasing differentiation of haptic color experiences, color relationships assume major significance. Haptic color relationships are determined by the emotional effects colors have on us. A blue within purple might have a lonely, sad effect, whereas a purple within a bright-yellow environment would create the mood of solemnity. A green close to a shrill yellow might mean fear, whereas it might calm us down if we place it close to a soft blue. Although much has been written on the emotional meaning and significance of color, color relationship will always be a highly subjective means of expression. In expressionistic art haptic color experiences receive their highest meaning.

Maitland Graves provides a brief summary of the conclusions on the psychological effect of color "reached by investigators and psychologists as a result of experiments upon thousands of people. . . . The warm colors, yellow, orange, and red, are positive and aggressive, restless, or stimulating, as compared to the cool violets, blues, and greens, which are negative, aloof, and retiring, tranquil, or serene. . . . Color preference is as follows, in the order named (pure colors): *a*. Red, *b*. Blue, *c*. Violet, *d*. Green, *e*. Orange, *f*. Yellow. . . . Pure colors are preferred to shades and tints when used in small areas. . . . In large areas, shades and tints are preferred to pure colors."[8]

Although these conclusions are based on "thousands of people," they have no general validity for teaching purposes. That they are based on thousands of people means only that the majority reacted to these colors in the way the summary shows. The haptically minded minority is neglected if we apply the results of this summary rigidly. In a classroom situation the haptically minded group may need more attention than the visually minded. In this case such summaries must be interpreted with great care.

In his "Characteristics and Symbolism of Color" Graves refers to historic and present-day symbolisms of colors. In his analysis of the majority of the colors, he provides interesting and valuable information. He discusses pleasant and unpleasant associations and emphasizes that such information is subjective and is not generally valid. He says, "Yellow, for example, is a sacred color, not only in China but also in European Christianity. On the other hand, it is sometimes used to signify treachery and deceit. This is confusing unless it is remembered that yellow is, and has been, loosely applied to many hues, tints, and shades, ranging from the clear and brilliant cadmium and lemon yellows, to the ochers and bilious greenish yellows. . . . Bright clear yellow is emblematic of the sun and is cheerful, gay, and lively. . . . The darker and the more neutralized yellows and greenish yellows are the most unpopular and disliked of all colors. These yellows are associated with sickness and disease, indecency, cowardice, jealousy, envy, deceit, and treachery. The yellow flag is flown on quarantined ships and sometimes hospitals. In tenth-century France, the doors of the houses of traitors and criminals were painted yellow, and Judas was pictured as clad in yellow garments. . . . Today the terms 'yellow dog' and 'yellow streak' convey the ideas of treachery and cowardice. Nevertheless, these yellows, although unpleasant by themselves, may be satisfactory and even beautiful when properly related with other colors."[9]

Valuable and important as these color associations may be for the proper knowledge and understanding of colors, color itself in art is meaningless unless related to its environment. And, again according to Graves, ". . . colors unpleasant by themselves may be satisfactory and even beautiful when properly related with other colors. That shows that there is no general validity or rule in color reactions in art, but that relationships determine their meaning just as they do in space and line."

Therefore instead of discussing the possible meanings of the single colors, we shall discuss the meaning of color relationships within a composition. Depending upon period and culture and artist personality, color relationship can be based on aesthetic or expressive assumptions.

In the visual and decorative arts color relationships are based mostly on aesthetic functions. Color relationships, therefore, are dependent upon the principles given in color harmony. These principles can best be understood if we compare them with music, especially with tonal music, in which the longing for resounding chords is one of the main driving forces. In some of the works of tonal music the interest in the work of art is increased by the dramatic tension under which sounds approach one another under different circumstances, until the longing for the chord is so great that the chord finally has to resound. Of course the type of experience underlying this "battle" is different with different works and composers.

In the representative arts we do not deal with different time sequences as we do in listening to music. We can see the whole picture simultaneously. In color, however, we can draw close parallels with music, if we regard the single colors as tones and a color harmony as a chord. In a picture, as in music, the resounding of a color harmony can be interrupted by colors that are interpolated in order to increase the tension or interest for the "resounding" color harmony. In the same way that rhythm in music is produced by the principle of repetition, it is also produced in color. In music as well as in color compositions the interest in repetitions is created by varying them, either by different emphasis in the intensity of tones (dynamics) or through different intervals (harmonics).

If the longing for the resounding of a chord is subordinated to the expressive quality, regardless whether it is produced by discords or chords, we deal with the type of music that can be compared with color compositions in which aesthetic are subordinated to expressive values. In this realm color relationships assume a different significance. Subjective value relationships dominate this type of color composition. There are no absolute bright or dull colors. Everything depends upon the meaning of color in relationship to its environment. We may compare this experience with a girl who looks beautifully dressed in her dull environment. As soon as she has to compete with others on the dance floor, she will be submerged in the mass of color and brightness. Bright colors may become overpowered by environmental influences. Bright colors may no more seem bright but monotonous when repeated by equally intensive colors.

The significance attached to color can be understood by imagining the feeling of a student who could not graduate but still has to sit in her beautiful evening dress among her graduate colleagues wearing their black baccalaureate gowns. If she had to paint this picture, the bright colors of evening dress would not assume the meaning of brightness or significance. Visually bright colors, then, do not necessarily imply emotional brightness. Colors receive their emotional content through the relationships in which they are represented. Since these relationships are an outcome of subjective experiences and association, color relationships in expressionistic art are highly individual.

## UNITY, OR COMPOSITION

Unity, or composition, in a work of art is the integration of all the previously mentioned properties in a sum total in which all compositional elements are interwoven into one consistent pattern. "The purpose of composition is to organize all the physical elements which make up a work of art into a coherent pattern, pleasing to the senses."[10] However, "pleasing to the senses" is a relative value judgment. We all know that many people would oppose our calling Picasso's mural "Guernica" pleasing to the senses. We have, however, a simple means to prove this "consistent pattern" by attempting to change the unity in a work of art. The greater the work of art, the less is the possibility of making the slightest change in any of its compositional elements. Any attempt to change any one of the compositional properties must subsequently result in disunity. A work of art contains the highest and most complete organization of its elements. In such an organization there is nothing superfluous for it represents the highest form of economy. Every part is related to the whole and the whole is related to every part. The foreground supports the background and the background brings out the foreground. If one can exist without the other, the work of art is incomplete.[11]

Recognizing this unity of composition as the highest form of organization and economy in which nothing can be changed without doing harm to the whole, the educator is better able to help the student in his drive for harmonious integration. He will no longer look exclusively for balance and rhythm, which are only some aesthetic properties in a composition, but will become aware of the integration of all elements and their expressive qualities. He will use as a criterion the possibility of changes as well as the necessity that each part is a part of the whole. He will furthermore steer toward this highest economy in which only the most necessary things are expressed. Necessary, however, also is a relative value judgment; necessary will vary with each artist. The educator will not succeed if he does not place the individual above rules, if he does not consider unity of composition the outcome of integrating personality with creation.

Fundamental to any aesthetic education is the recognition that the aesthetic product is only a record of the degree to which the senses have developed and have been brought into harmonious relationship with the external world. If the senses have been refined and cultivated, it will be revealed in the aesthetic product.

## Aesthetics for the Consumer

Aesthetic considerations are by no means limited to those who produce works of art. The consumer, too, uses his aesthetic sense, though it may be that he often does so unconsciously. The selection of utensils, accessories, clothing, furniture, homes—the list is endless, for it includes all of the means by which man has shaped his environment and what he has elected to preserve—has shaped and determined the character of our visual world. These choices reflect both cultural and individual differences. We can tell a great deal about a society from those artifacts that are uncovered by archaeologists. We have discussed the effects of today's society upon architecture, reflecting our own confusion and fear (see Chapter 2). The differences of "taste" as seen in our individual choices may be more a reflection of our personality than of any learning of the proper rules of color harmony, rules of form, or knowledge of particular styles.[12] This does not imply that we are static beings, for as Frank Sibley has said, ". . . there is no doubt that our ability to notice and respond to aesthetic qualities is cultivated and developed by our contacts with parents and teachers from quite an early age."[13]

*Exposure to, and awareness of, some of the variety of forms available in contemporary art* (see Figure 106) *should be considered as important in education as exposure to ideas and forms in scientific or political thinking.* We certainly need to know a great deal more about how ". . . different kinds of art affect different kinds of persons in different kinds of situations."[14]

Obviously, social and practical considerations are important in our selection of home, institutions, factories, and parks, but the form these take, the character of an urban renewal project, the voting of monies, may rest upon the aesthetic judgment of those who have had no exposure to aesthetic education beyond what may have been absorbed from their own environment. The blight that constantly faces us (see Figure 107) needs to have careful and thorough consideration, for it is only through education that art can bring sanity and truth to what man produces, to what man is.

RELATED ACTIVITIES

1. Find examples of utensils, vases, or household accessories that are functionally well designed, though inexpensive and available at a local store. Compare these with poorly designed items of comparable price. Explain the reasons for saying some are better designed than others, relating this to materials, function, and manufacture.

2. Make a series of lines which are expressive of being sleepy, angry, sad, militant, happy, and so forth. List these words and draw the corresponding

**Figure 107.** The common recurrence of such surroundings as these reflects a society's lack of concern with aesthetic sensitivity.

lines in random order in two columns. How many people can match the expressive word with the intended line? Can you draw any conclusions as to the individualistic interpretation or universality of meaning of such expressive lines?

3. Collect examples of texture and pattern as seen in nature. Design a display of such natural patterns, capturing some of the feeling for pattern in the display itself.

4. Visit public and private buildings of various styles and of as many eras as possible. Be aware of the influences of different cultures: European, Asian, Mediterranean, and so forth. Discuss the various factors influencing the building of a particular structure. List some of the influences and considerations important in planning buildings for today.

5. Make a study of the effect and meaning of color. Cite an example where color is used in each of the following ways: decoratively; dynamically;

**Figure 106.** Students should be aware of contemporary developments in art, such as this example of housing and home furnishings. (Furniture and fabric from Herman Miller, Inc.)

dramatically; expressively; atmospherically; bound up with form; abstractly.

6. Select examples of paintings that are related to a particular period of art. Explain why these are representative of their time, referring to subject matter, technique, and mode of representation.

NOTES

1. Kenneth Beittel, "Appreciation and Creativity," *Research Bulletin,* The Eastern Arts Association, **V,** No. 1 (1954).

2. Herbert Read, *Education Through Art* (London: Faber & Faber, Ltd., 1943), pp. 274, 275.

3. Conrad Fiedler, *On Judging Works of Visual Art,* tr. Henry Schaefer-Simmern (Berkeley: University of California Press, 1949).

4. Victor D'Amico, *Creative Teaching in Art,* rev. ed. (Scranton, Pa.: International Textbook Co., 1953).

5. R. G. Wiggin, *Composing in Space* (Dubuque, Iowa: William C. Brown Company, 1949).

6. Compare with M. Schoen, *Art and Beauty* (New York: The Macmillan Company, 1942).

7. Jay Hambidge, *Dynamic Symmetry* (New Haven: Yale University Press, 1923).

8. Maitland Graves, *The Art of Color and Design* (New York: McGraw-Hill Company, Inc., 1941), p. 256.

9. *Ibid.,* p. 259.

10. Read, *op. cit.*

11. Thomas Munro, "Powers of Art Appreciation and Evaluation," *The Fortieth Yearbook of the National Society for the Study of Education* (Bloomington, Ill.: Public School Publishing Co., 1941), pp. 323–348.

12. Earl W. Linderman, "The Relation of Art Picture Judgment to Judge Personality," *Studies in Art Education,* **III,** No. 2 (Spring 1962), p. 46 ff.

13. Frank Sibley, "Aesthetic Concepts," *Philosophy Looks at the Arts,* ed. Joseph Margolis, (New York: Charles Scribner's Sons, 1962), p. 84.

14. Thomas Munro, "The Psychology of Art: Past, Present and Future," *Journal of Aesthetics and Art Criticism,* **XXI,** No. 3 (Spring 1963), p. 268.

# 12

# The Gifted Child

A FIFTH grade teacher was standing in the front of her room looking through a large stack of paintings, which had just been picked up off the floor where they had been drying. She was saying how much her children enjoyed their art experiences. That is, all but one child, "The one in the back row that needs the haircut," she said, nodding toward the one boy who looked as if he could stand a bath. She began thumbing through the paintings. "Aren't some of these lovely?" Most of them looked tightly drawn and carefully colored. Suddenly she came upon one that was full of color, painted very directly, and apparently with a lot of feeling. It was a large head outlined in strong purple with a red background, looking somewhat like one of Rploualt's paintings. She looked up and, shrugging her shoulders, said, "See, always this crude scribbling, no talent at all!"

It is fairly obvious that this teacher had certain likes and dislikes in art, which she was using to evaluate children's drawings. The fact that the boy needed a haircut and a bath may also have influenced her judgment. At any rate, what one teacher might look upon as being outstanding, another teacher might consider a mess. Not only do we have individual differences in what teachers like, and what parents like, but we also find that what was liked fifty years ago may not be looked upon as being outstanding in the field of art today.

The standards of aesthetic beauty change. Not very long ago the ultimate in beauty was embodied in the Golden Age of Greece. We found that schools and post offices were made to look like Greek temples. Venus de Milo was looked upon as the classic form of beauty, Greek motifs adorned our houses, and even bird baths were perched on top of sawed-off columns. Today, however, our society has different standards of beauty. A modern home looks more representative of Asian culture than of any European counterpart. Primitive African sculpture is now looked upon as being beautiful. With constantly changing aesthetic standards, undoubtedly we will have new forms of beauty in the next fifty years. We would be on shaky ground, then, to pick out from a fifth grade class a gifted child by looking at his paintings. Fifty years hence, one who is now a fifth grader may be responsible for changes in our aesthetic taste.

Occasionally we hear of a child who is outstanding in art and yet does not seem very intelligent. This may be quite natural. A child who is frustrated in subjects such as reading, writing, or arithmetic, and is pointed to as being slow, may turn to art for a release of his frustrations, because in art there are no right or wrong answers. Some children will excel in sports for this reason. If a child gets satisfaction from drawing, and is rewarded for his efforts, he will certainly continue to try to gain recognition. As we have seen in earlier chapters, in discussing the drawings of children up to age ten, there is a positive relationship between intelligence and their drawings. This relationship may be more in terms of perceiving and thinking about details than about the organization of these parts. The intellectually gifted child tends to scribble earlier than normal and continues to advance through the developmental stages more rapidly than the normal child. Certainly intelligence tests usually administered in schools do not give any indication of artistic giftedness. As has been pointed out by Torrance, the creative child may be the one whom the teacher considers less desirable or at least not as well understood;[1] Getzels and Jackson have given us evidence that children can be highly creative

**Figure 108.** The intense concentration of this ten-year-old boy is typical of the involvement of the gifted child in his creative activity.

without being highly intelligent.[2] There may be particular qualities in *children* that show their potential much more accurately than do their drawings. The child who does not conform to the characteristics generally expected from his classmates may indeed be the gifted child.

Just as we have seen that expression grows out of, and is a reflection of, the total child, we find that the gifted child also expresses his thoughts, feelings, and interests in his drawings and paintings. Observant children show their knowledge of their environment in their creative expressions. A ten-year-old who is concerned with the mechanical operation of parts, gears, levers, and pulleys will work through these relationships in his drawings. Note the intense concentration shown in Figure 108. Much thought and planning has gone into the details of the operation of the wings and the joining of the various struts in his plan for an airplane (see Figure 109). That this looks little like an adult concept of a plane has little relevance here. Each child reveals his capabilities and involvement, although these may in some cases bear little relationship to "beauty."

While every child, regardless of where he stands in his development, should first of all be considered as an individual, the gifted child makes us doubly aware of this responsibility. In fact, his highly developed sensitivity within his special field of interest not only makes him often appear different from others but may also keep him from participating in general activities less important to him. To do justice to the gifted child is not only vital to this society, but is an important educational principle. It is indeed one of the most difficult tasks, for what is generally true of developmental characteristics does not necessarily apply to a child of such

**Figure 109.** This plan for a working model of an airplane, drawn by a ten-year-old boy, may not be aesthetically pleasing to an adult, but the boy's thinking through of the functions of the various parts shows an inventive awareness of mechanical details.

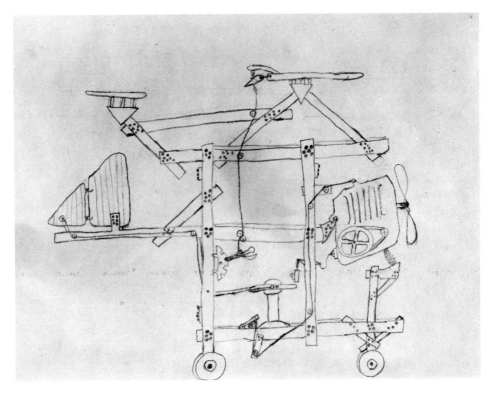

individuality. Motivations effective for the group might be frustrating to the gifted individual. Mediums and procedures considered thwarting may become vital parts of expression. Paper sizes considered restricting for the average child may become just the ideal area for the gifted child's particular kind of expression. Quite apart from the aesthetic message, it is this deviation from the average that is the most potent contribution of the gifted child to education, for without it the danger is great of falling into educational stereotypes such as "Draw big." "Don't use crayons because they are a restricting medium." "Size of the paper should be at least——." All this advice becomes mere prescription, a type of academicism, which we would not accept elsewhere.

## The Individual Case

Let us discuss two specific cases of especially gifted children, Bobby and Sandra. What is it that distinguishes these children from the average child? Five major factors stand out among the many to be considered:

1. Fluency of imagination and expression.
2. The highly developed sensibility (in certain areas, especially to movement and space).
3. The intuitive quality of imagination.
4. Directness of expression.
5. The high degree of self-identification with subject matter and medium.

### FLUENCY OF IMAGINATION AND EXPRESSION

The most obvious characteristic in this specific case appears to be the freedom with which Bobby adapts his ability to the diverse situation with which he is dealing. This constant change in which one element grows out of the other seems to be not only one of the important factors of the talent of this specific case but, as J. P. Guilford and W. Lambert Brittain in their independent studies on creativity found,[3] it may be a general criterion for creativeness, regardless of where it is applied. In looking at Figure 110, the eye is almost directed from one event to the other, from one movement to the next. It becomes quite evident that the drawing developed as the imagery "expanded." It was not a preconceived whole, but went quite fluently from one figure to the other almost as the fight

**Figure 110.** A drawing by Bobby, aged seven, shows a strong feeling for action and rhythm. He worked with pencil and crayon on small, lined paper.

developed. Such fluency of ideas is an important part of any creative process.[4] The especially gifted individual has it to a higher degree than is usually found. This spontaneity of expression and the resulting ability to take advantage of the given situation in developing new ones can be seen in drawings of the gifted. The mind never stands still. The imagery expands with the creative process like a chain reaction. In early childhood this fluency of imagination deals mainly with the continuously developing responses toward subject matter and the flexible use of concepts, called schemata. In the drawing "Indians Pursuing a Russian" (Figure 111) Bobby obviously started with the fleeing Russian and then, as it were, the pursuit began—the Indian close to him followed, he gave rise to the next Indian using a different motion and method of pursuit, and then the fourth swiftly following the third. Had the paper been larger, others would have followed with the same fluency of imagination and the same flexibility in the use of the concepts for horses and Indians. That the sequence was according to the pursuit of the Russian can clearly be seen from the overlapping pencil marks of the horses "covering" parts of those following. This great inventive power of building up a situation out of continuous chain reactions of stimuli to new and changing responses to subject matter and form is a highly significant criterion of the gifted. As the child grows older the same "chain reaction" also develops in the use of materials and techniques. With the growing awareness toward the art product, he is able to take continuous advantage of accidental or other technical achievements as the artist does. However, it is quite obvious that directing the child's attention to this developing technique at a time when he has no such desires would only interfere with his spontaneous unconscious approach.

However unconsciously, the child makes highly sensitive use of the material. It is here where we have to revise some of our preconceived ideas. Both children discussed use the pencil in its intrinsic quality with such intense self-identification that it can scarcely be replaced by any other material. Furthermore, it is *their* means to express *their* sensibilities. To deprive them of these means or to divert them to others might be frustrating. Sandra, in her "Galloping Horses Followed by a Dog" (Figure 112), uses the pencil line with such a fluency, sensitivity, and certainty that we would have difficulty in finding such expression on a conscious, artistic level. Bobby, too, never seems to have the need of drawing over a line again, so certain is he of his expression and the use of his medium.

### THE HIGHLY DEVELOPED SENSIBILITY

The child's aunt tells us: "When I drove Bobby back to his house,

**Figure 111.** "Indians Pursuing a Russian," drawn by Bobby. Rhythm and action, seen in horses and flying arrows, appear meaningful in this drawing.

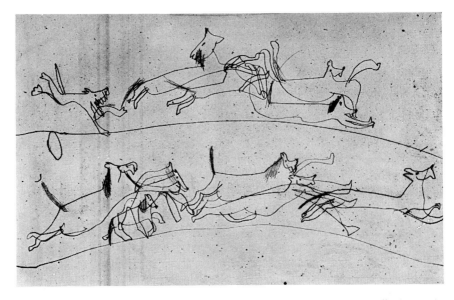

**Figure 112.** "Galloping Horses Followed by a Dog," drawn by Sandra, aged five. This drawing is made with pencil on news-print.

we saw some boats and some trains. I asked him to draw a picture of the boats and the trains and send them to me. He replied, to my astonishment, 'I can't. I only draw things that are moving fast in my pictures.'" This sensibility toward movement and rhythm can readily be seen as one of the outstanding characteristics in Bobby's drawings. Sensibilities toward various experiences are not always equally developed in the gifted. On the contrary, a certain highly developed area of experience may even characterize the gifted. In the case of Bobby it is first of all movement and to a lesser degree color. In Sandra it is movement only. She never wants to use color. But both have in common the high degree of sensibility for spatial distribution and organization. The gifted child flexibly adapts this sensitivity for organization to different situations. If he needs the whole area for his battleground or the story, the organization spreads over the whole sheet (see Figure 110). However, if the directional movement is important for expression, it determines the organization. As we can readily see, movement, rhythm, content, and organization become an inseparable entity. Such integration of thinking, feeling, and perceiving is part and parcel of any creative process. The gifted only has it to a much higher degree. One merely has to look at the "Galloping Horses Followed by a Dog" by Sandra, a five-year-old, to realize the degree of sensibility toward motion and rhythm, the almost unrestricted use of the pencil line, the incarnation of movement; or at the beautiful masterly rhythm of the arrows and the tomahawk in the drawing "Indians Pursuing a Russian" by Bobby. The meaningful is in such perfect relationship to the meaningless or background area that any change would disturb the harmonious relationship.

## THE INTUITIVE QUALITY OF IMAGINATION

Imagination may merely serve the purpose of recalling events, either directly or associatively. It may, however, also be used as a vehicle for new adventures into the unknown, bringing into existence constellations or events that have not existed before. It is this intuitive quality of imagery that is an important part of every creative act. In the gifted individual it is present to a high degree. It is seen in the great inventive power of Bobby in creating his almost Picasso-like symbols for human expression and movement, particularly in the boat scene (see Figure 113), as well as in the spontaneity and variability of five-year-old Sandra's fleeing horses. It is documented in the great diversity of spatial symbolisms. Both children

**Figure 113.** "Boat Fight," drawn by Bobby. The schema for his figures is flexibly used.

**Figure 114.** "The Peter Pan Story," drawn by Sandra. The action spreads over the whole sheet of paper. Although Sandra is five, she uses an X-ray type of drawing, more typical of seven-year-olds.

create the "space" in which their action takes place with a lordly autonomy, as if they were the Creator themselves. One has only to compare the ingenious inventiveness of using base-line symbols in the five reproductions to realize the great intuitive power of the two gifted children. Such intuitive imagery must be expressed; it must be translated into concrete form. This is the main difference between fantasy and art. As soon as fantasy is translated into some form of expression through the intuitive power of the creator, it ceases to be mere fantasy. Educationally this is of great significance because it answers the often-placed question of how far we should go in motivating the fantasy of children without overstimulating them. We cannot go too far as long as the child translates his feelings into concrete and factual material. It is the intuitive quality of the imagery of the gifted that does not stop without this great fulfillment.

**DIRECTNESS OF EXPRESSION**

From the child who expresses his lack of confidence in the often-heard phrase "I can't draw" to the directness seen in the expression of the gifted, is a wide range of reactions that constitute the atmospheres of our classrooms. What makes Bobby and Sandra so sure of their expression? The answer to this has important educational implications, for it is quite obvious that it is neither the ability to come close to external reality nor a special skillful dexterity that can be detected in Sandra's or Bobby's work. "I can't draw" is then no indication of a child's lack of skill or his inability to portray external reality. In fact, Bobby has given us the answer in his conversation with his aunt when he said, "I only draw things that are moving fast in my pictures." With this he indicated that if no basic experience affected him, he could not draw it. If, however, an experience is in tune with his desire for expression, he draws it with such certainty and directness that we do not doubt for a second the convincing quality of *his* expression. The creator gives it its own life with its independent intrinsic qualities. Bobby and Sandra create with a conviction and directness of expression that are especially developed in the gifted.

### THE HIGH DEGREE OF SELF-IDENTIFICATION

For Bobby as well as for Sandra the subject matter is extremely important. They live in it to such a degree that all the consistency of organization and expression is guided by the intensity of the emotional and physical participation in the experience during the creative process. Indeed, we get this vital feeling when looking at every detail Bobby has created. Most of all one can get it from the sequence with which he produced his drawings. He almost went kinetically through the whole action. All this is impossible without an intense identification of the self with the depicted experience. Indeed, without some identification no creative activity is possible. Bobby had extreme self-identification with his subject matter—the holding of a dagger, the riding on the horse, the shooting of the arrow, the jumping of a dog, the fleeing of the horses—and also had an intense feeling for the medium. The pencil had almost become a continuation of the body. It is no longer a separate means but is a part of it. Bobby and Sandra, as it were, live and breathe through their pencil.

## Educational Implications

The question arises, What can the art teacher or parents contribute to the growth of the gifted child? Bobby and Sandra have developed their world of expression on the basis of high sensibilities and experiences that were most meaningful to them. Any forcing of new material such as poster paint upon these children might cause confusion. As long as their expression satisfies their needs, there is no reason to introduce a change. However, these children are rapidly growing, and having a variety of materials at their disposal may eventually lead to other kinds of expression. There is some indication that a variation of paper sizes would be welcomed as the desire for more details and space grows. According to his father, Bobby loves to tell interesting stories about his drawings. Such verbalization may lead to more insight and greater concentration and enrichment of his areas of interest. As Sandra grows, in addition to the great movement she will also want more characterization of parts, or swifter movements with broader strokes. All this is purely speculative, for motivating the gifted is intensely personal.

Although we have discussed two children in detail, there should be no implications that the gifted child is always easy to recognize. A study of children's art abilities at the Cleveland Museum of Art reported that those children judged as having special art ability differed from those with average ability only in degree.[5] For many children in a classroom there may be a very small difference between those gifted in art and those not gifted. To put this in another way, individual attention and encouragement may make the difference between being gifted and not being so. The teacher, then, plays a vital role in contributing to the development of artistic ability in those children with whom he works.

Usually when we think of children gifted in art, we mean children who show some ability to draw and paint. In the professional world of art, however, we find very few artists actually making a living by drawing and painting. A much larger number become architects, textile designers, art historians, ceramists, teachers, interior designers, sculptors, advertising designers, and so forth. There are certainly large differences in these fields, and a child who enjoys working with objects and wooden blocks may be just as gifted as the child who is able to draw well. It might be well to consider every child as being potentially gifted.

In the elementary school we rarely find any program aimed specifically at providing an enriched background for the child gifted in art. However, some school systems do try to identify and encourage gifted children to take art at the high school level.[6] An enriched program in art often includes a bus trip to a local art museum, a trip to a print shop, and the opportunity to work with a great number of materials. The artistically talented youngsters are usually called upon to exhibit their talents for the school in making posters and charts, and at the junior high and senior high level as scenery painters for the Christmas play or as workers on the school yearbook. It can certainly be argued that trips to museums and design studios could certainly stimulate interest in those children who are supposedly not gifted. The additional work of making posters or painting scenery may be of little real value to the children themselves except to keep them busy.

It would appear that high school is the logical place for a full development of artistic talent within our school system. But such is rarely the case. Usually only one youngster in ten takes any art beyond the junior high school level. Among those who take art are the students who are prodded into the course by the high school counselor so that they will maintain enough interest to finish high school, those students who look upon art as an inoffensive way to spend time, and of course the high school athlete who has to pass at least one course. Therefore, the high school art teacher has to deal with a large range of abilities, and the gifted student may be in the minority. We also find unhappy circumstances that tend to push the gifted student into the more academic courses to insure acceptance into college. Certainly one of the outstanding needs of today is that of providing for those students gifted in art a truly exciting program that will stimulate and encourage a new, different kind of thinking, a new approach to art that will make it a fundamental part of the program for the gifted.

At the end of this discussion it should be re-emphasized that *every child is potentially gifted*. To divide children into "gifted" and "not gifted" would be absurd, for the very foundation of our philosophy is the development of all potential creative abilities in every child, regardless of where he presently stands, regardless of his background, and regardless of our own personal bias or taste.

## RELATED ACTIVITIES

1. Check to find an elementary school that divides its classes according to achievement levels. Compare the drawings of children in the "fast" classes with those in the "slow" classes. Are there any differences in method of representation? Number of details used?

2. Interview several people who are recognized artists in business, in industry, or free-lance. What influenced their choice of career? At what age did they decide to enter the art field? To what extent was the public school art program helpful or influential in their vocational choice?

3. Compare the quantity and quality of drawings from several children you

consider gifted with several you do not consider gifted in art. List the differences in drawings. Plan experiences you think would be of value to the gifted children. Would these be of value for those not gifted?

4. Work with a class of third grade youngsters. Plan one lesson emphasizing environment: trees, homes, school, and so forth. Plan a second lesson that emphasizes the imaginative: dreams, make believe animals, strange creatures. Do the same children seem gifted for both lessons? Are there qualities of giftedness that cannot be easily judged?

5. Pick out one child who does not appear gifted in art. Over a period of several months give special attention to his art performances. Show an interest in his products, encourage him, praise changes in his expression, exhibit his paintings, show him you enjoy what and how he draws, give him confidence to explore new materials, ask him if he would like to be an artist. After the experimental period compare his products with those done previously. Do you still consider him not particularly gifted?

## NOTES

1. E. Paul Torrance, *Guiding Creative Talent* (Englewood Cliffs, N.J.: Prentice-Hall, Inc., 1962).

2. Jacob W. Getzels and Philip Jackson, *Creativity and Intelligence* (New York: John Wiley & Sons, Inc., 1962).

3. J. P. Guilford, R. C. Wilson, and P. R. Christiensen, "A Factor-Analytic Study of Creative Thinking, II. Administration of Tests and Analysis of Results." *Reports from the Psychological Laboratory,* The University of Southern California, No. 8, 1952. Also W. Lambert Brittain, "Experiments for a Possible Test to Determine Some Aspects of Creativity in the Visual Arts" (Unpublished doctoral dissertation, The Pennsylvania State University, 1952).

4. See the discussion on creativity in Ch. 1.

5. Thomas Munro, *Art Education: Its Philosophy and Psychology* (New York: Liberal Arts Press, 1956), pp. 209–236.

6. The University of the State of New York, *56 Practices for the Gifted* (Albany: The State Education Department, 1958), p. 95.

# 13

# Summary of All Stages

Art education has tremendous potential for the understanding of children and for the promoting of their creative growth. Every child is unique. Knowing the stages of his creative growth in relation to his general development allows us to motivate him toward his greatest achievement and personal fulfillment. An attempt has been made to put into outline form some of the factors involved in the development of creative expression. These outlines are simplified and should be used only as a reminder of the differences and similarities existing among children. For every stage are listed certain procedures and media that are most appropriate; these as well as an outline of the progression of creative expression are summarized.

Some of the most important concepts the authors hoped to convey cannot be put into outline form. Sensitivity to children and an understanding of the importance of the creative act need to be experienced rather than memorized. We must recognize that our knowledge is worthless unless we can develop within children the self-confidence to utilize art as a means of imaginative self-expression according to individual needs. Through such creative experiences our youth may lead more unified and better-adjusted lives.

SUMMARY. SCRIBBLING STAGE—TWO TO FOUR YEARS

| Characteristics | Human Figure | Space | Color | Design | Motivation Topics | Materials |
|---|---|---|---|---|---|---|
| (1) Disordered. Kinesthetic experience. No control of motions. | None. | None. | No conscious approach. Use of color for mere enjoyment without any intentions. | None. | Through encouragement. Do not interrupt or discourage or divert child from scribbling. | Large black crayon. Smooth paper. Poster paint. Finger paint only for maladjusted children. Clay. |
| (2) Controlled. Repeated motions, establishment of coordination between visual and motor activity. Control of motions. Self-assurance of control through deviations of type of motions. | None. | None, or only kinesthetically. | Same as above. | None. | Same as above. | Same as above. |
| (3) Naming. Change from kinesthetic to imaginative thinking. Mixing of motions with frequent interruption. | Only imaginatively by the act of naming. | Purely imaginatively. | Color used to distinguish different meanings of scribbling. | None. | In the direction of the child's thinking by continuing the child's story. | Colored crayons. Poster paint. Clay, felt-nibbed pen. |

# SUMMARY. PRESCHEMATIC STAGE—FOUR TO SEVEN YEARS

| Characteristics | Human Figure | Space | Color | Design | Motivation Topics | Materials |
|---|---|---|---|---|---|---|
| Discovery of *relationship* between drawing, thinking, and environment.<br><br>Change of form symbols because of constant search for definite concept. | Circular motion for head, longitudinal for legs and arms. Head-feet representations develop to more complex form concept. Symbols depending on active knowledge during the act of drawing. | Self as center, with no orderly arrangement of objects in space: "There is a table, there is a door, there is a chair." Also emotional relationships: "This is *my* doll." | No relationship to nature.<br><br>Color according to emotional appeal. | No conscious approach. | Activating of passive knowledge related mainly to self (body parts). | Crayons, clay, tempera paints (thick), large bristle brushes, large sheets of paper (absorbent). |

## SUMMARY. SCHEMATIC STAGE—SEVEN TO NINE YEARS

| Characteristics | Human Figure | Space | Color | Design | Motivation Topics | Materials |
|---|---|---|---|---|---|---|
| Formulation of a definite concept of man and environment. | Definite concept of figure depending on active knowledge and personality, through repetition: schema. | First definite space concept: base line. | Discovery of relationship between color and object; through repetition: color schema. | No conscious design approach. | Best motivation concentrates on action, characterized by *we, action, where*. | Colored crayons. |
| Self-assurance through repetition of form symbols, schemata. | Deviations expressing experiences can be seen in— | Discovery of being a part of environment: important for cooperation and reading. | Same color for same object. | | Topics referring to— | Colored chalks. |
| In pure schema no intentional experience is expressed, only the thing itself: "the man," "the tree," etc. | (1) Exaggeration of important parts. | Base line expresses— <br>(1) Base. <br>(2) Terrain. | Deviation of color schema shows emotional experience. | | (1) Time sequences (journeys, traveling stories). | Tempera, poster paint. |
| | (2) Neglect or omission of unimportant parts. | Deviations from base line express experiences. Subjective space: | | | (2) X-ray pictures (inside and outside are emphasized), factory, school, home, etc. | Large paper. |
| Experiences are expressed by deviations from schema. | (3) Change of symbols. | (1) Folding over (egocentric). | | | | Bristle and hair brushes. |
| | | (2) Mixed forms of plan and elevation. | | | | Clay: |
| Use of geometric lines. | | (3) X-ray pictures. | | | | (1) Synthetic |
| | | (4) Space-time representations. | | | | (2) Analytic. |

## SUMMARY. STAGE OF DAWNING REALISM—NINE TO ELEVEN YEARS

| Characteristics | Human Figure | Space | Color | Design | Motivation Topics | Materials |
|---|---|---|---|---|---|---|
| Gang age. | Attention to clothes, (dresses, uniforms), emphasizing difference between girls and boys. | Removal from baseline expression. | Removal from objective stage of color. | First conscious approach toward decoration. | Self-awareness stimulated by characterization of different dresses and suits (professions). | Paper cutting. |
| Removal from geometric lines (schema). | | Overlapping. Sky comes down to base line. | Emphasis on emotional approach to color. | | | Crayons. |
| | Greater stiffness as result of egocentric attitude, and the emphasis on details (clothes, hair, and so forth). | Discovery of plane. | Subjective stage of color. Color is used according to subjective experience. | Acquaintance with materials and their function. | Cooperation and overlapping through group work. | Poster paint. |
| Lack of cooperation with adults. | | Filling in space between base lines. | | | | Flat, colored chalk. |
| Greater awareness of the self and of sex differences. | Tendency toward realistic lines. | | | | Subjective cooperation through type of topic: "We are Building a House." | Clay. |
| | | Difficulties in spatial correlations as result of egocentric attitude and lack of cooperation. | | | | Papier-mâché. |
| | Removal from schema. | | | | | Wood. |
| | | | | | Objective cooperation through team work. | Collage materials. |
| | | | | | | Metal. |
| | | | | | | Prints. |

## SUMMARY. PSEUDO-NATURALISTIC STAGE—ELEVEN TO THIRTEEN YEARS

| Characteristics | Human Figure | Space | Color | Design | Motivation Topics | Materials |
|---|---|---|---|---|---|---|
| Developed intelligence, yet unawareness. Naturalistic approach (unconscious). Tendency toward visual- or nonvisual-mindedness. Love for dramatization and action. | Joints. Visual observation of body actions. Proportions. Emphasis on expression by nonvisually minded. | Urge for three-dimensional expression. Diminishing sizes of distant objects. Horizon line (visually minded). Environment only when significant (nonvisually minded). | Changes of color in nature for distance and mood (visually minded). Emotional reaction to color (nonvisually minded). | First conscious approach to stylizing. Symbols for professions. Function of different materials, with related designs. | Dramatic actions in environment. Actions from imagination and posing (with meaning, like scrubbing). Proportions through emphasis on content. Color moods. | Water color. Gouache (water color and tempera). Poster paint. Bristle brush. Hair brush. Clay. Linoleum. Papier-mâché. Textiles. Wood. |

## SUMMARY. CRISIS OF ADOLESCENCE—THIRTEEN TO SEVENTEEN YEARS

| Characteristics | Human Figure | Space | Color | Design | Motivation Topics | Materials |
|---|---|---|---|---|---|---|
| Critical awareness toward environment. Three groups:<br><br>(1) *Visual type*: Intermediaries: eyes. Creative concern: environment, appearance.<br><br>(2) *Haptic type*: Intermediary: body. Creative concern: self-expression, emotional approach to subjective experiences.<br><br>(3) In-betweens: Reactions are not definite in either direction. Creative concern: abstract. | *Visual Type*: Emphasis on appearance, proportion. Light and shadow. Depiction of momentary impressions. Naturalistic interpretations of objective validity.<br><br>*Haptic Type*: Emphasis on inward expressions. Emotional qualities. Proportion of value. Individual interpretations. Depiction of character. | *Visual Type*: Perspective representations. Apparent diminution of distant objects. Atmosphere. Mood. Three-dimensional qualities. Light and shadow. Horizon line.<br><br>*Haptic Type*: Perspective of value with relation to the self. Value relationship of objects. Baseline expressions. | *Visual Type*: Appearance of color in nature. Color reflections. Changing qualities of color in environment, according to distance and mood. Analytic attitude. Impressionistic.<br><br>*Haptic Type*: Expressive, subjective meaning of color. Local color when significant. Color changes with emotional and psychological significance. | *Visual Type*: Aesthetic interpretation of form, balance, and rhythm. Decorative quality of design. Emphasis on harmony.<br><br>*Haptic Type*: Emotional design of abstract quality. Functional design. Industrial design. | Visual *and* haptical stimulations. Environment *and* figure. Appearance *and* content. Posing, with interpretations. Sketching. Sculpture. Graphics. Design. Painting. Mural. | Sketching in crayon, oil paint, tempera, conté, watercolor. Easel painting. Mural. Sculpture in clay, plaster, etc. Casting. Wood. Metal. Stone. Graphics. |

## SUMMARY. ADOLESCENT ART—THIRTEEN TO SEVENTEEN YEARS

| Characteristics | Human Figure | Space | Color | Design | Motivation Topics | Materials |
|---|---|---|---|---|---|---|
| Ambition. Energy. Romantic ideals. Introspection. Peer-group pressure. Sexual awakenings. | Action. Participation. Self-identification or empathy. Clothing. Costume. Dance and rhythm. | Visual perspective or perspective of value. | Sophisticated. Not necessarily naturalistic. | As integral part of function. In furniture, clothing, ornament, architecture, home style, site, landscaping, interior decoration). Appreciation. Abstract. Cartoons. | Self, home, community, nature, industry. Explore materials rather than emphasize technical excellence. Develop sensitivity. Excursions. | Any material that contributes to further growth or adult use. All previous materials, plus photography, ceramics, wood (constructing and carving). Natural materials. |

# Selected References

ALSHULER, Rose H., and Hattwick, La Berta W. *A Study of Painting and Personality of Young Children*, 2 vols. Chicago: University of Chicago Press, 1947.

ANDERSON, Harold H. (ed.). *Creativity and Its Cultivation*. New York: Harper & Row, Publishers, 1959.

ANDREWS, Michael F. (ed.). *Aesthetic Form and Education*. Syracuse: Syracuse University Press, 1958.

ARNHEIM, Rudolph. *Art and Visual Perception*. Berkeley: University of California Press, 1954.

BANNON, Laura. *Mind Your Child's Art*. New York: Farrar, Strauss & Cudahy, Inc., 1952.

BARKAN, Manuel. *A Foundation for Art Education*. New York: Ronald Press Co., 1955.

————. *Through Art to Creativity*. Boston: Allyn & Bacon, Inc., 1960.

BLAND, Jane Cooper. *Art of the Young Child.* New York: Simon & Schuster, Inc., 1957.

BURKHART, Robert C. *Spontaneous and Deliberate Ways of Learning.* Scranton, Pa.: International Textbook Co., 1962.

CANE, Florence. *The Artist in Each of Us.* New York: Pantheon Books, 1951.

COLE, Natalie Robinson. *The Arts in the Classroom.* New York: John Day Company, Inc., 1940.

CONANT, Howard, and Randall, Arne. *Art in Education.* Peoria, Ill.: Chas. A. Bennett Co., Inc., 1959.

D'AMICO, Victor. *Creative Teaching in Art.* Rev. ed. Scranton, Pa.: International Textbook Co., 1954.

————— and Wilson, Frances. *Art for the Family.* New York: Museum of Modern Art, 1956.

DEFRANCESCO, Italo L. *Art Education, Its Means and Ends.* New York: Harper & Row, Publishers, 1958.

DEWEY, John. *Art as Experience.* New York: G. P. Putnam's Sons, 1934.

ELLSWORTH, Maud, and Andrews, Michael F. *Growing with Art.* Chicago: Benjamin H. Sanborn & Co., 1951.

ERDT, Margaret H. *Teaching Art in the Elementary School.* New York: Holt, Rinehart & Winston, Inc., 1962.

FARBER, Seymour, and Wilson Roger (eds.). *Conflict and Creativity.* New York: McGraw-Hill Company, Inc., 1963.

GAITSKELL, Charles D. *Children and their Art.* New York: Harcourt, Brace & World, Inc., 1958.

————— and Gaitskell, Margaret. *Art Education in the Kindergarten.* Toronto: Ryerson Press, 1952.

GETZELS, Jacob W., and Jackson, Philip. *Creativity and Intelligence.* New York: John Wiley & Sons, Inc., 1962.

GRAVES, Maitland. *The Art of Color and Design.* New York: McGraw-Hill Company, Inc., 1941.

GRÖZINGER, Wolfgang. *Scribbling, Drawing, Painting.* London: Faber & Faber, Ltd., 1955.

GRUBER, Howard E., Terrel, Glenn, and Wertheimer, Michael (eds.). *Contemporary Approaches to Creative Thinking.* New York: Atherton Press, 1962.

HARRISON, Elizabeth. *Self Expression Through Art,* Toronto: W. J. Gage and Co., 1951.

HORN, Joicey. *Young Artists.* New York: Longmans, Green and Co., 1961.

International Bureau of Education. *Education and Art.* Paris: UNESCO, 1955.

—————. *Teaching of Art.* Paris: UNESCO, 1953.

JEFFERSON, Blanche. *Teaching Art to Children.* Boston: Allyn & Bacon, Inc., 1959.

KEILER, Manfred. *Art in the Schoolroom*. Rev. ed. Lincoln: University of Nebraska Press, 1955.

———. *The Art in Teaching Art*. Lincoln: University of Nebraska Press, 1961.

KELLOGG, Rhoda. *What Children Scribble and Why*. Palo Alto: National Press Books, 1959.

KEPES, Gyorgy. *The Language of Vision*. Chicago: Paul Theobald and Co., 1945.

KNUDSEN, Estelle, and Christensen, Ethel. *Children's Art Education*. Peoria, Ill.: Chas. A. Bennett Co., Inc., 1957.

LINDSTROM, Miriam. *Children's Art*. Berkeley: University of California Press, 1957.

LOGAN, Frederick. *Growth of Art in American Schools*. New York: Harper & Row, Publishers, 1955.

LOWENFELD, Viktor. *The Nature of Creative Activity*. London: Routledge and Kegan Paul, Ltd., 1952.

———. *Your Child and His Art*. New York: The Macmillan Company, 1956.

MARGOLIS, Joseph. *Philosophy Looks at the Arts*. New York: Charles Scribner's Sons, 1962.

MATTIL, Edward L. *Meaning in Crafts*. Englewood Cliffs: Prentice-Hall, Inc., 1959.

MAYER, Ralph. *The Artist's Handbook of Materials and Techniques*. New York: Viking Press, 1957.

McFEE, June King. *Preparation for Art*. San Francisco: Wadsworth Publishing Co., 1961.

McILVAIN, Dorothy. *Art for the Primary Grades*. New York: G. P. Putnam's Sons, 1961.

MENDELOWITZ, Daniel. *Children Are Artists*. Stanford: Stanford University Press, 1953.

MIEL, Alice (ed.). *Creativity in Teaching*. San Francisco: Wadsworth Publishing Co., 1961.

MOHOLY-NAGY, Laszlo. *Vision in Motion*. Chicago: Paul Theobald and Co., 1947.

MUNRO, Thomas. *Art Education: Its Philosophy and Psychology*. New York: Liberal Arts Press, 1956.

———. *The Arts and Their Interrelations*. New York: Liberal Arts Press, 1956.

——— and Read, Herbert. *The Creative Arts in American Education*. Cambridge: Harvard University Press, 1960.

NAUMBURG, Margaret. *Schizophrenic Art: Its Meaning in Psychotherapy*, New York: Grune & Stratton, Inc., 1950.

OTT, Richard. *The Art of Children*. New York: Pantheon Books, 1952.

PIAGET, Jean. *Judgment and Reasoning in the Child*. Paterson, N. J.: Littlefield, Adams and Co., 1959.

READ, Herbert. *Education through Art*. New York: Pantheon Books, 1958.
————. *Icon and Idea*. Cambridge: Harvard University Press, 1956.

REED, Carl. *Early Adolescent Art Education*. Peoria, Ill.: Chas. A. Bennett Co., Inc., 1957.

RILEY, Olive. *Your Art Heritage*. New York: McGraw-Hill Company, Inc., 1954.

SCHAEFER-SIMMERN, Henry. *The Unfolding of Artistic Activity*. Berkeley: University of Calif. Press, 1950.

SMITH, Paul (ed.). *Creativity: An Examination of the Creative Process*. New York: Hastings House, 1959.

STEIN, Morris I., and Heinze, Shirley. *Creativity and the Individual*. Glencoe, Ill.: Free Press of Glencoe, Inc., 1960.

TAYLOR, Calvin W. (ed.). *Research Conference on the Identification of Creative Scientific Talent*. Salt Lake City: University of Utah Press, 1955, 1957, and 1959.

TORRANCE, E. Paul. *Guiding Creative Talent*. Englewood Cliffs: Prentice-Hall, Inc., 1962.

WICKISER, Ralph L. *An Introduction to Art Education*. Yonkers, N. Y.: World Book Company, 1957.

WINSLOW, Leon Loyal. *The Integrated School Art Program*. New York: McGraw-Hill Company, Inc., 1949.

ZIEGFELD, Ernest. *Art in the College Program*. New York: Columbia University Press, 1953.

# Index